IMAGES
of America

PANAMA CITY BEACH

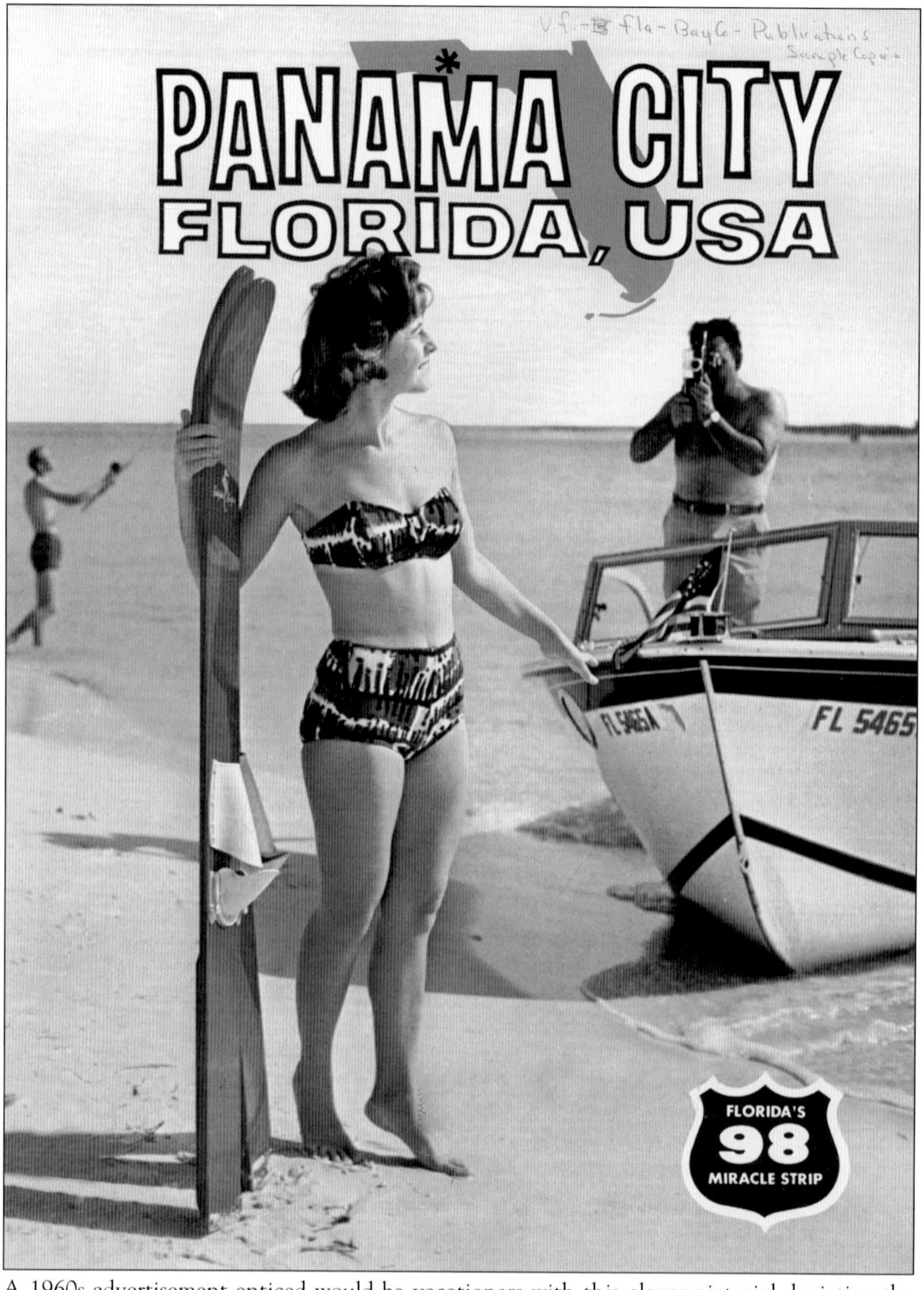

A 1960s advertisement enticed would-be vacationers with this clever pictorial depicting the many activities encountered on a visit to Panama City Beach. Note that the names Panama, Panama City, and Panama City Beach were often used interchangeably when referring to the beach area. (Courtesy Bay County Library.)

IMAGES
of America

PANAMA CITY BEACH

Jan Smith
Foreword by Rebecca Brown Saunders

ARCADIA
PUBLISHING

ISBN 978-0-7385-1700-1

Published by Arcadia Publishing
Charleston, South Carolina

Printed in the United States of America

Library of Congress Catalog Card Number: 2004108900

For all general information contact Arcadia Publishing at:
Telephone 843-853-2070
Fax 843-853-0044
E-mail sales@arcadiapublishing.com
For customer service and orders:
Toll-Free 1-888-313-2665

Visit us on the Internet at www.arcadiapublishing.com

To Doug, who made it all possible.

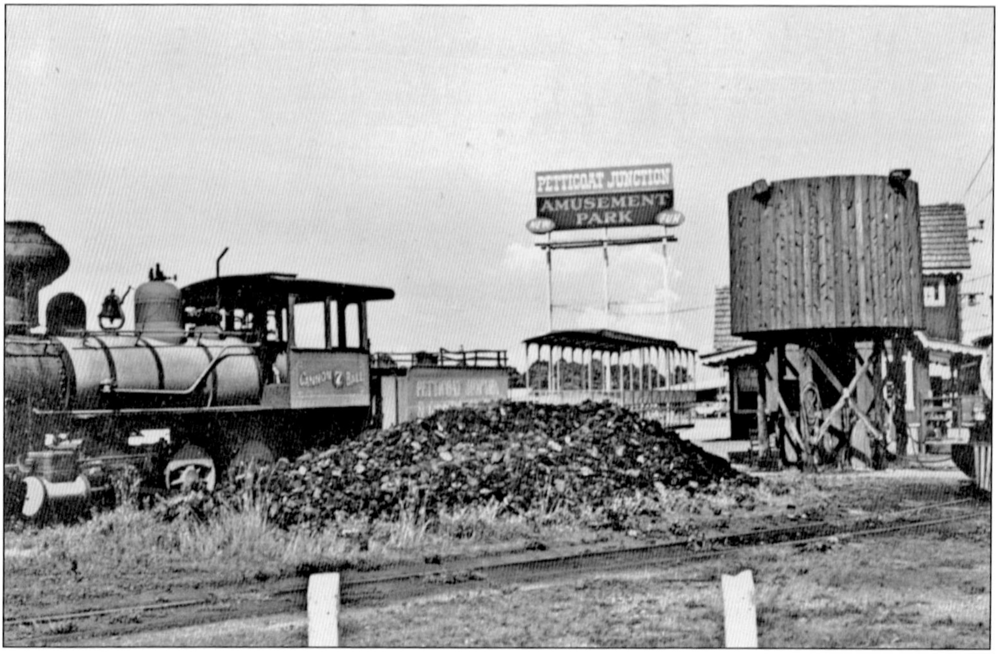

Named after a popular 1960s TV show, Petticoat Junction Amusement Park flourished from 1963 to 1984. An integral part of the Long Beach Resort entertainment complex, the park satisfied the public's desire for more diverse activities at the beach.

Contents

ACKNOWLEDGMENTS

The author would like to thank the following individuals and organizations for their generosity of spirit and assistance in preparing this book: Bay County Library; Bud Creel; Dick Doerr; Florida State Archives; Sam Fuchs; Paul Goulding; Richard and Deborah Gregg; Ed Hickey; Carolyn Insley; Jimmie Jones Family; Shannon Knight; Koplin Family; Lark Family; Long Beach Resort; Walt Lumpkin; John Metcalf; Jim Miller; Robert Morton; Museum of Man in the Sea; Panama City Beach Restaurants; Patronis family; Kay Pledger; Capt. Andy and Celia Redmond; Reynolds, Smith & Hills CS, Inc.; Doug, Jason and Scott Smith; James Stevenson; John van Etten; Venture Out; Louie Walker; J.D. Weeks; Bill and Ruth Wharton; and Panama City Beach Convention and Visitor's Bureau.

Special thanks go to Rebecca Saunders and Anita Lucas of the Bay County Library, without whom this book could not have been written, and Barbie Langston at Arcadia Publishing, whose patience and tutelage will long be remembered.

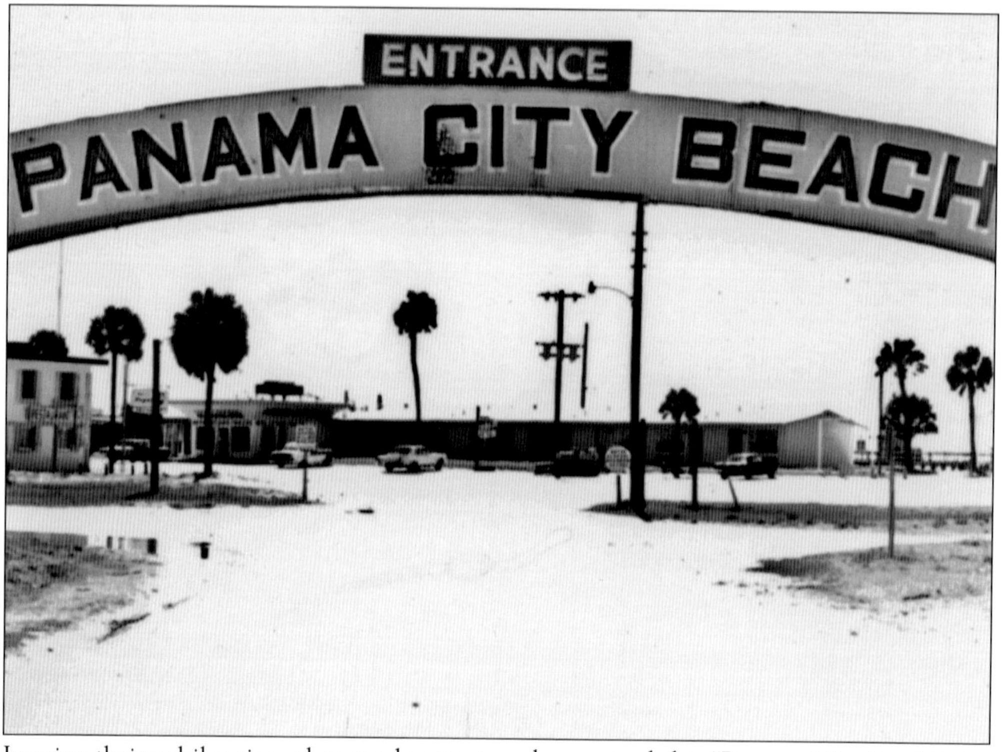

Imagine their exhilaration when road-weary travelers spotted this "Panama City Beach" sign welcoming them to their vacation destination. Part of a beachfront motel complex, the familiar arch symbolized family fun and relaxation. (Courtesy Bay County Library.)

Foreword

I am pleased to have been asked to write a forward for Jan Smith's book on Panama City Beach. She has worked closely with Anita Lucas and myself in the Local History Room of the Bay County Public Library and used information and photographs in the library collection. She also has contacted many citizens of the area, and they have shared photographs and information with her.

Panama City Beach has seen many changes over the years, from the homesteads of the 1920s that cost about $1.25 per acre to the look of the beach during the 1940s to 1980s. In 2004, the beach is changing again to the high-rise condominium look. Change in every walk of life is inevitable, but it is also wonderful to remember the way it was.

In the 1940s and 1950s, my family owned a cottage at Laguna Beach, and I have fond memories of the time we spent at the cottage and the several-block trek we made to the beach with our inner tubes, blankets, and other stuff needed for an outing on the beautiful, white-sand beaches of Bay County.

Jan Smith's book will be a wonderful reminder of how the beach has looked over the years, and it will bring back memories of years past for all who have witnessed the growth of this area. So sit back, relax, and enjoy the memories that this book will bring to mind.

—Rebecca Brown Saunders

INTRODUCTION

The completion of the Hathaway Bridge across St. Andrews Bay, coupled with the opening of the Gulf Coastal Highway (US 98) in May 1929, provided motorists with access to the Panama City Beaches and the once-secluded peninsula. The area seemed poised on the brink of discovery, and property was purchased with an eye toward future development. Although the Great Depression put a dent in the tourism business, visionaries like Walter Sharpless, J.E. Churchwell, Gideon Thomas, Harry Edwards, and the Lahan family were undeterred.

In the early 1930s, J.E. Churchwell purchased Sharpless' Long Beach Pavilion property and constructed Long Beach Resort; Gid Thomas along with his daughter Claudia and her husband Angus (A.W.) Pledger built the Panama City Beach Hotel on 100 acres that they acquired in 1932. Harry Edwards opened Larkway Villas while the Lahans developed the Laguna Beach area. All shared a common vision: attract vacationers to Panama City Beaches and the area would prosper.

Officially opened to the public in 1936, the anticipated flood of tourism proved to be little more than a trickle of visitors from nearby Southern states: Alabama, Georgia, and Louisiana. Wealthy Easterners from the Mid-Atlantic had already adopted Miami, on Florida's East Coast, as their favorite vacation venue. The land boom was a bust. As Marlene Womack reveals in her must-read history, *Along the Bay*, "the Lahan Development Company offered lots from $100–$600 and urged investors to 'profit while you play' . . . but vacationers still had no great desire to purchase beach lots."

During World War II, Panama City Beach served a dual role as a military observation site, from which the Gulf could be scanned for potential enemy invasion, and as a place of rest and relaxation for servicemen weary from the duties of war. After the war, many former soldiers, sailors, and airmen from all over the country remembered the Gulf's beautiful beaches, and as husbands and fathers of the 1950s, they returned to vacation with their families.

In 1953, Panama City Beach was created as its own entity. In the 1960s, four separate resort communities—Panama City Beach, Edgewater, Long Beach, and West Panama City Beach—merged to become the City of Panama City Beach. Today, there are two municipalities: Panama City Beach, and the City of Panama City Beach on the peninsula.

A 40-year span, from the 1950s through the early 1990s, saw increased development and the phenomenon of "mom and pop" motels along the beach. Amusement parks opened on a grand scale to keep kids of the television generation entertained. Goofy Golf, with its wacky sculptures, was started by Leo Koplin in 1958. Koplin's Tombstone Territory on the Miracle Strip and Churchwell's Petticoat Junction at Long Beach Resort were both named after TV shows of the era. The Miracle Strip Amusement Park with its "metal monsters" was erected by the Lark family as was Ship-Wreck Island Water Park. The Coconut Creek Golf/Maze filled another niche, as did Jungle Land, which had its own "volcano" and haunted house. Golf courses like Signal Hill, Holiday Golf Club, and Hombre were built, and new restaurants surfaced to keep the masses fed. Bars and clubs provided food, drink, and nightly entertainment. The beach area had at last come into its own.

Although high-rise condominiums were slow in arriving at Panama City Beach, by the year 2003, they were being built in record number, replacing many of the "mom and pop" motels and restaurants with huge structures of concrete and steel. The gigantic cranes that line the beach today foretell the future for Panama City Beach. It's doubtful that the original founders would have ever imagined such enormous growth, but they probably would have been pretty pleased to be proved right.

One

Early Times

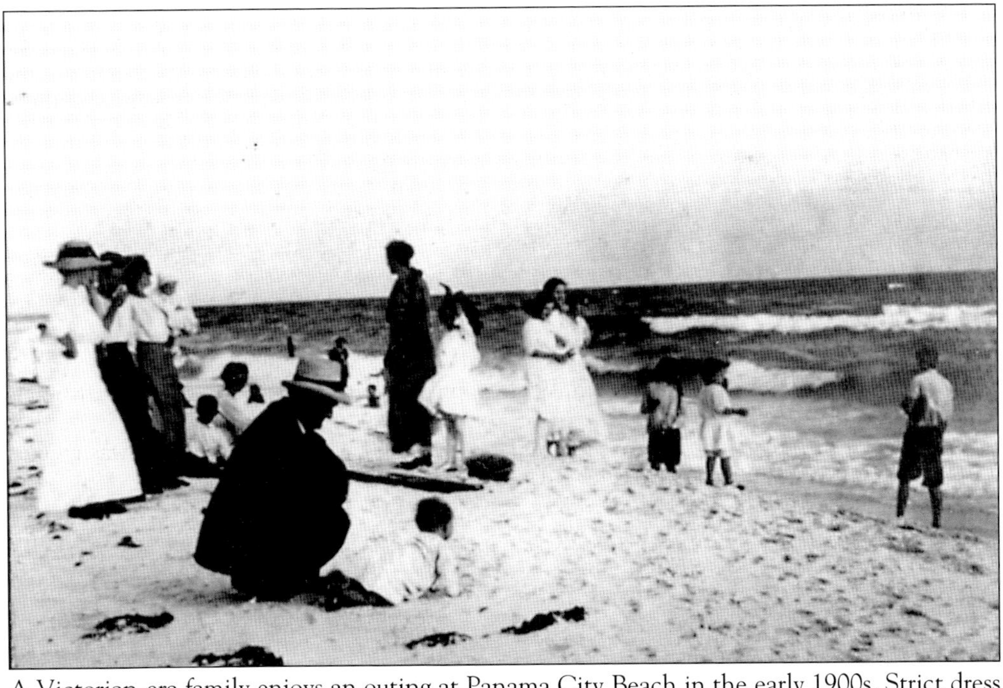

A Victorian-era family enjoys an outing at Panama City Beach in the early 1900s. Strict dress codes were adhered to, even at the beach. Note the pristine white dresses and stockings worn by the girls while the man kneeling in the foreground appears formally attired. (Courtesy Bay County Library.)

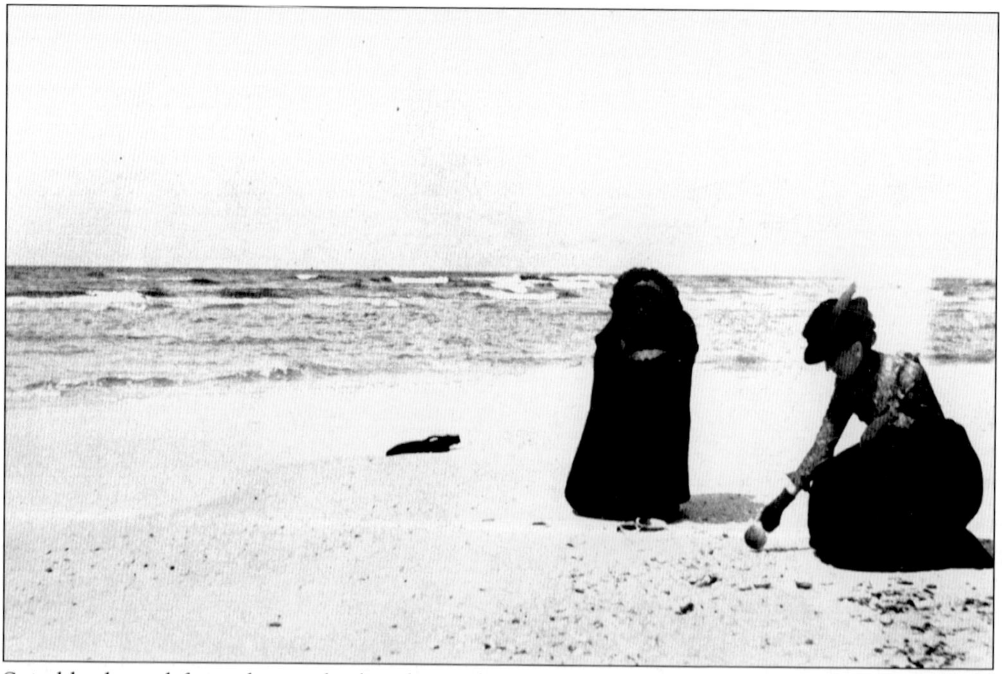

Suitably dressed for a day at the beach—at least by Victorian standards—these two women search for shells at the water's edge. Although they must have sweltered, their long sleeved dresses, feathered hats, and ladylike gloves were considered appropriate garb for women *c.* 1900. (Courtesy Bay County Library.)

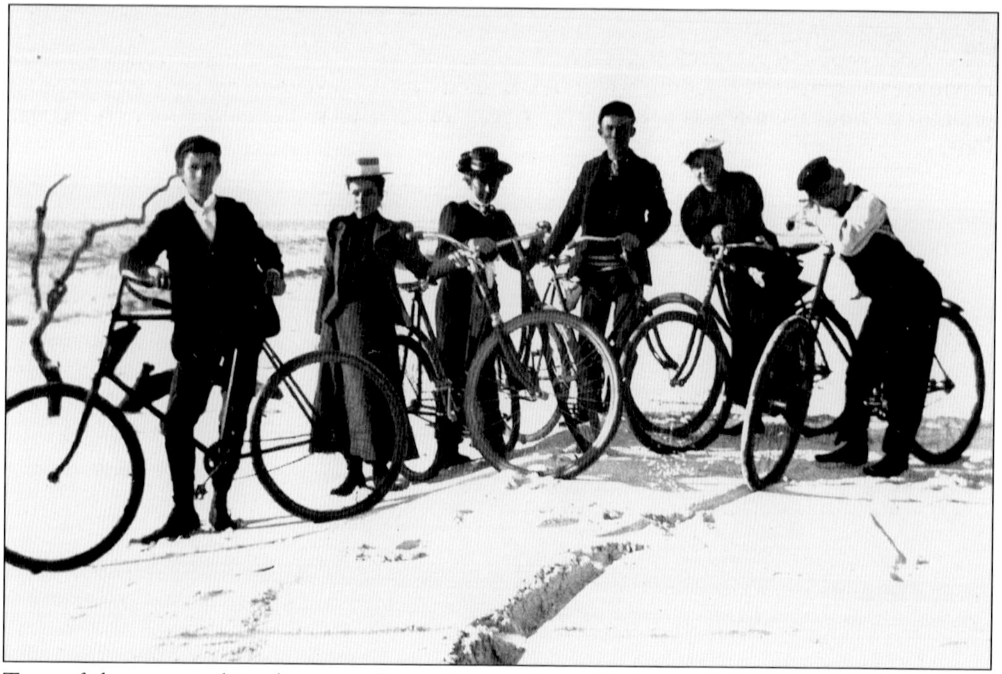

Turn-of-the-century bicyclists pose for a photo and a well-deserved rest before resuming their ride along the beach. Marta Maxon is third from the left all others are unidentified. (Courtesy Herman Jones and Bay County Library.)

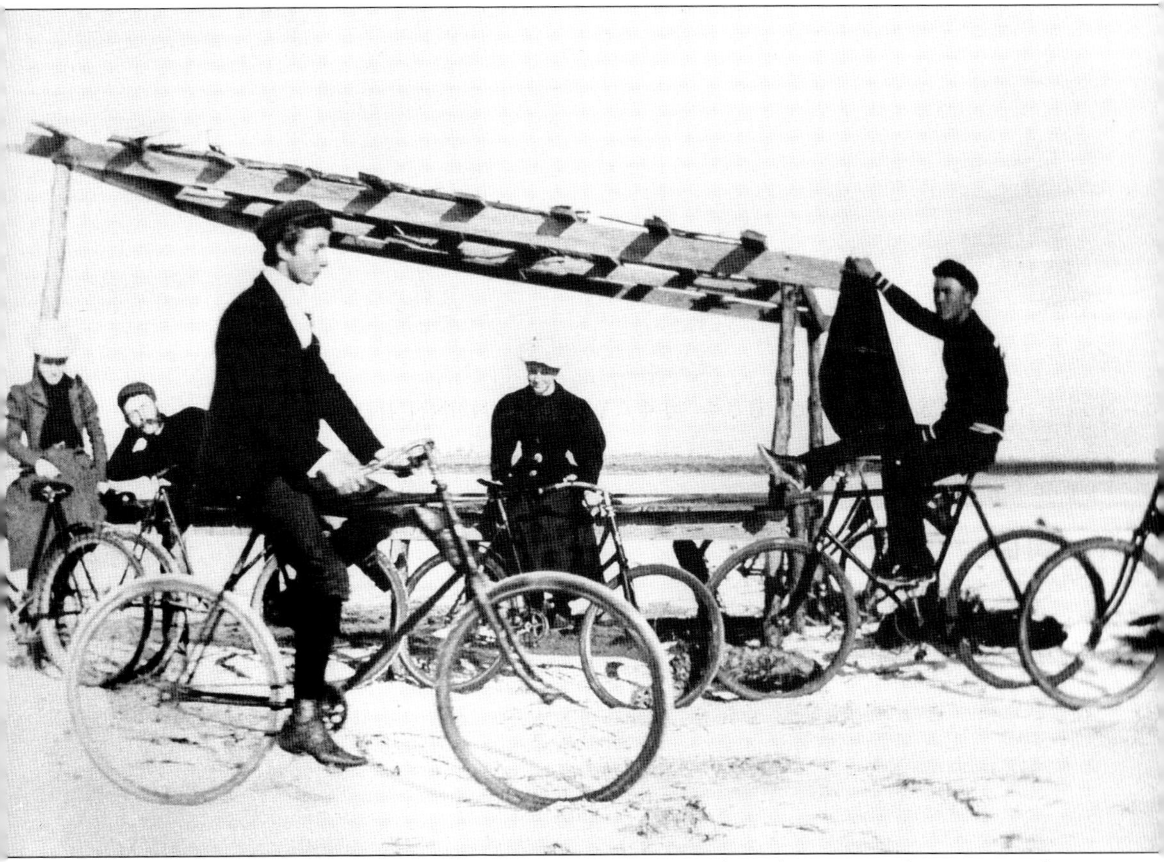

Having reached their destination, cyclists relax and enjoy the bicycling antics of a group member prior to building a palm-leaf sanctuary as protection from the hot sun, *c.* 1900. (Courtesy Herman Jones and Bay County Library.)

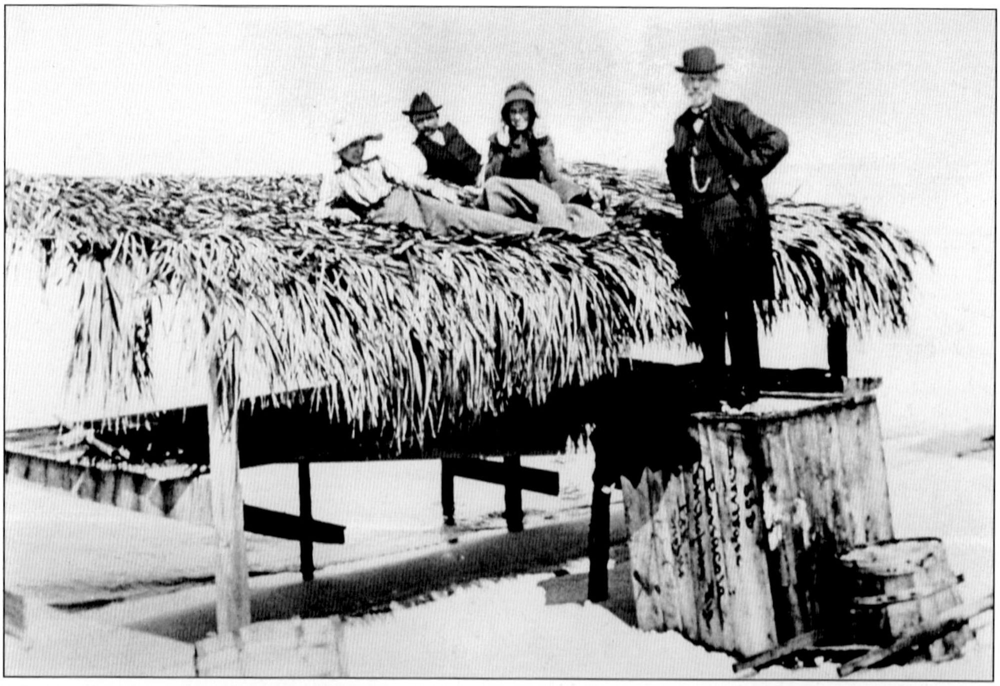

Obviously pleased with their efforts, two women and a man sit atop a newly constructed palm-branch "cabana" at the water's edge, *c.* 1900. Another man stands on a large wooden crate by the structure. (Courtesy Herman Jones and Bay County Library.)

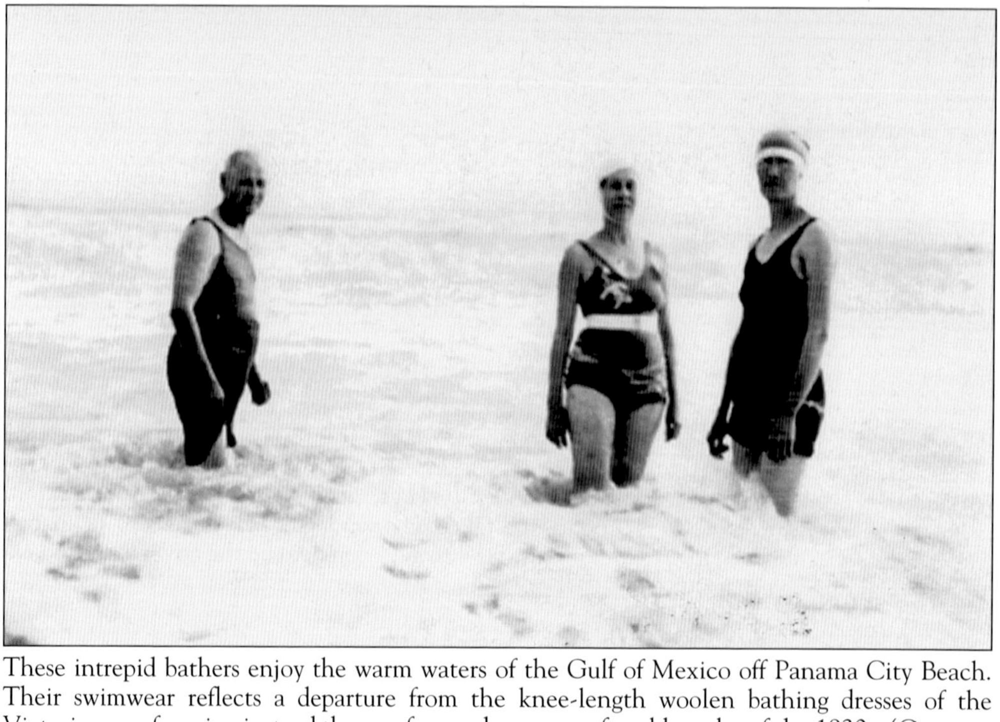

These intrepid bathers enjoy the warm waters of the Gulf of Mexico off Panama City Beach. Their swimwear reflects a departure from the knee-length woolen bathing dresses of the Victorian era, favoring instead the carefree and more comfortable styles of the 1920s. (Courtesy Bay County Library.)

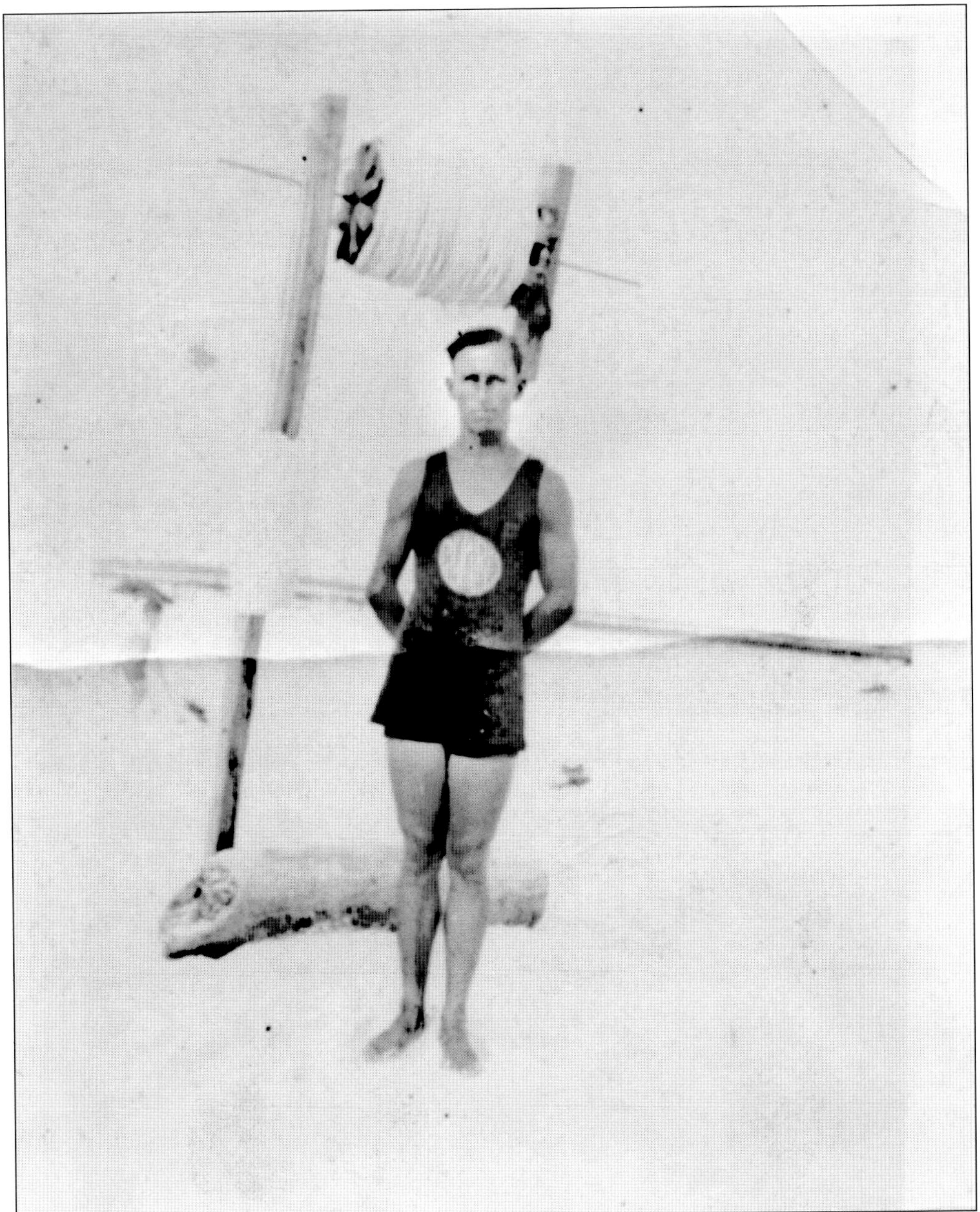

William L. Stevenson Sr. is pictured here on Shell Island, where he worked as a lifeguard in 1926. He was 19 years old when this photo was taken. His son James Stevenson was a Panama City Beach lifeguard in the late 1960s and early 1970s and is featured on the cover of this book. (Courtesy James Stevenson.)

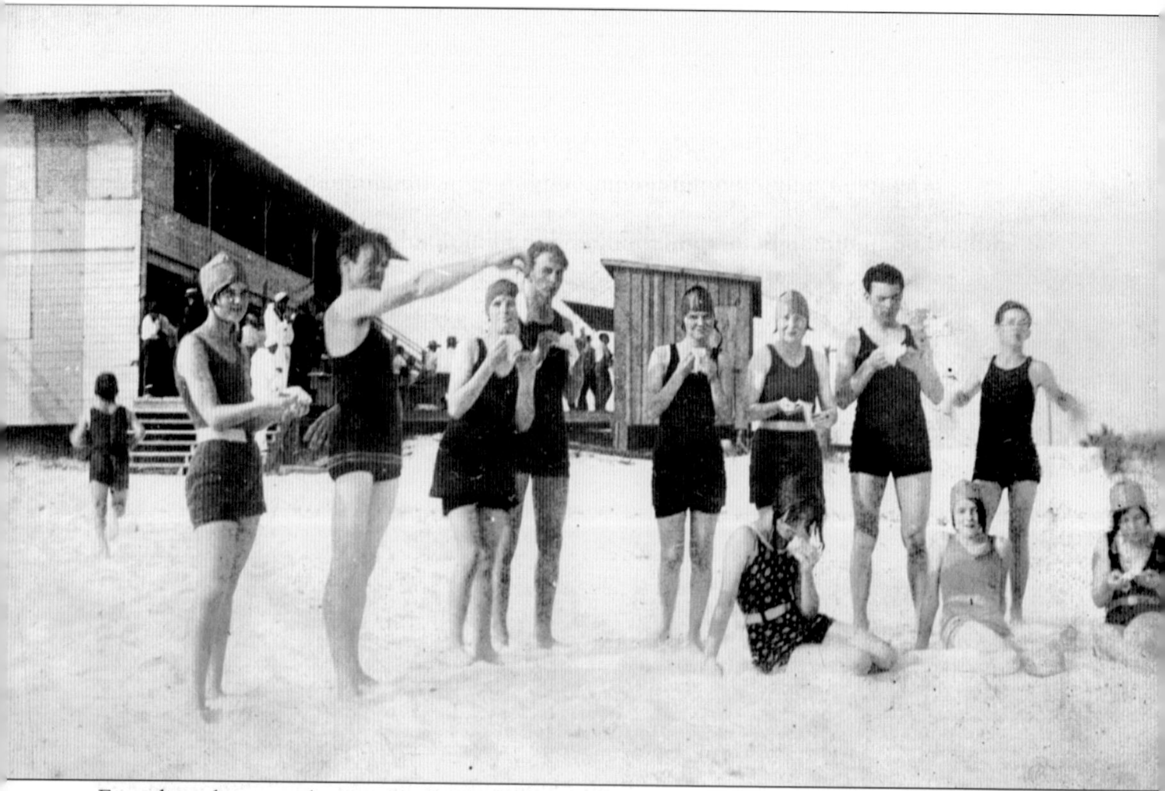

Friends gather together on Shell Island for good times at the Pavilion, one of the first tourist attractions along the beach. Pictured here are, from left to right, Margorie Douglas, Francis Orr, Florrie Williams, Curtis McCall, Janie Hutton, Helen Ellis, and David Davidson. The others are unidentified. (Courtesy Florida State Archives.)

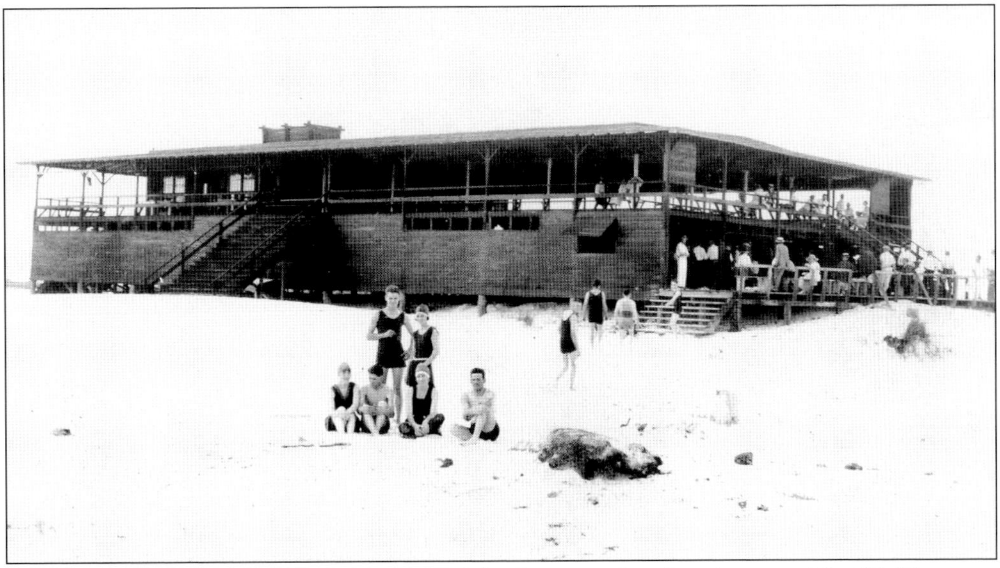

One of the first to realize the potential of the Panama City beaches was Mr. W. Sherman, who built the Pavilion at what was then known as Lands End, near the St. Andrew's Bay Pass. In 1926, Walter Sharpless purchased the Pavilion and had it moved via ox cart to his property at Long Beach. Renamed the Long Beach Pavilion, it became a popular attraction for day-trippers who visited the area by boat. The upper level featured a dance hall, while the beach level was reserved for concession stands, dressing rooms, and bathing suit rentals. (Courtesy Bay County Library.)

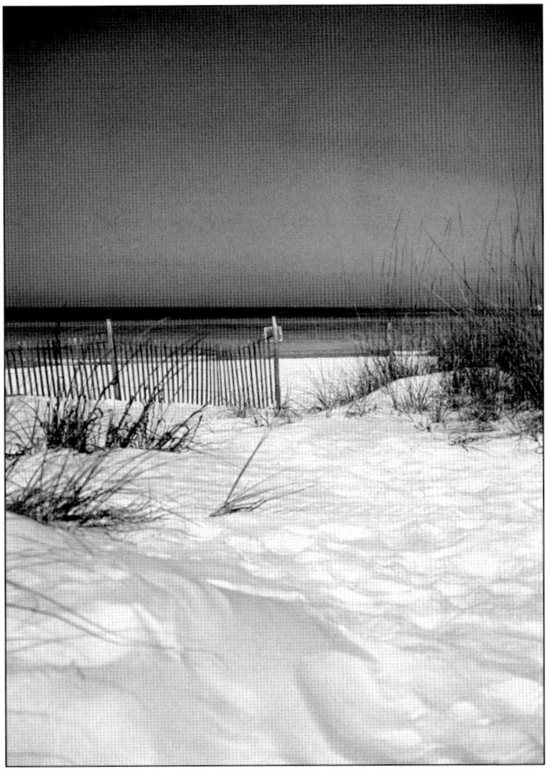

Shell Island is pictured as it appears today, with its pristine, white-sand beaches and crystal-clear water. The area is now an aquatic preserve, in association with St. Andrew's State Park. (Courtesy Panama City Beach Convention and Visitors Bureau.)

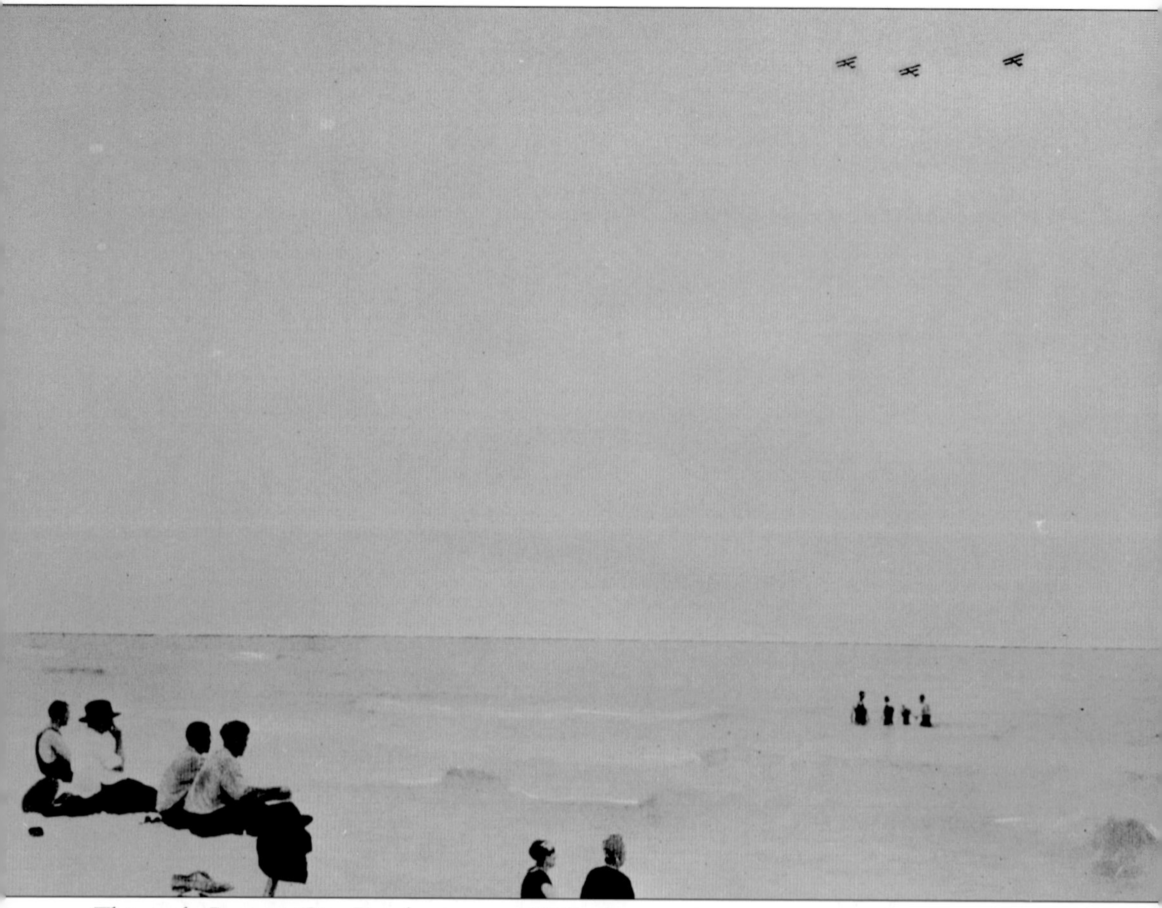

This early Panama City Beach scene, *c.* 1912, shows swimmers enjoying the warm waters of the Gulf of Mexico. Note the Victorian-era bathing costumes of the women seated in the foreground. (Courtesy Florida State Archives.)

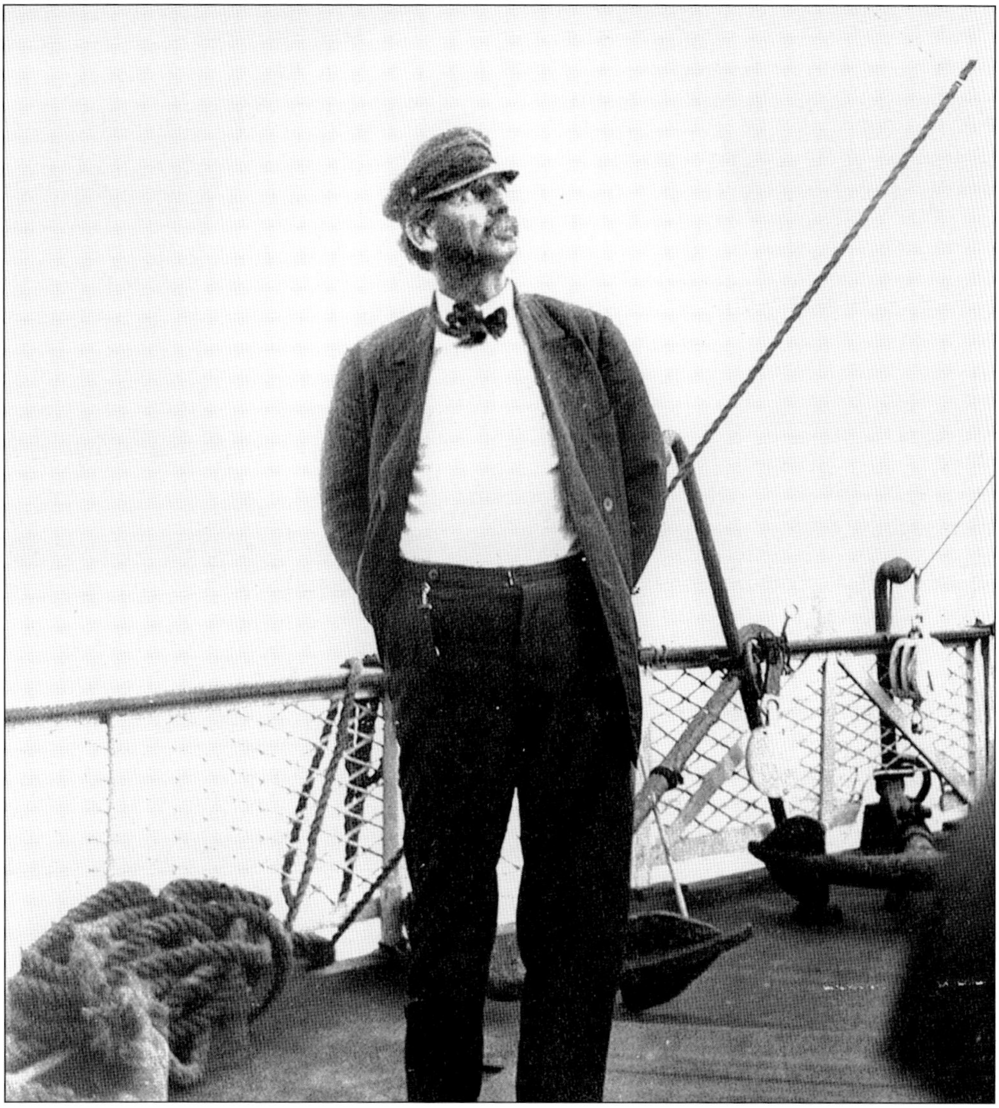

Capt. Willis Barrow navigated the USS *Tarpon* along the Gulf Coast from 1903 to 1937. Ever mindful of the *Tarpon*'s reputation for reliability, even in the harshest of weather, Captain Barrow was known to boast that "God makes the weather and I make the trip." (Courtesy Bay County Library.)

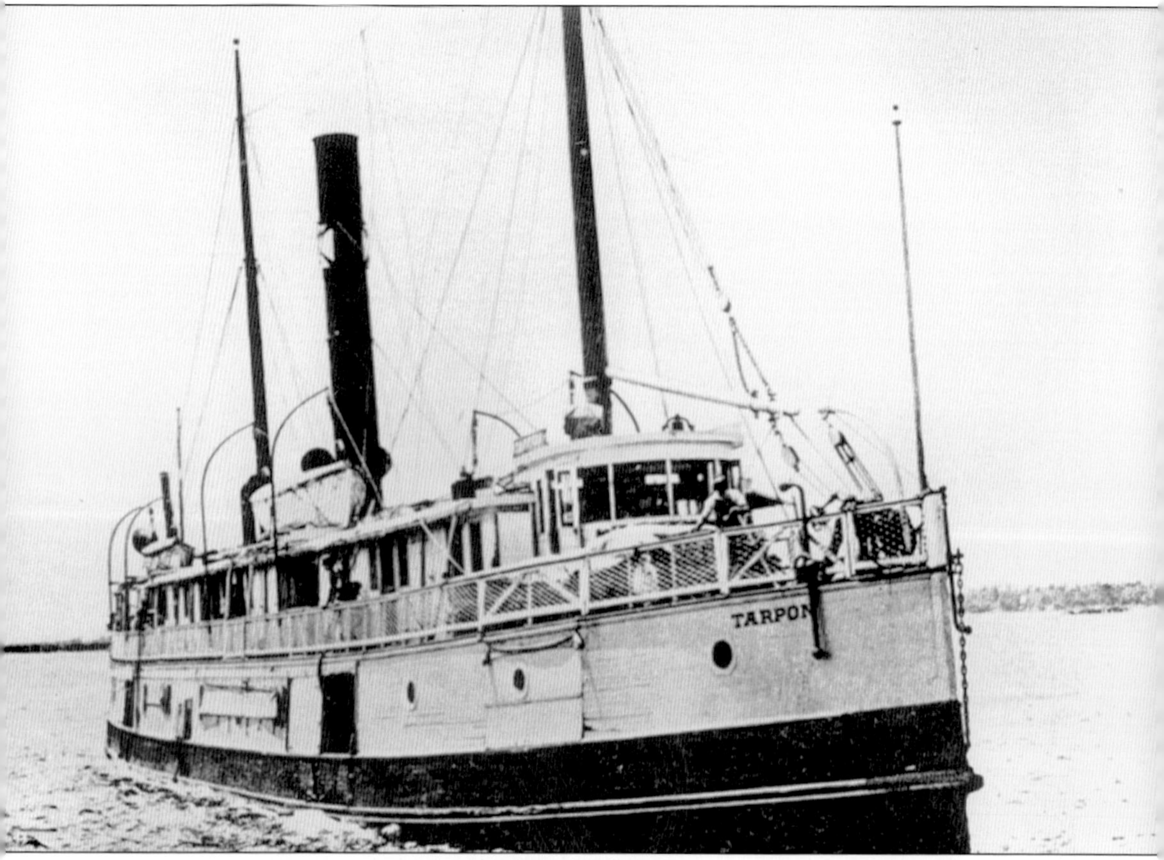

Constructed in 1887, the *Tarpon* sank in September 1937, just weeks before her 50th birthday. Purchased in 1902 by the Pensacola, St. Andrews, and Gulf Steamship Company and captained by Willis Barrow, the steamer serviced Mobile, Pensacola, Panama City, St. Andrews Bay, Apalachicola, and Carrabelle. With few paved roads or bridges, trade between the gulf's coastal communities was dependent on water-bound travel. Here, the USS *Tarpon* docks at one of her ports of call, enabling passengers to disembark and goods to be delivered. (Courtesy Bay County Library.)

Two

THE "DISCOVERY"

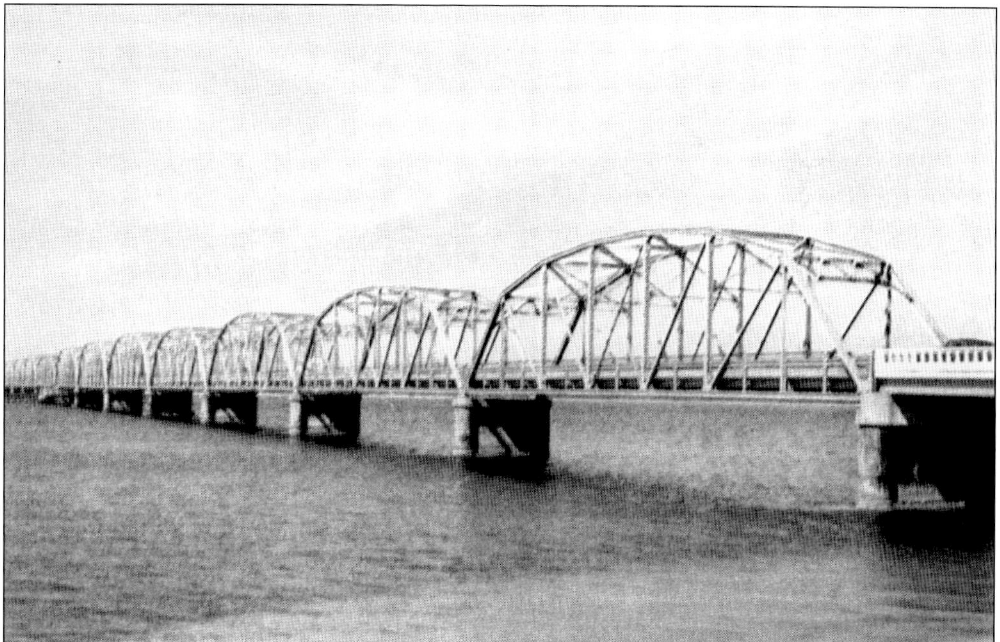

Originally called the St. Andrews Bay Bridge but later renamed for Dr. F. Hathaway, head of the Florida State Roads Department, the Hathaway Bridge opened for business in 1929. The new bridge connected Panama City with the beaches and paved the way for development of the beach area. (Courtesy Bay County Library.)

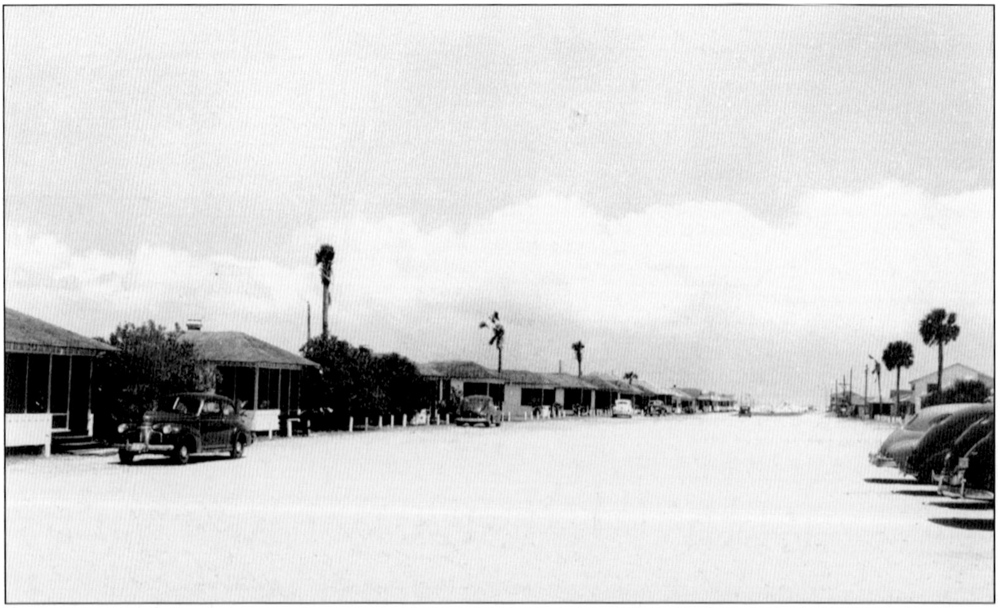

J.E. Churchwell purchased the Pavilion in 1932, renamed it Long Beach Resort, and erected several rental cottages nearby, along with an artesian well for drinking water. Churchwell would later expand Long Beach Resort to include the Hang Out, a dancehall; a skating rink; and Petticoat Junction, an amusement park. (Courtesy Bay County Library.)

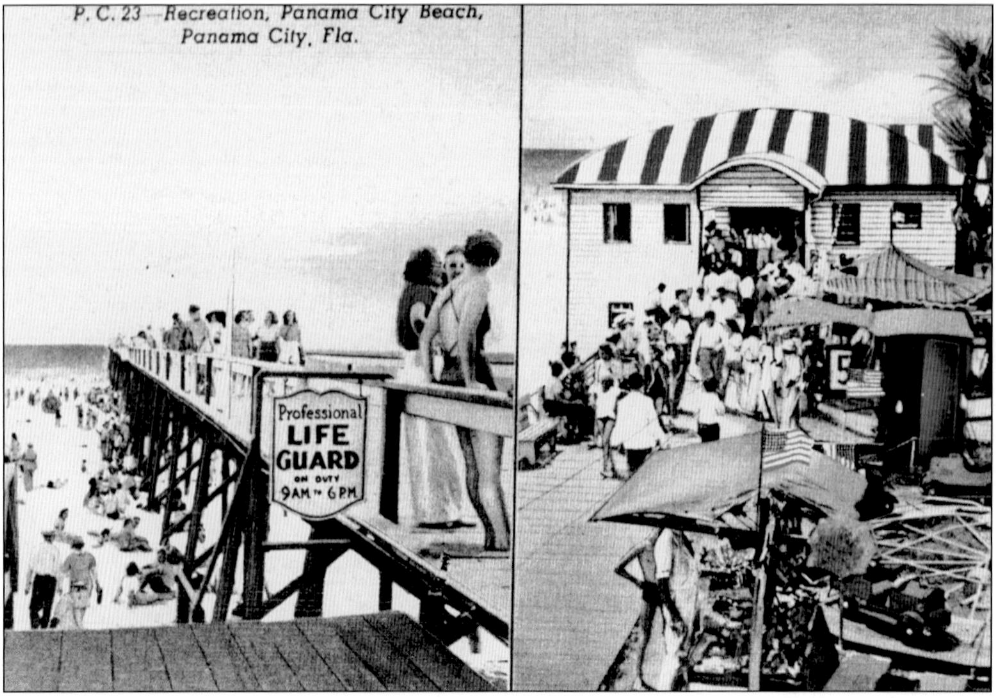

This postcard shows the Casino (on right), which became part of the Long Beach Resort when it was moved from what is now known as Shell Island. The Pier (on left) enabled tourists to walk out over the sand and water without getting their feet wet. (Courtesy Bay County Library.)

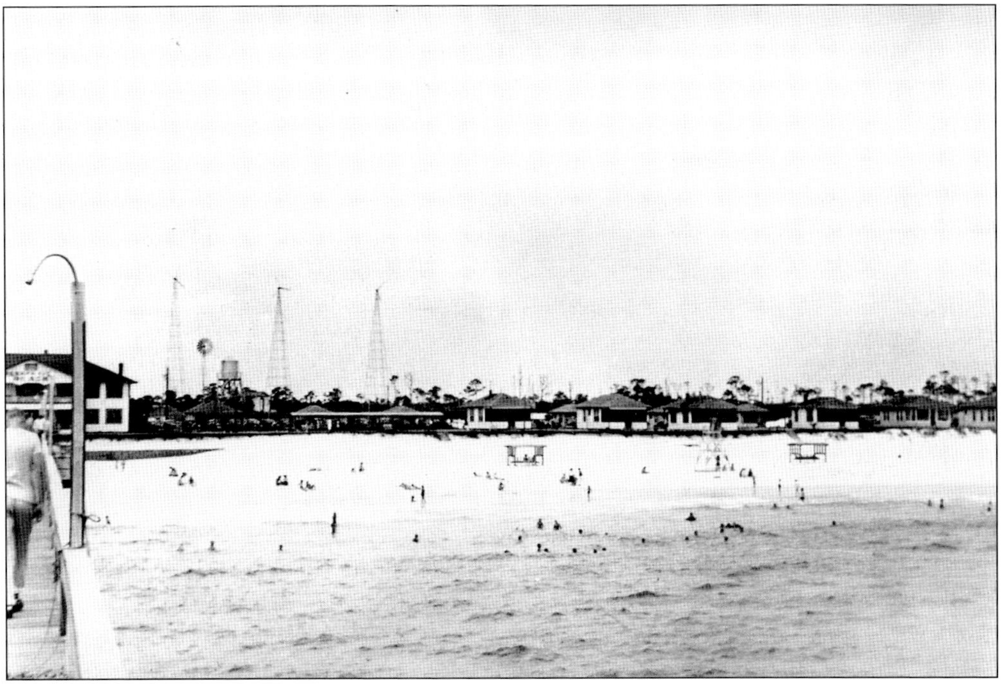

An aerial view of Panama City Beach in the 1960s shows nary a high-rise along the beach. Note the Long Beach Resort water tower in background. (Courtesy Dick Doerr.)

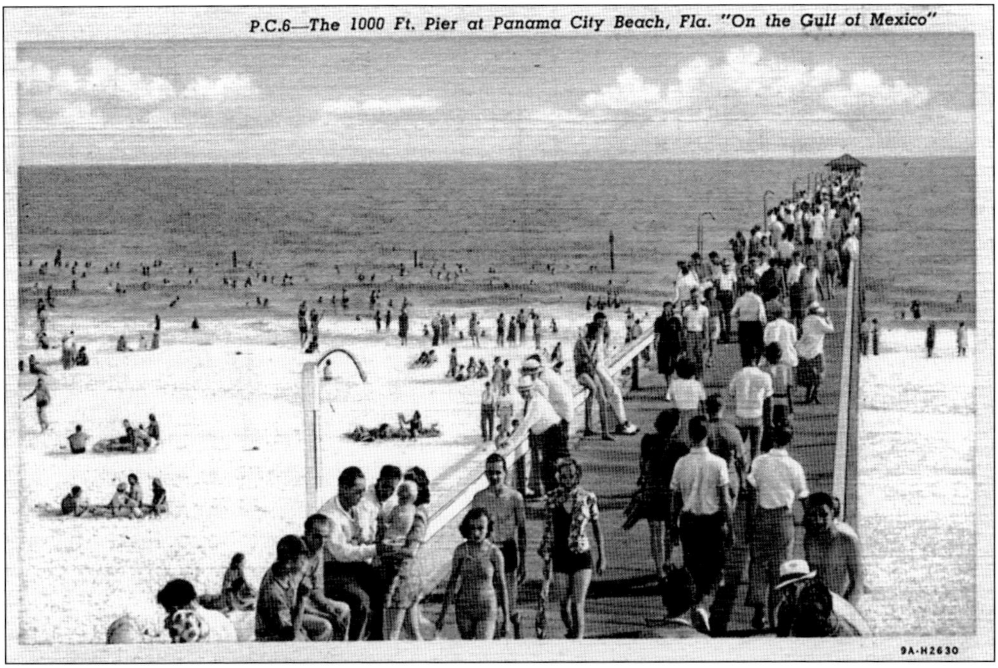

Sent to a daughter in New Jersey, this postcard features an artistic rendering of the "1000 Ft. Pier" at Panama City Beach as it looked in 1951. Inscription reads, "It looks good but is too cold for this on front . . . Love, Mother and Dad."

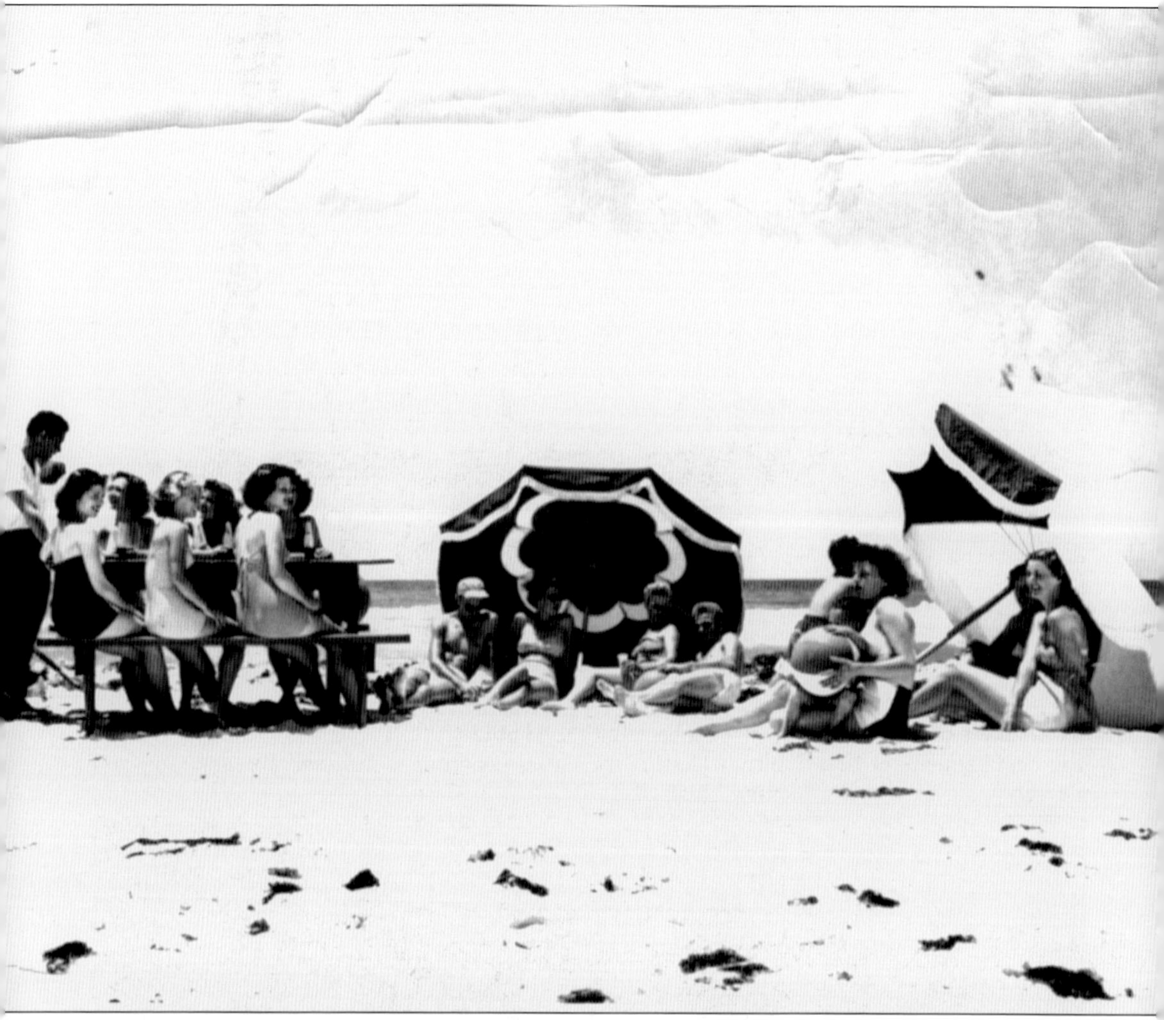

This photo, taken for the U.S. Army by Sgt. L.V. Pelham, shows a happy group enjoying the beach on a summer's day. It may have been used as part of a public-relations promotion for the army. (Courtesy Bay County Library.)

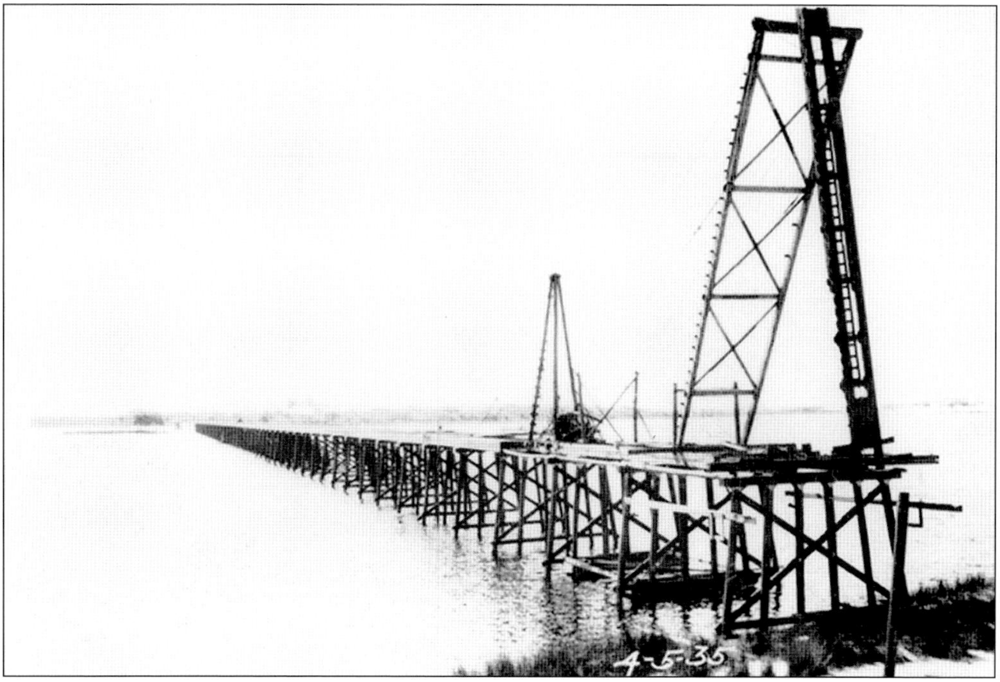

Completed in 1935, the Powell Lake Bridge (also known as the Philips Inlet Bridge) was built to the west of the Panama City beaches on U.S. Highway 98. Its construction helped boost the development of Fort Walton, Destin, and other beach areas between Panama City and Pensacola. (Courtesy Bay County Library.)

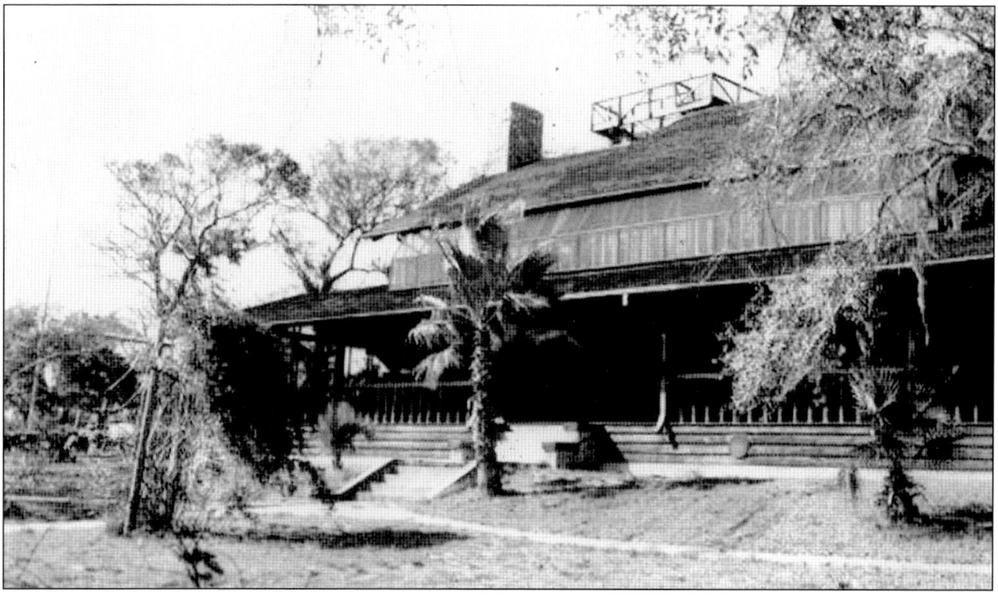

Once owned and operated by the Avondale Mills of Alabama for use by its vacationing employees, Camp Helen is now a Florida State Park. The Lodge at Camp Helen and surrounding cottages have been preserved, offering visitors a glimpse of vacation life in the 1940s. Camp Helen has over 183.5 acres devoted to fishing, camping, boating, and hiking. Karl Holland took this photograph in November 1956. (Courtesy Bay County Library.)

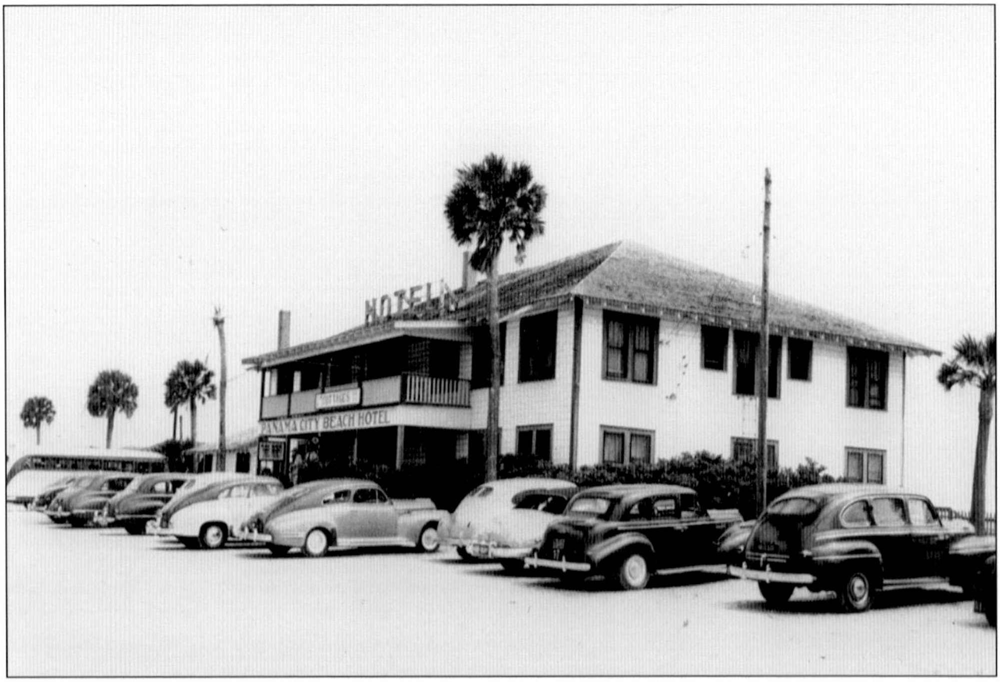

In 1932, Gideon Thomas, along with his daughter and son-in-law, purchased 104 acres next to Long Beach Resort. The original Panama City Beach property consisted of cottages, a two-story hotel, a windmill, and the famous 1,000-foot pier. (Courtesy Bay County Library.)

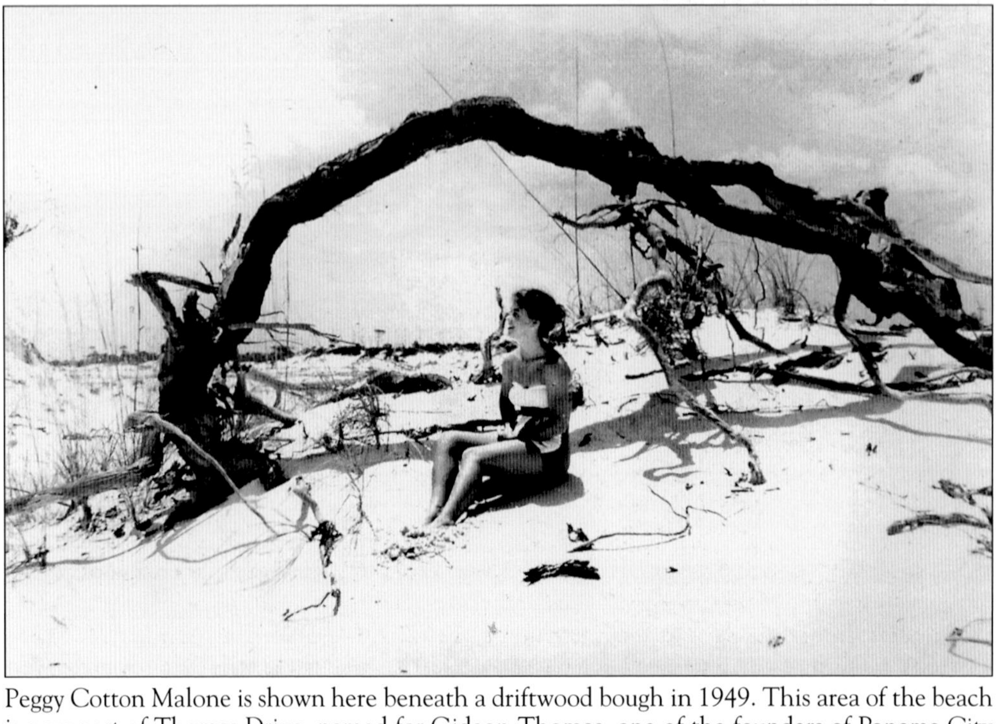

Peggy Cotton Malone is shown here beneath a driftwood bough in 1949. This area of the beach is now part of Thomas Drive, named for Gideon Thomas, one of the founders of Panama City Beach. Mrs. Malone is employed by Bay County Library. (Courtesy Bay County Library.)

Three

LONG BEACH RESORT

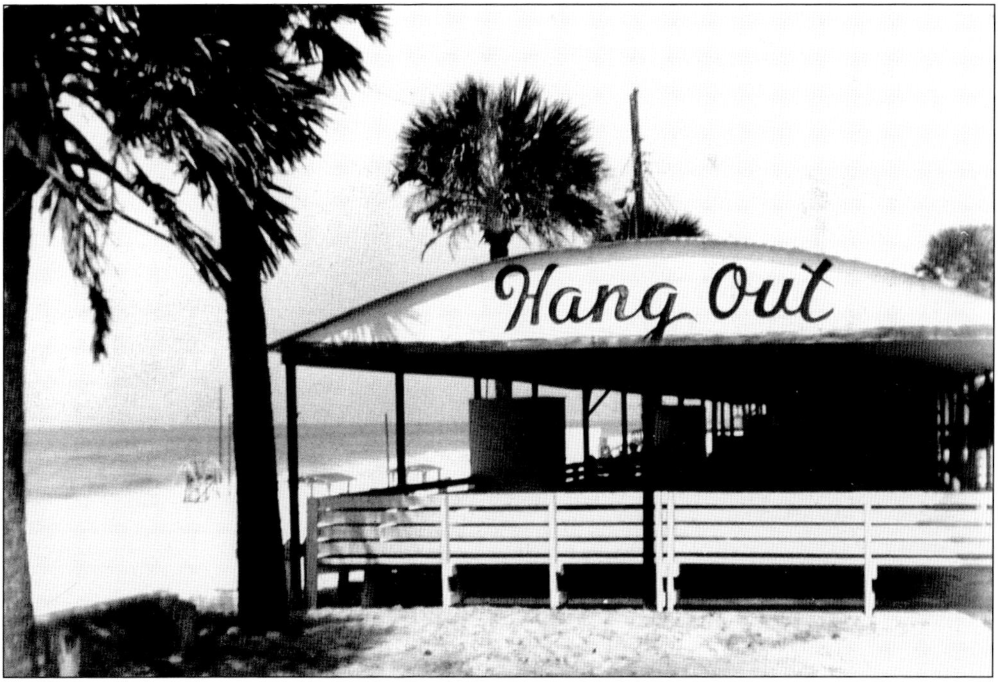

Originally built by J.E. Churchwell as a dance pavilion for young and old alike, the Hang Out was quickly adopted by the teenage set as "their" place at Long Beach Resort. Many a summer romance had its start at the Hang Out as dancers bopped, twisted, swayed, and rocked to the popular tunes of the 1950s and 1960s. (Courtesy Bay County High School, Class of 1953.)

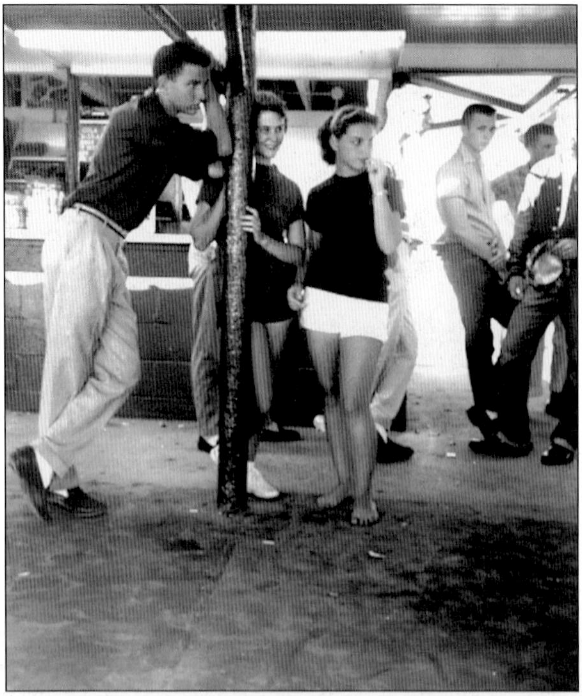

The Hang Out at Long Beach Resort was a favorite spot for teenagers to meet, dance, and listen to music. From left to right are unidentified, Susan Jones, Donna Hazen, Charles Pumphrey, and Donald Pumphrey. Jimmie Jones took the photo in the late 1950s. (Donated to Bay County Library by Susan Moore and Nelson Jones.)

Dancing to the beat of beach music, these young people may well have been perfecting the steps of the "PC," a dance that originated in Panama City Beach. Another popular dance, the "Shag," had its origins in Myrtle Beach, South Carolina, but quickly made its way to the Panhandle. (Courtesy Bay County Library.)

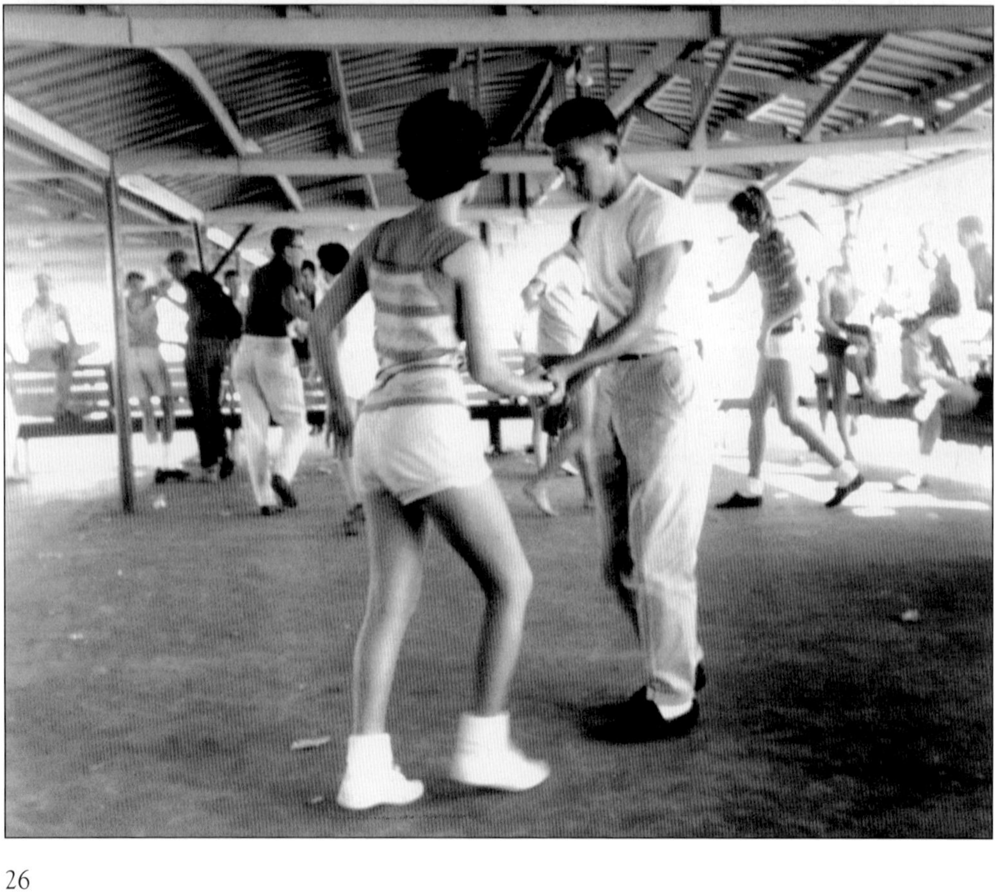

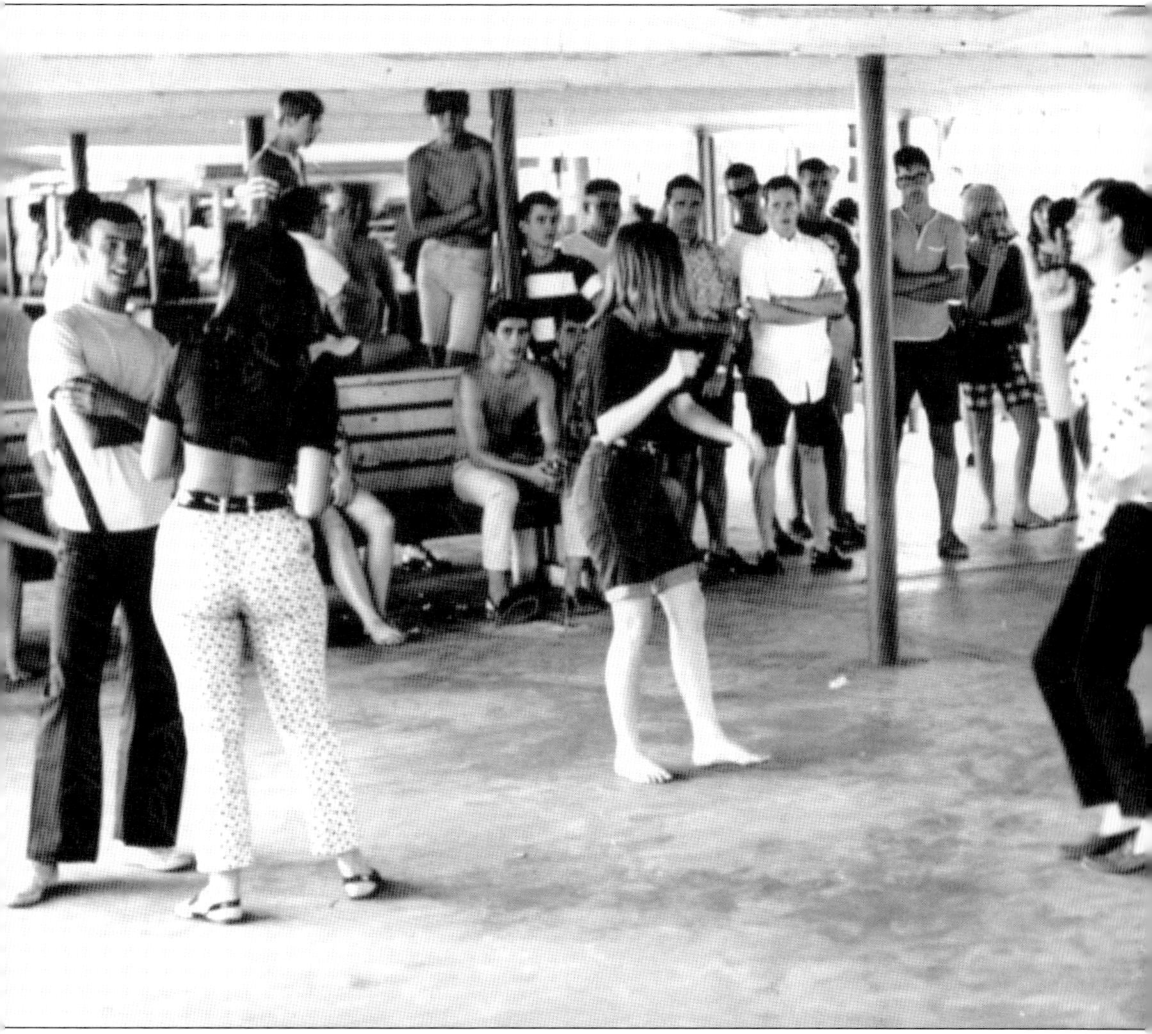

Dancers take to the floor at Long Beach Resort. Many a vacationing teen whiled away the summer dancing and listening to music at the Hang Out. Bob Hargis took this photo in 1958. (Courtesy Bay County Library.)

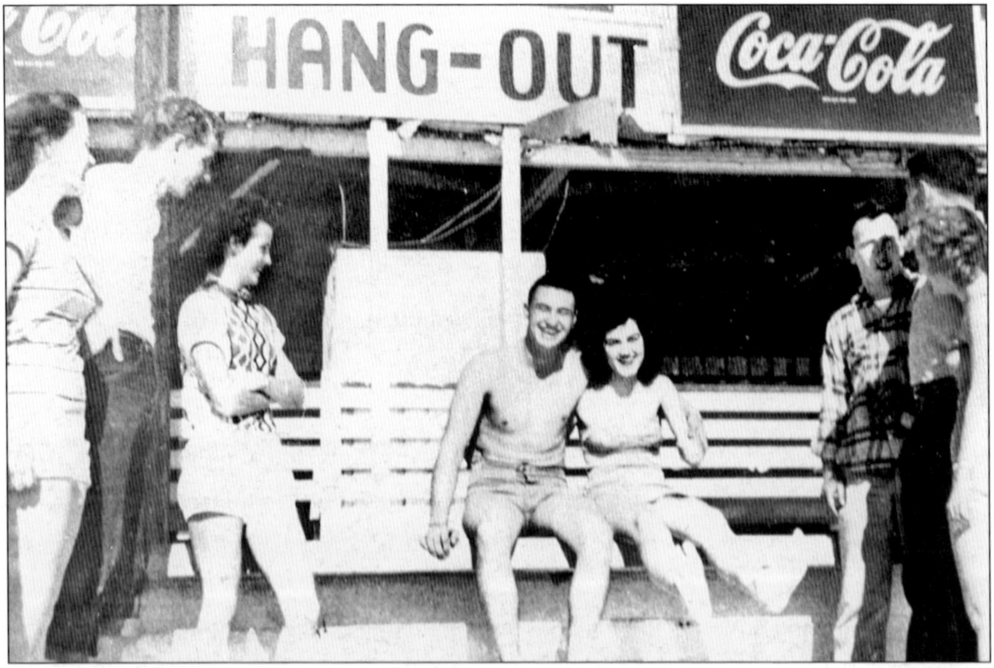

Friends reveling in a day spent together at Long Beach Resort's "Hang Out" are, from left to right, unidentified, Tommy Doss, Betty Chancey, Glen Bush, Gwen Anderson, Hulon Mitchell, and two unidentified, *c.* 1960. (Courtesy Bay County Library.)

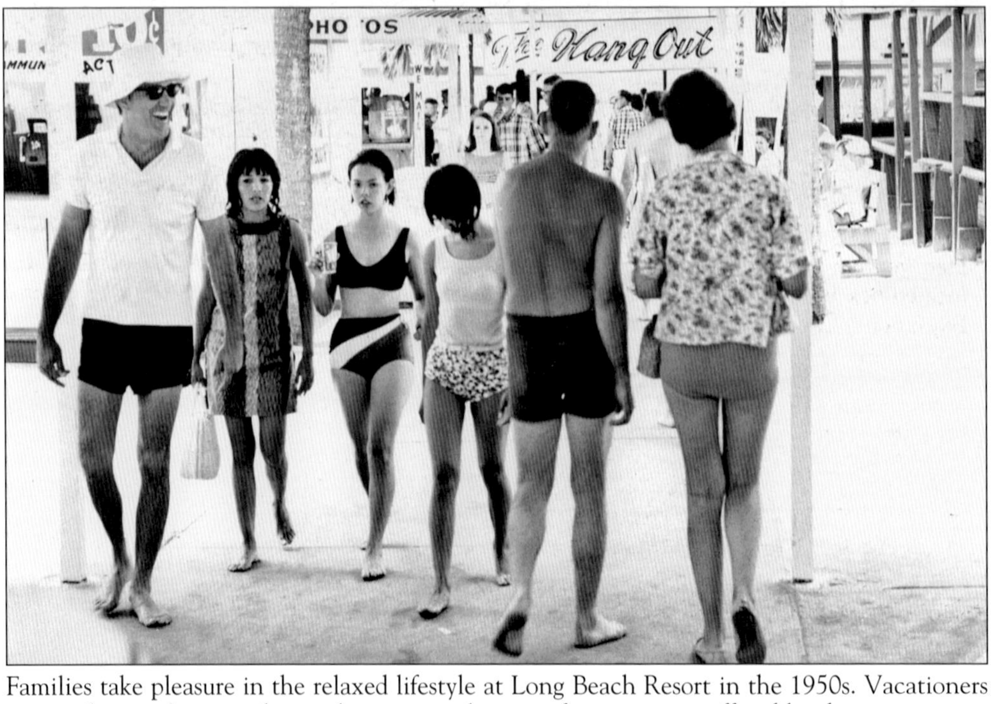

Families take pleasure in the relaxed lifestyle at Long Beach Resort in the 1950s. Vacationers returned year after year due to the scope and range of amusements offered by the resort; every member of the family could find some kind of fun for his or her enjoyment. (Courtesy Bay County Library.)

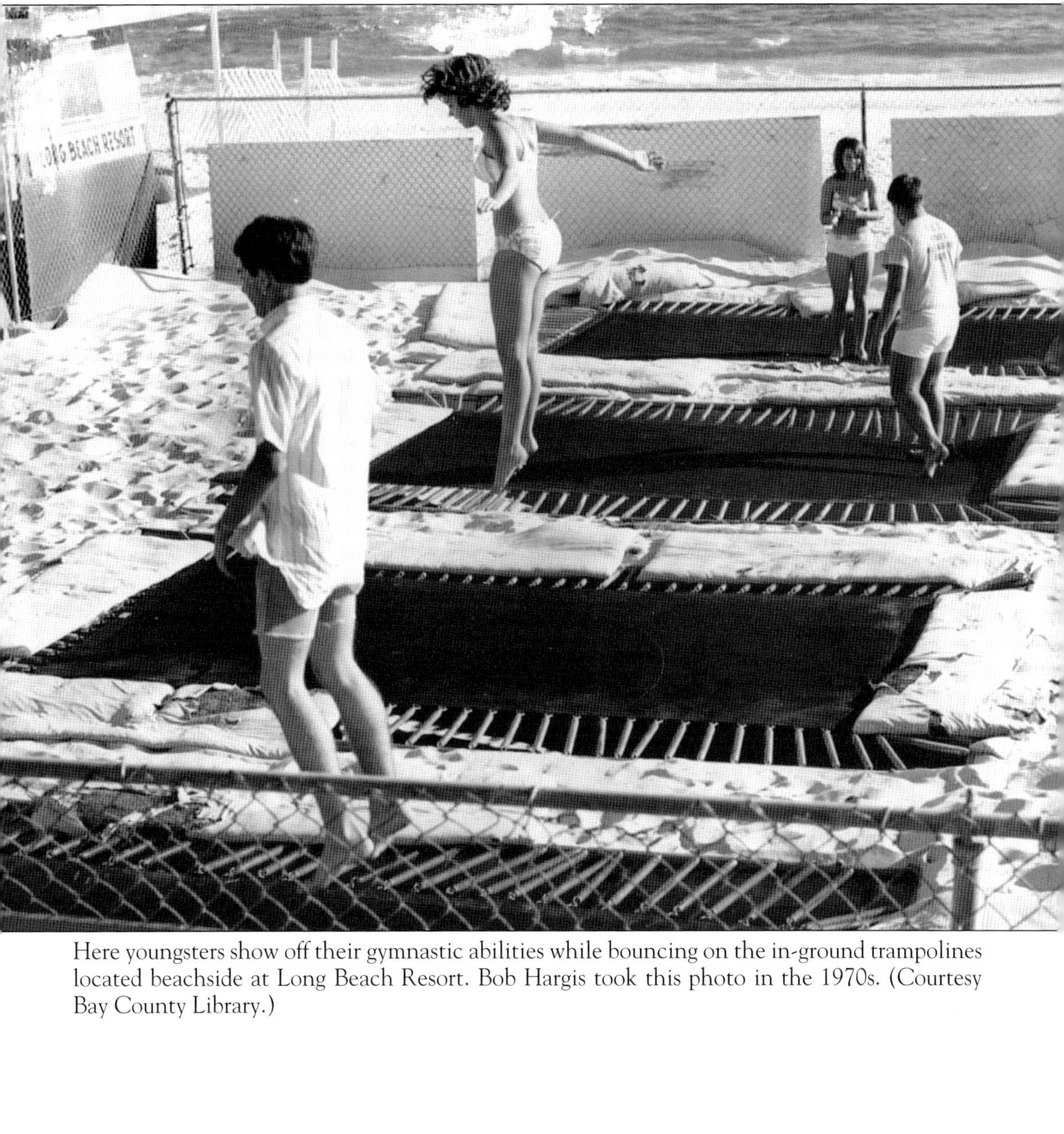

Here youngsters show off their gymnastic abilities while bouncing on the in-ground trampolines located beachside at Long Beach Resort. Bob Hargis took this photo in the 1970s. (Courtesy Bay County Library.)

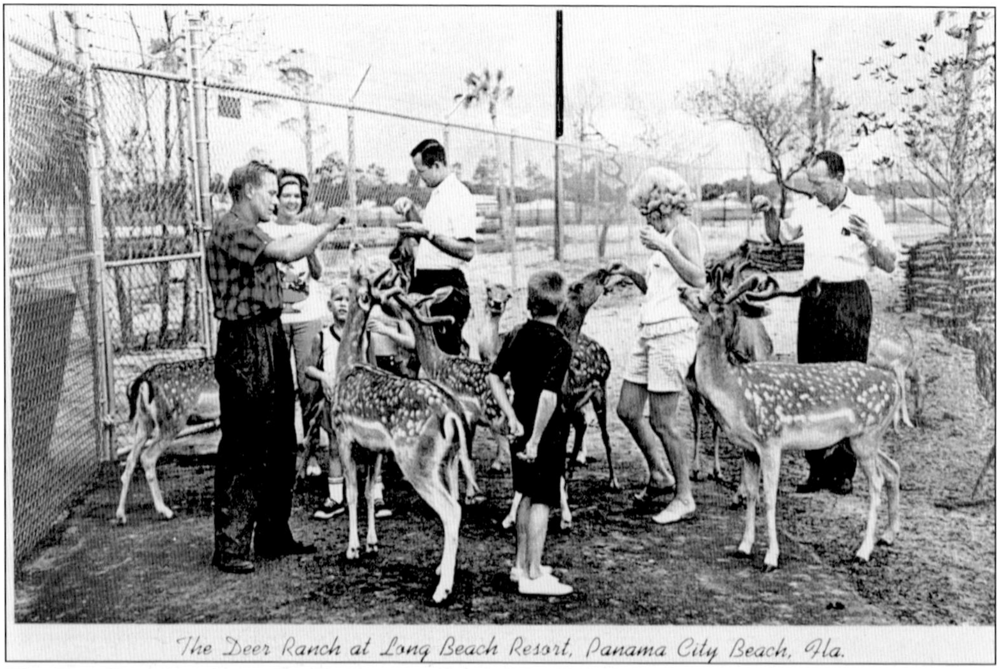

The Deer Ranch at Long Beach Resort provided fun-filled entertainment for the whole family and a nice change of pace from the daily routine of swimming and sunbathing. This postcard dates from July 1964. (Courtesy Bay County Library.)

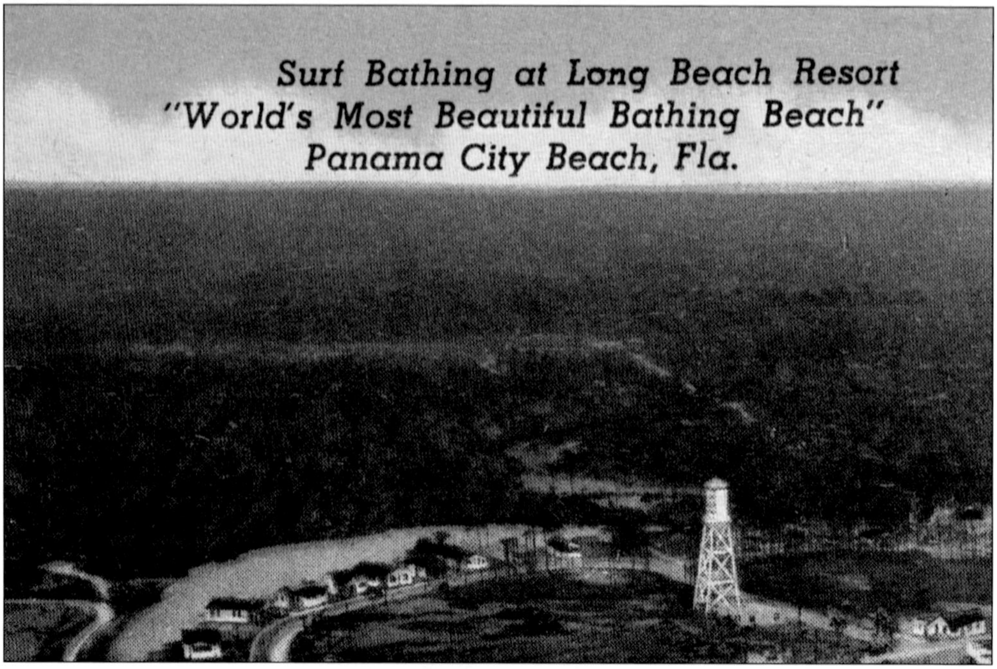

A postcard from the private collection of noted author and history buff J.D. Weeks offers a perspective on the magnitude of the Long Beach Resort's holdings during its heyday as a vacation destination. (Courtesy J.D. Weeks.)

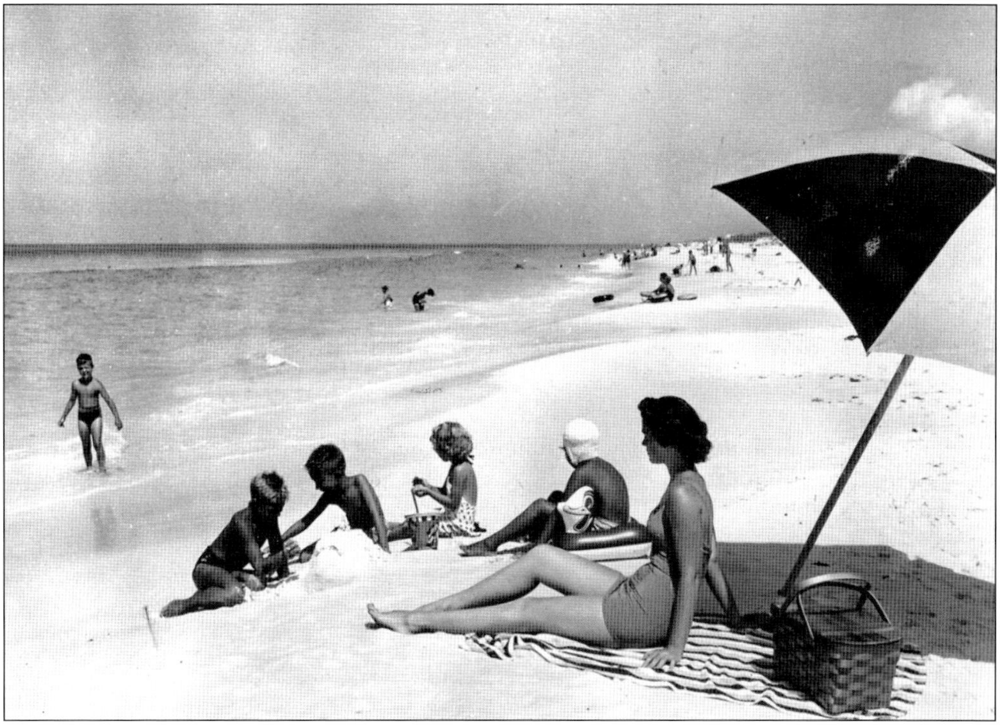

Children enjoy the warm, emerald-green waters of the Gulf of Mexico as their mother looks on. This scene was photographed at Long Beach Resort in the 1950s. (Courtesy Bay County Library.)

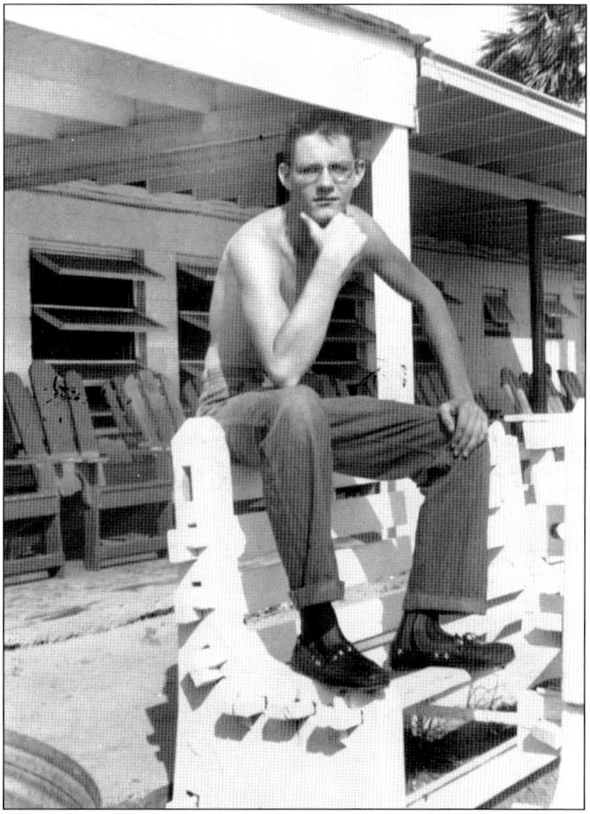

J.D. Weeks was staying at the Bessemer Cottages just east of Long Beach Resort when this photo was taken in the 1950s. He is pictured here sitting in front of the cottages. (Courtesy J.D. Weeks.)

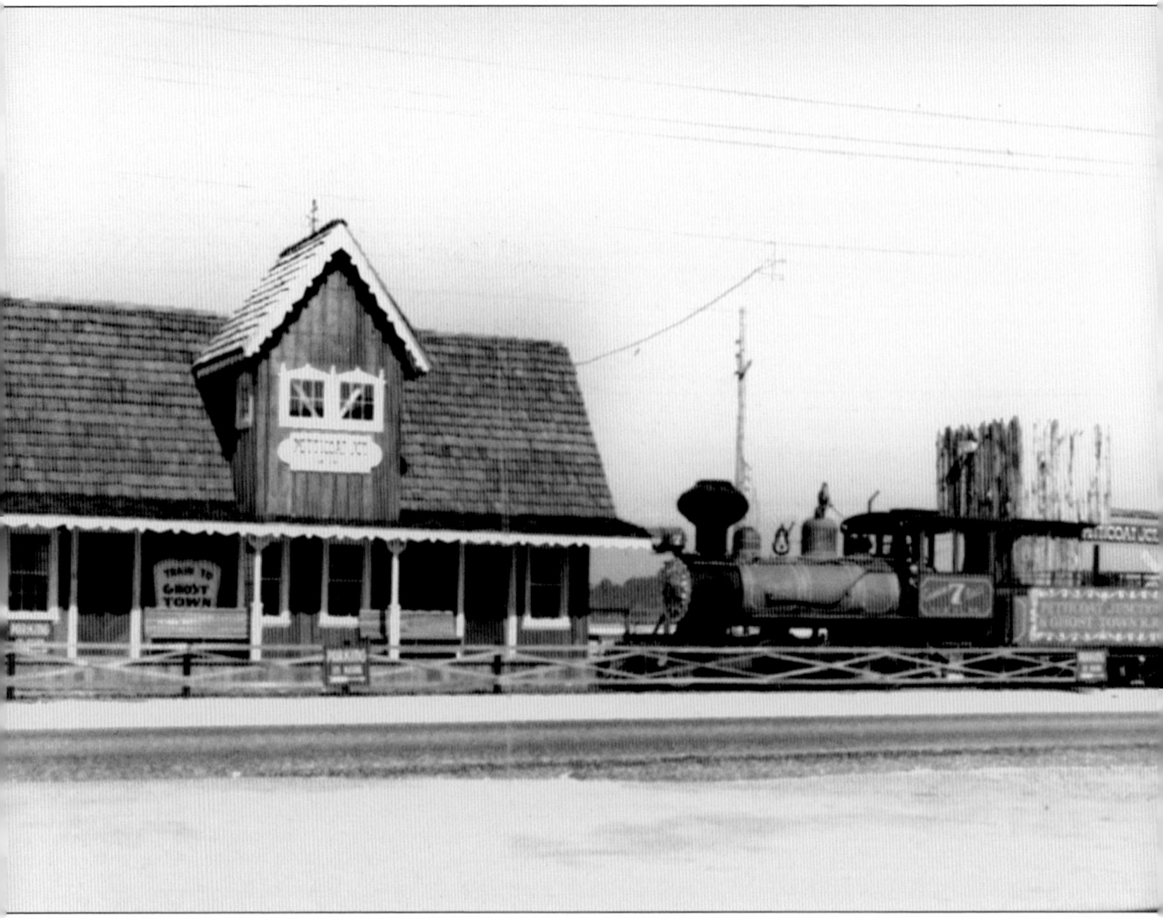

Named after a popular TV show, Petticoat Junction featured steam engines, a rollercoaster called the Tornado, a flume, a ghost town, an arcade, and a merry-go-round. The Cannonball steam engine is shown in this 1964 photo. (Courtesy Bay County Library.)

Gloria Southall and Leatrice Jackson from Hueytown, Alabama, are seen here in 1947, soaking up some sun in front of Long Beach Resort. (Courtesy Florida State Archives.)

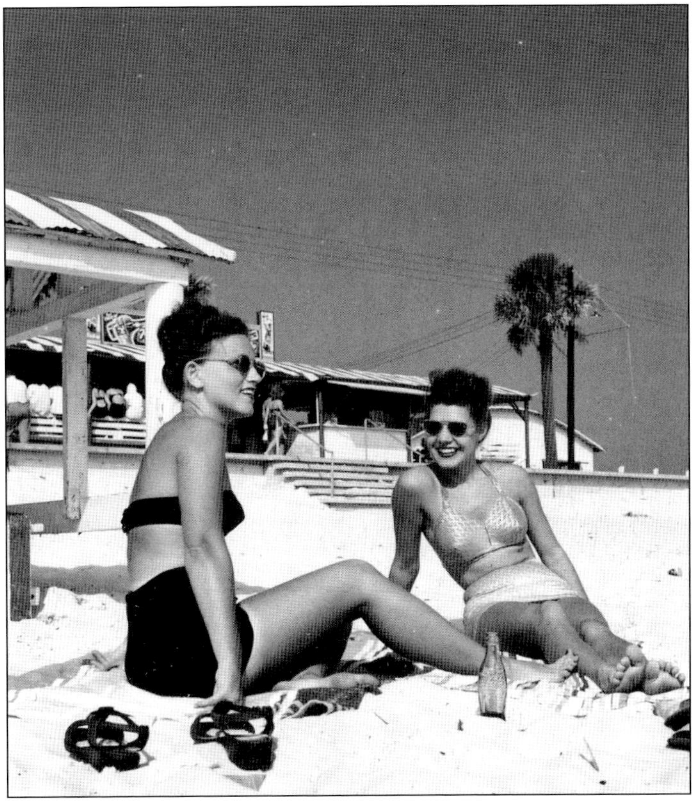

His friends are more interested in his new 1955 Chevrolet, but J.D. Weeks can still get a hug from friend Joann Jackson. The two are pictured here in the 1950s at a Spring Break gathering. J.D.'s sister Bobbie is standing at the left of the car. An avid postcard collector and active grandfather, J.D. and his family still retain strong ties to the Panama City Beach area. (Courtesy J.D. Weeks.)

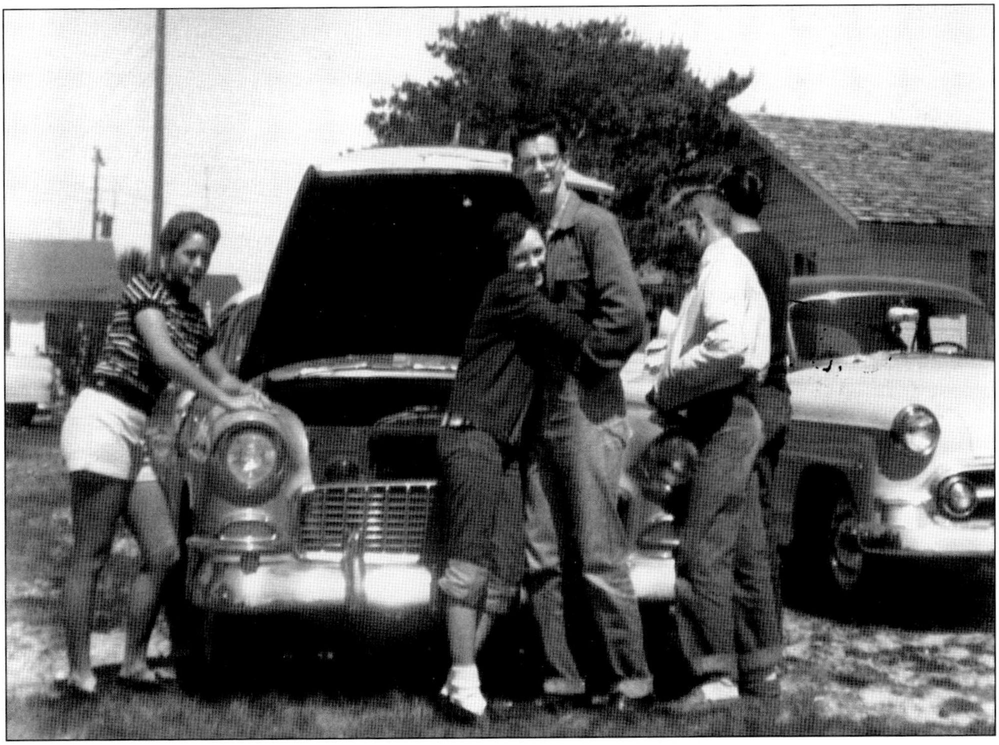

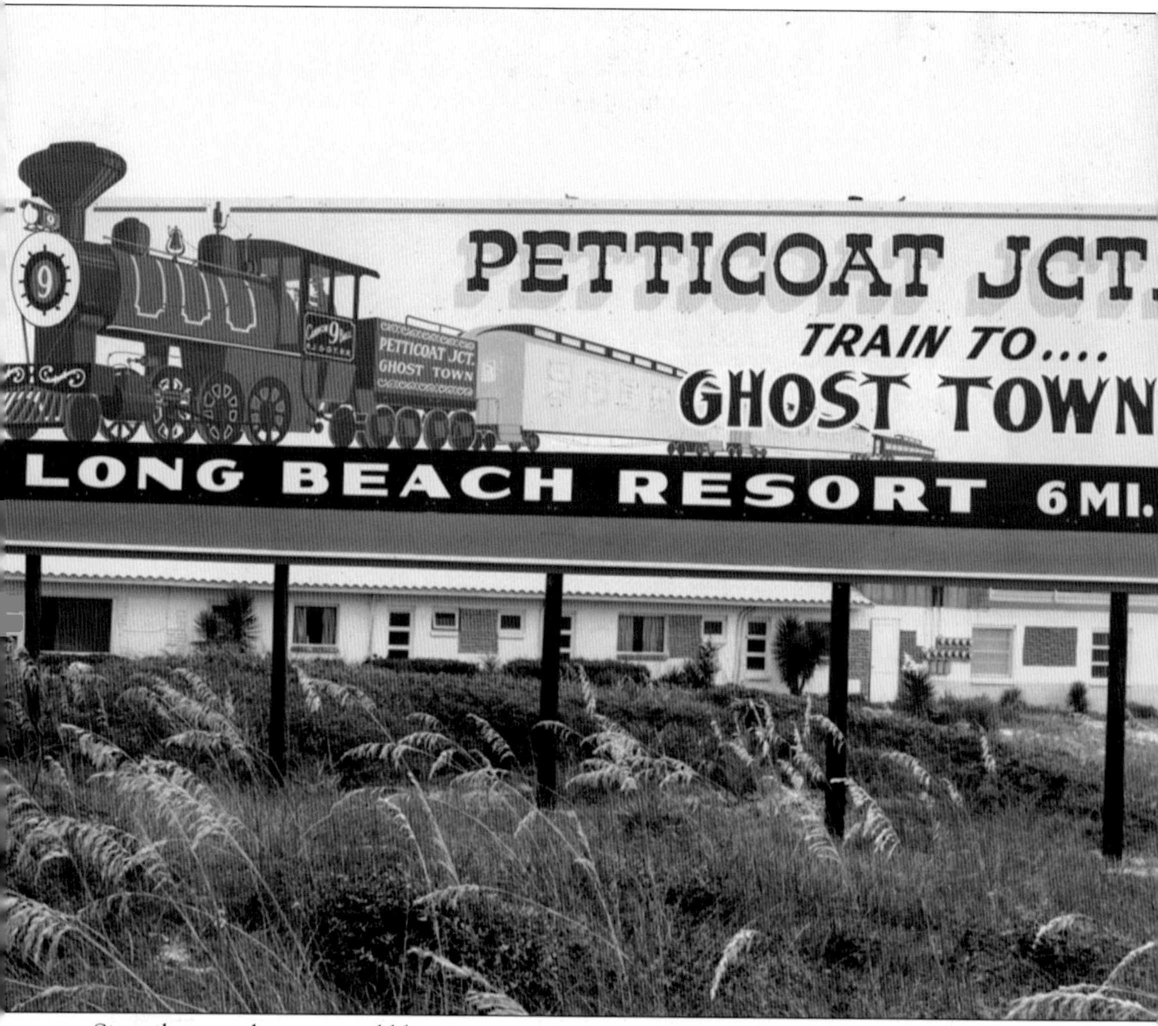

Six miles must have seemed like an eternity to youngsters anxious to ride the train at Petticoat Junction amusement park. Owned and operated by the Churchwell family from 1963 to 1984, the park was sold and its contents auctioned off in 1985. (Courtesy Bay County Library.)

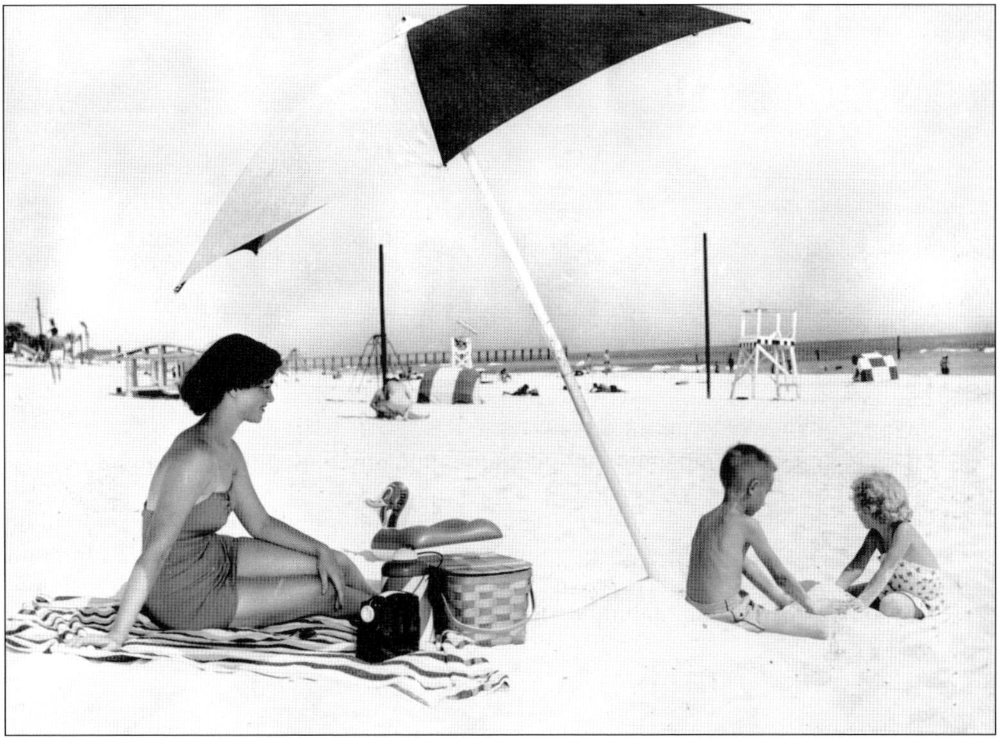

Charles Barron took this 1954 photo of his wife and daughter, Kathleen (with an unidentified friend), on a picnic at Long Beach Resort. (Courtesy Florida State Archives.)

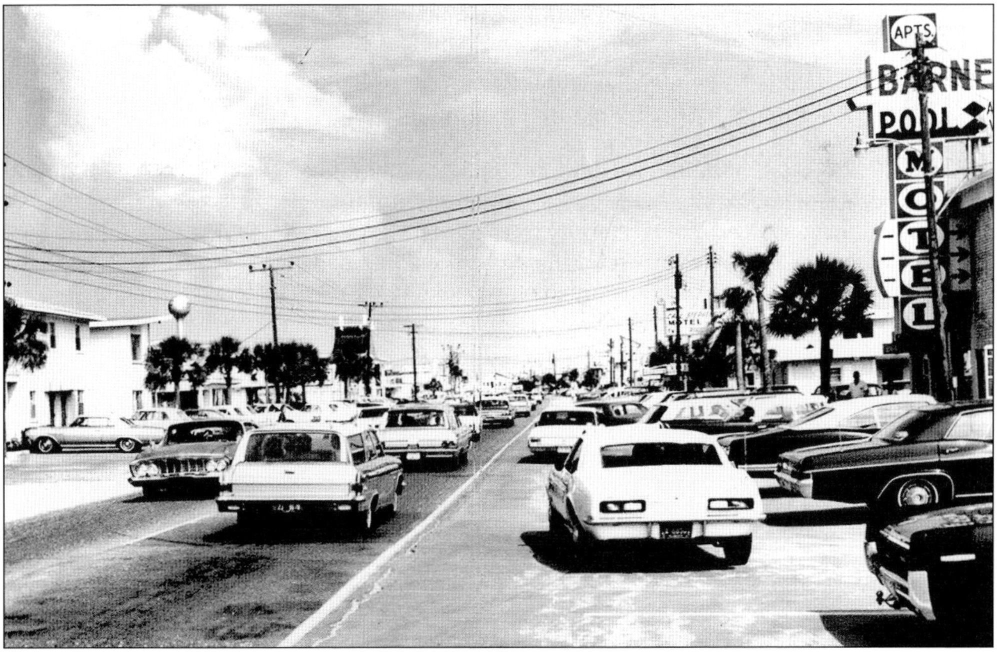

It is a busy time on Front Beach Drive, looking east from Long Beach, as this photograph clearly shows—it looks like Spring Break is underway. Note the station wagons in the "lineup," forerunners of today's pickups and SUVs. (Courtesy Bay County Library.)

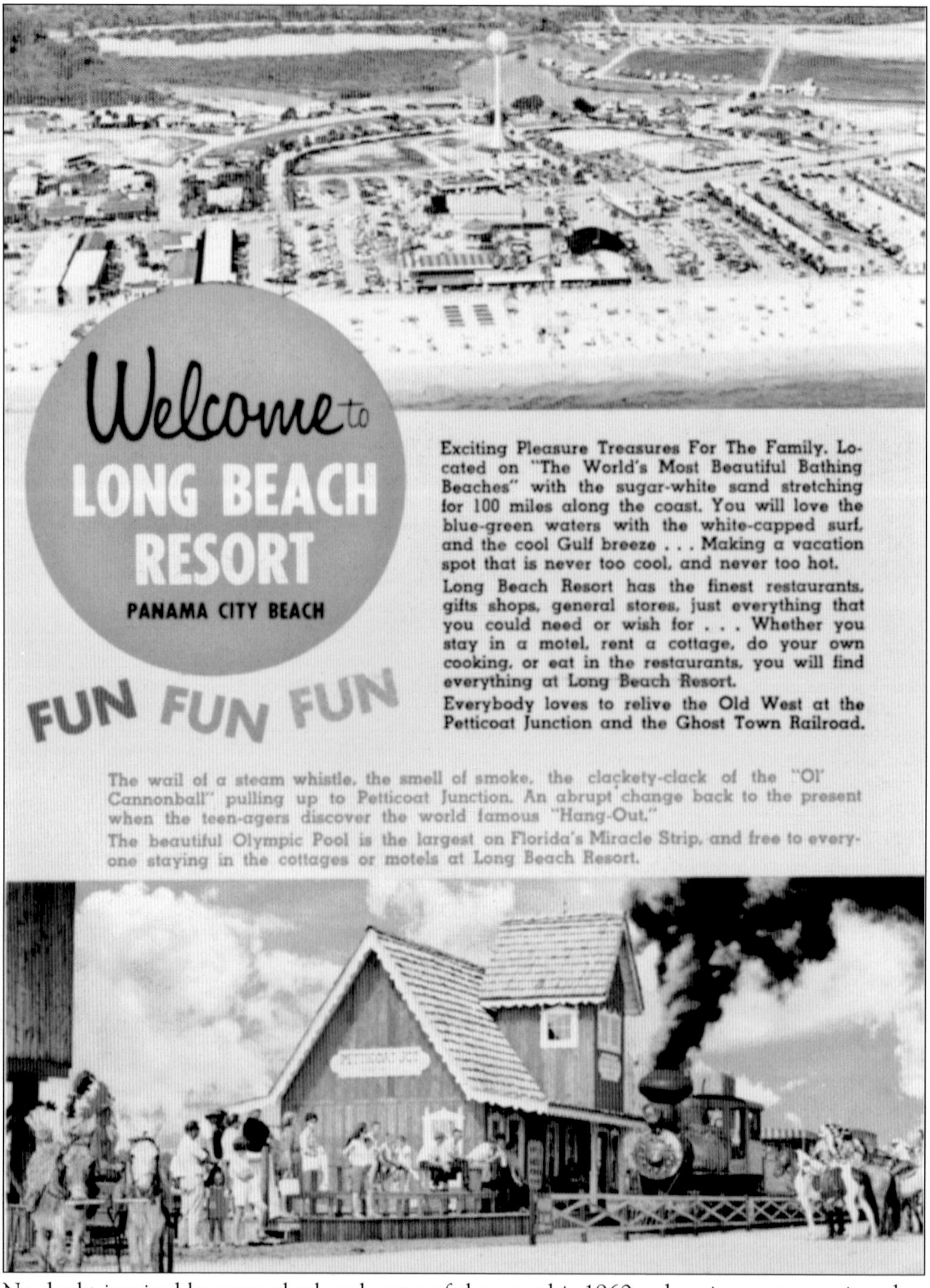

No doubt inspired by a popular beach song of the era, this 1960s advertisement promises that visitors will have "fun, fun, fun" while vacationing at Long Beach Resort.

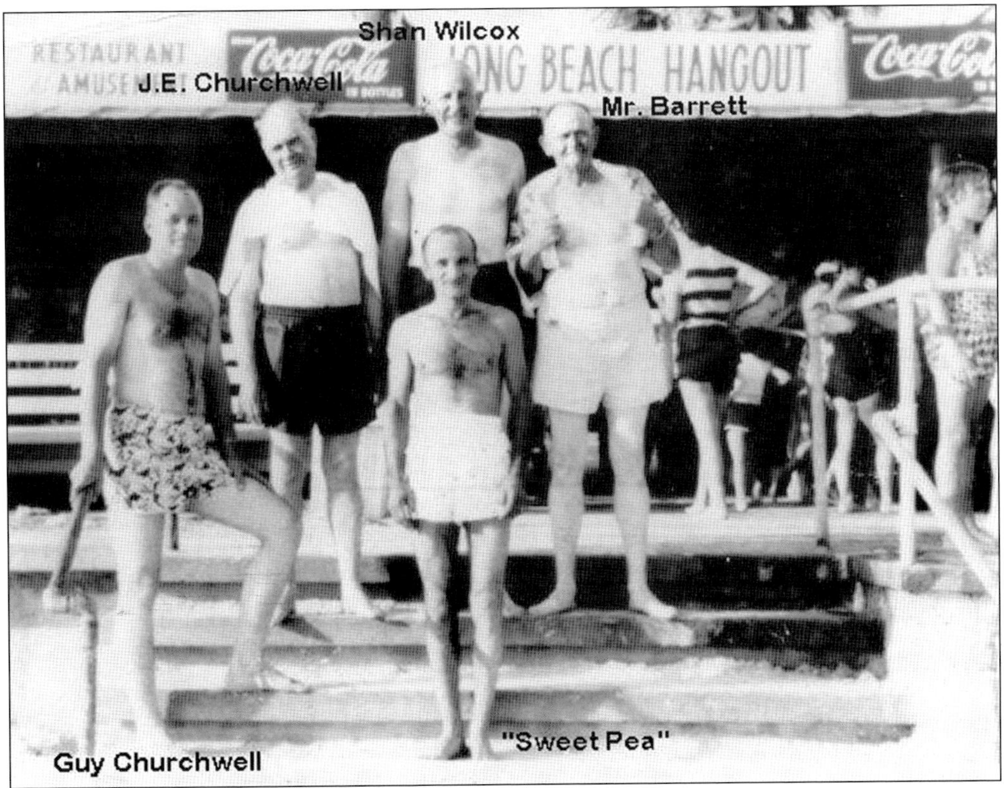

Pictured here in the 1950s are five men who contributed greatly to the success of Long Beach Resort: (from left to right) Guy Churchwell, Long Beach Resort founder; J.E. Churchwell; Shan Wilcox, who leased the amusement concession property from the Churchwells; Mr. Barnett; and "Sweet Pea," who ran the hot dog stand at Long Beach Resort. (Courtesy J.D. Weeks.)

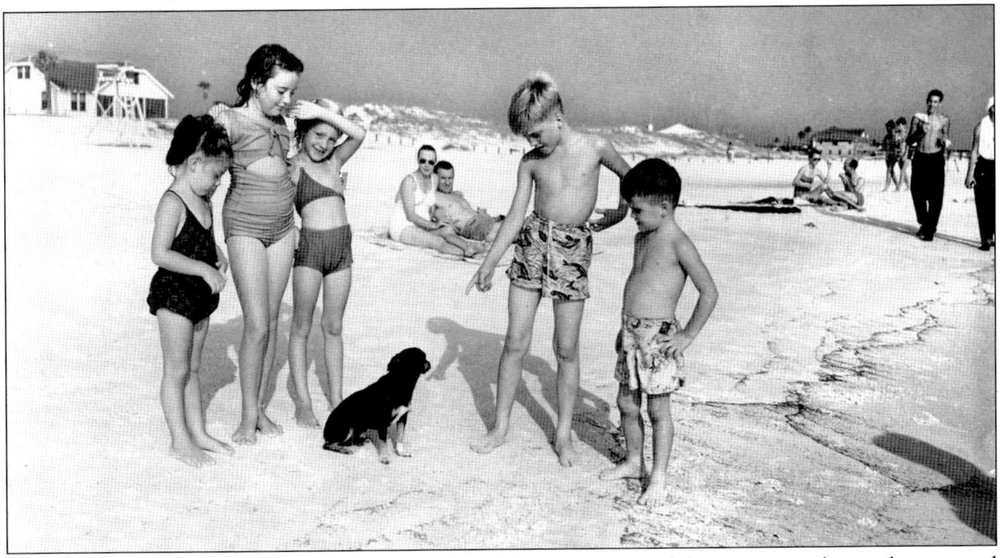

Carol, Jeannette, and Martha Webb from Birmingham, Alabama, are obviously amused by the antics of the Wallach boys (Ross and Michael) and their dog, Butch. This scene was photographed on August 30, 1947, at Long Beach Resort. (Courtesy Florida State Archives.)

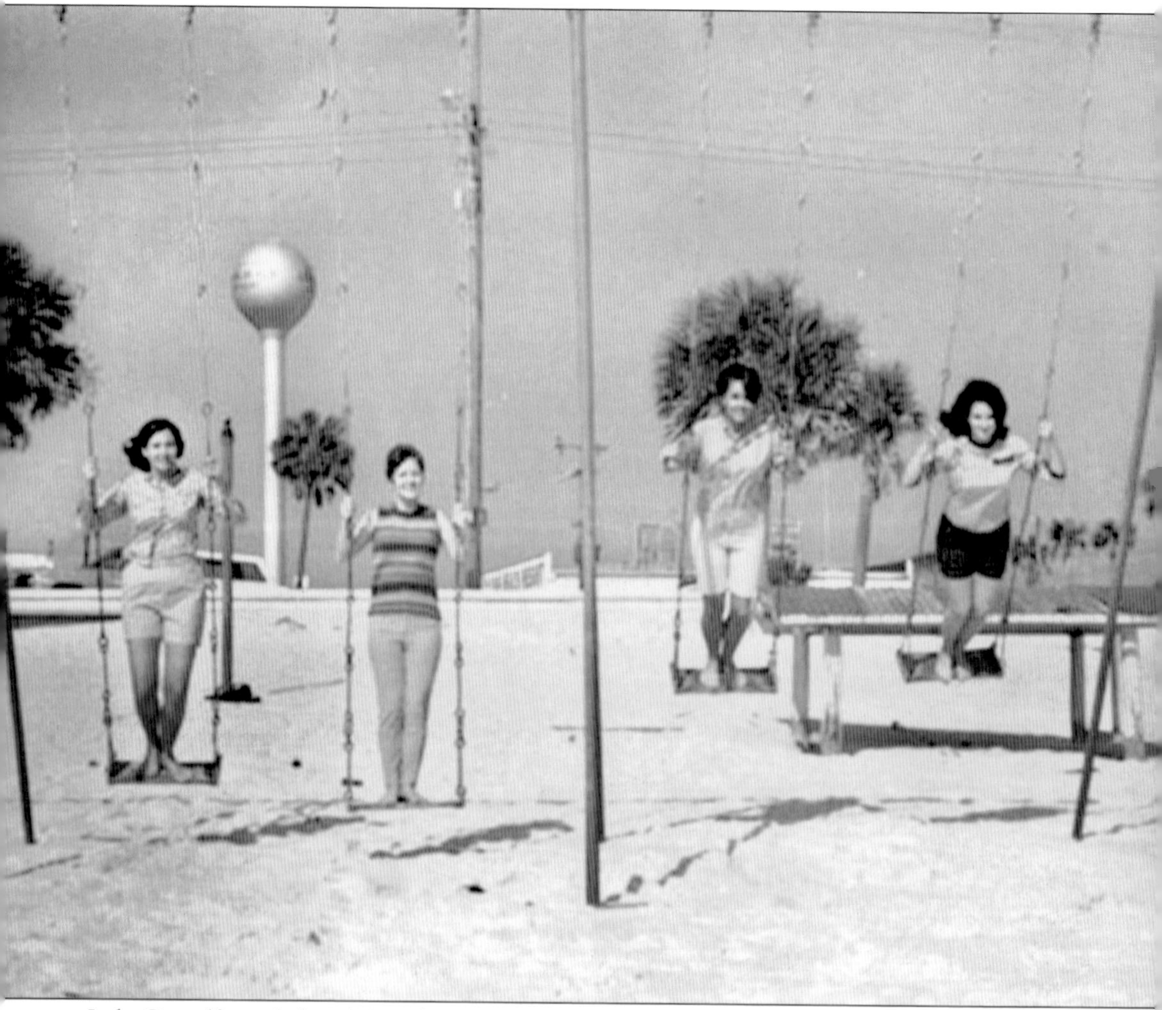

Judy Gore (far right) and friends are pictured on the swings behind Long Beach Resort. Bob Hargis took the photo. (Courtesy Bay County Library.)

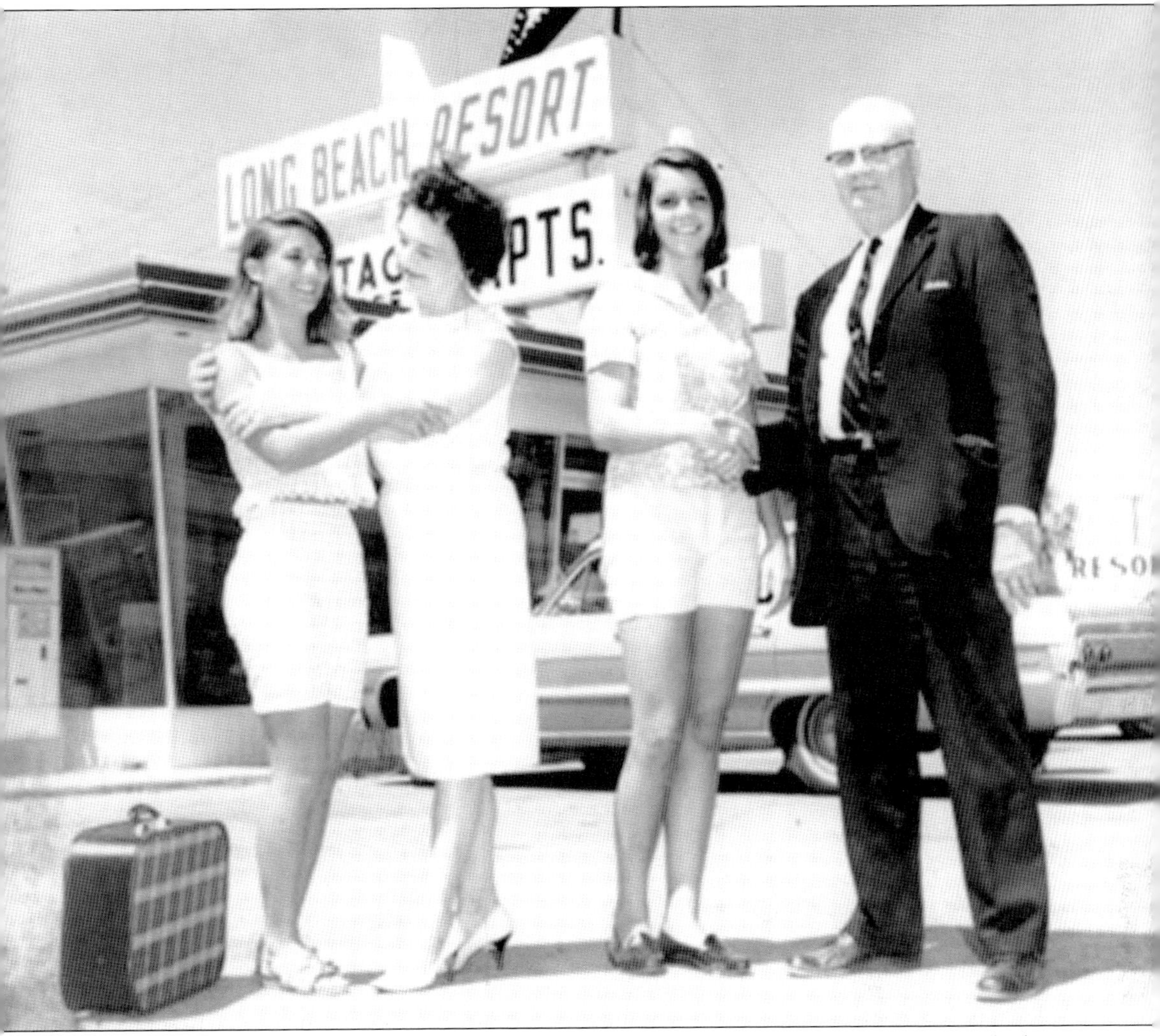

Mr. and Mrs. J.E. Churchwell are pictured in the 1960s outside Long Beach Resort with their guests. (Courtesy Bay County Library.)

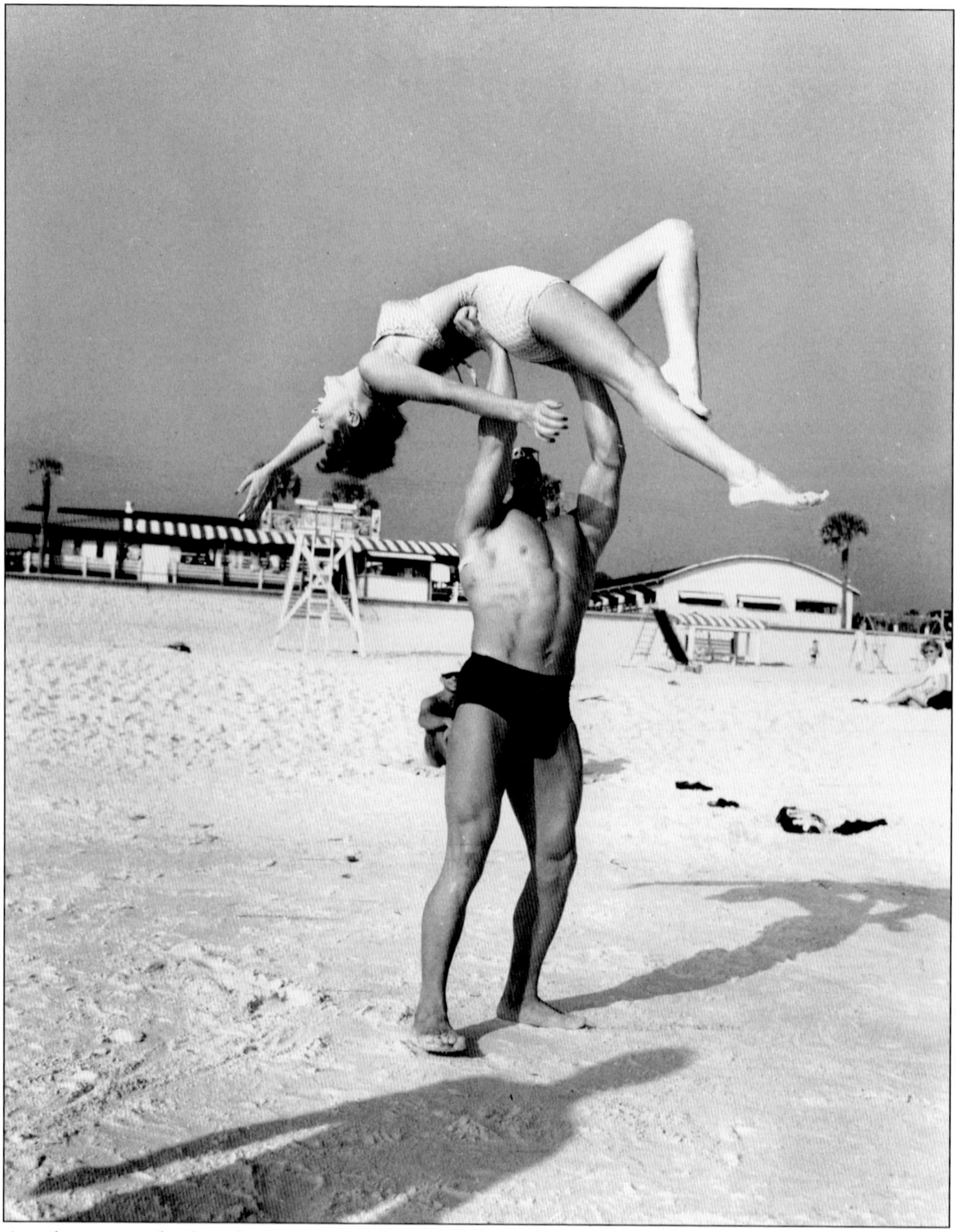

Acrobatics on the beach were a popular pastime in the 1940s and 1950s. Here Phil King lifts Leatrice Jackson of Hueytown, Alabama, overhead *c.* 1947. (Courtesy Florida State Archives.)

Four

Life at the Beach

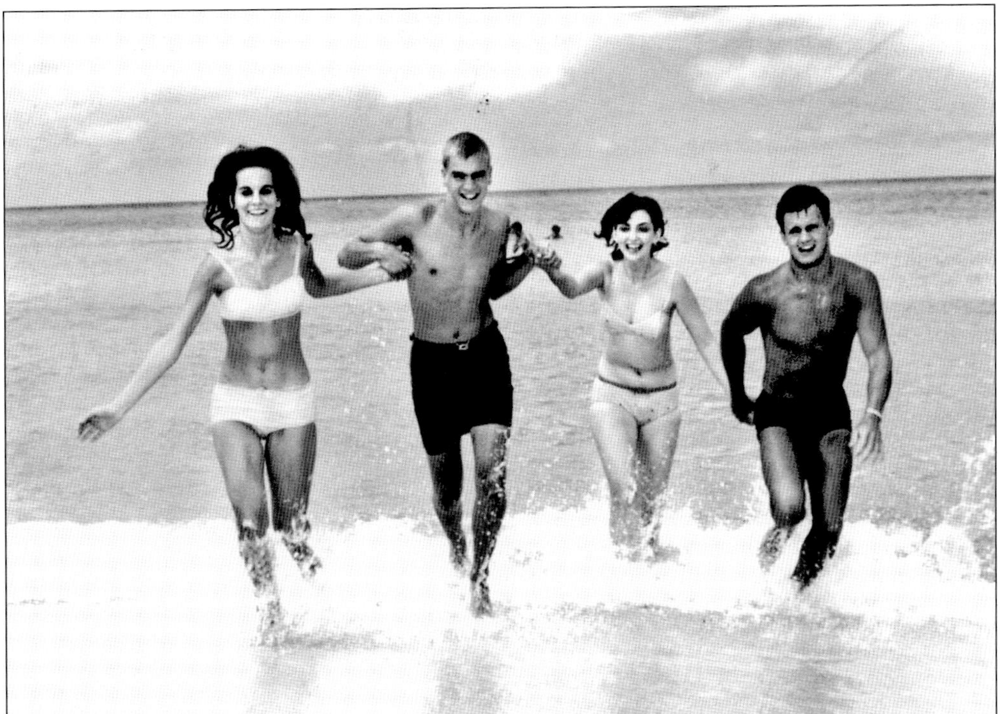

Four exuberant young people emerge from the Gulf. Bob Hargis took this photo in the early 1960s for *Beachweek* magazine. (Courtesy Bay County Library.)

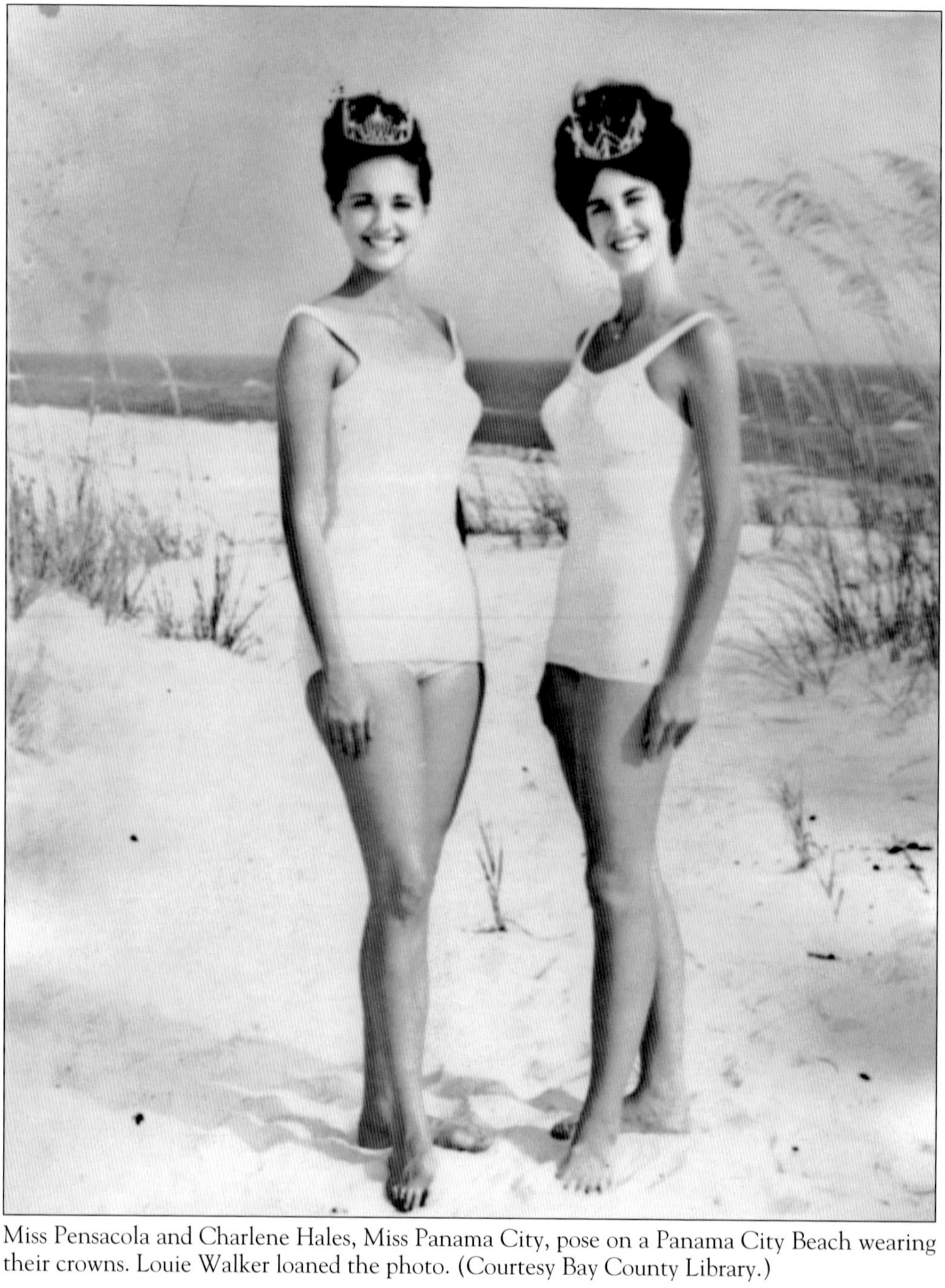

Miss Pensacola and Charlene Hales, Miss Panama City, pose on a Panama City Beach wearing their crowns. Louie Walker loaned the photo. (Courtesy Bay County Library.)

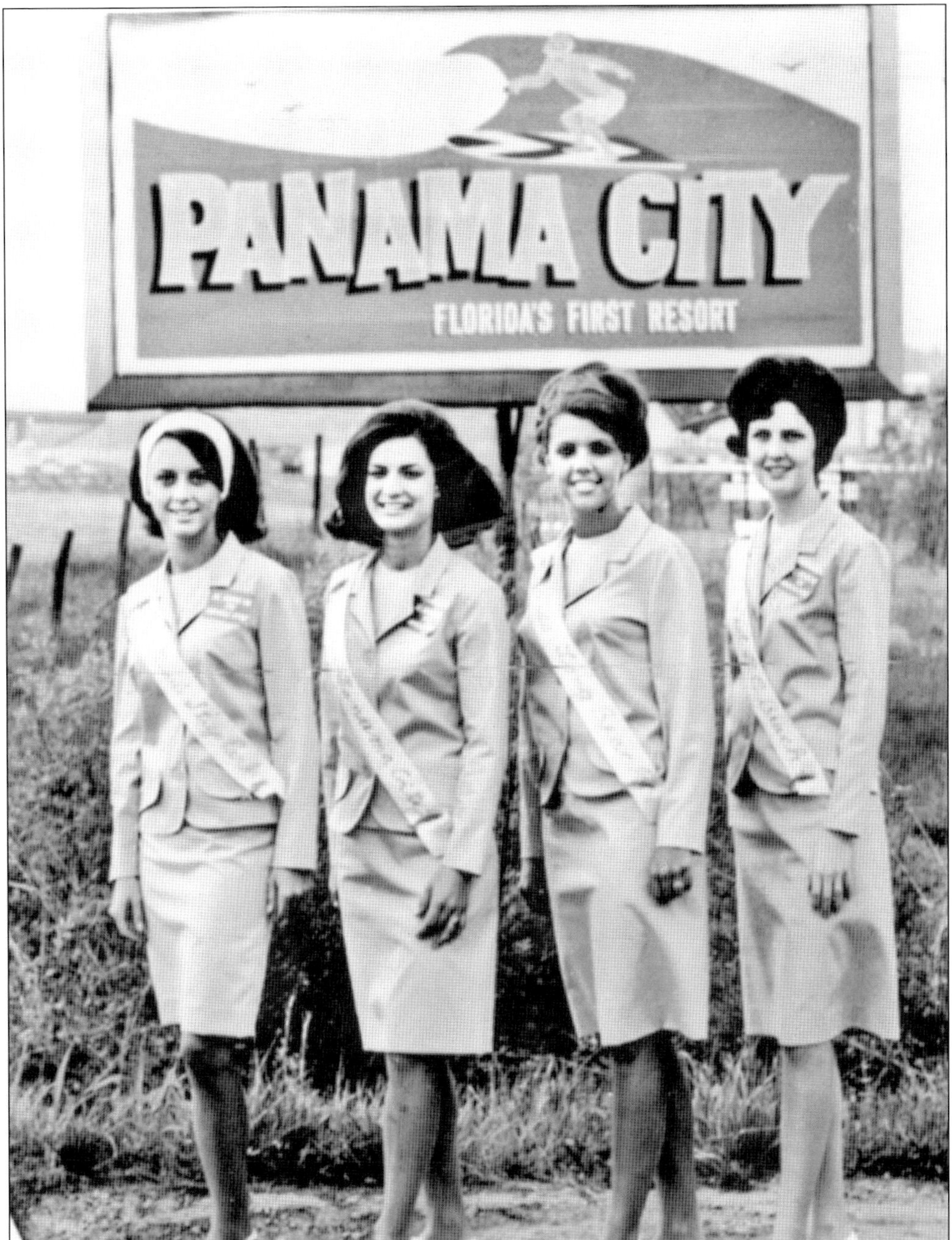

Beauty queens posing for photographer Bob Hargis in the 1970s are, from left to right, Miss Miracle Strip, Miss Panama City, Miss Long Beach, and Miss West Panama City. (Courtesy Bay County Library.)

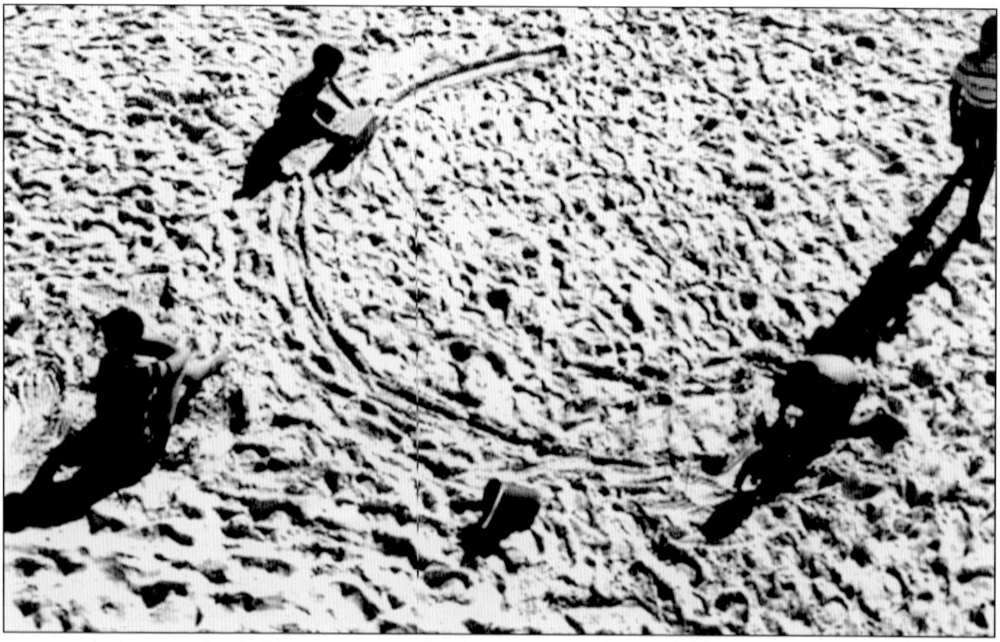

Intent on their work, children busily make designs in the sand with their beach toys at Panama City Beach. Bob Hargis took this photo in the 1970s. (Courtesy Bay County Library.)

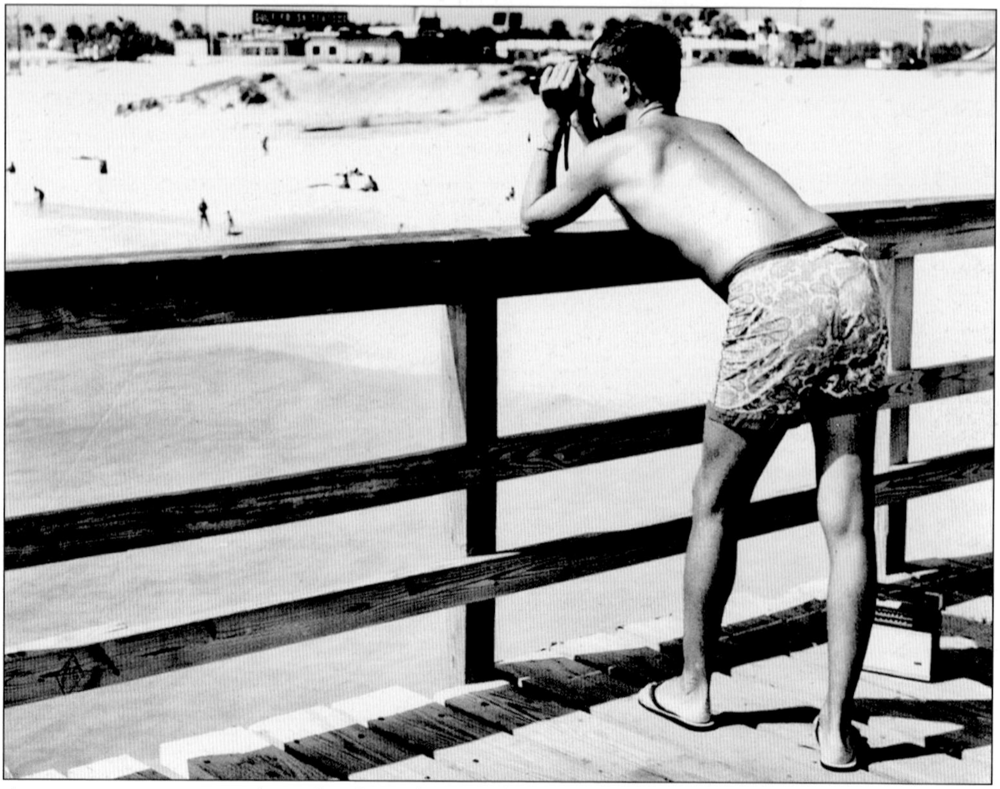

A summer visitor views the sights from the pier through binoculars. Gulf Fresh Seafood is in the background. Bob Hargis took the photo in 1960. (Courtesy Bay County Library.)

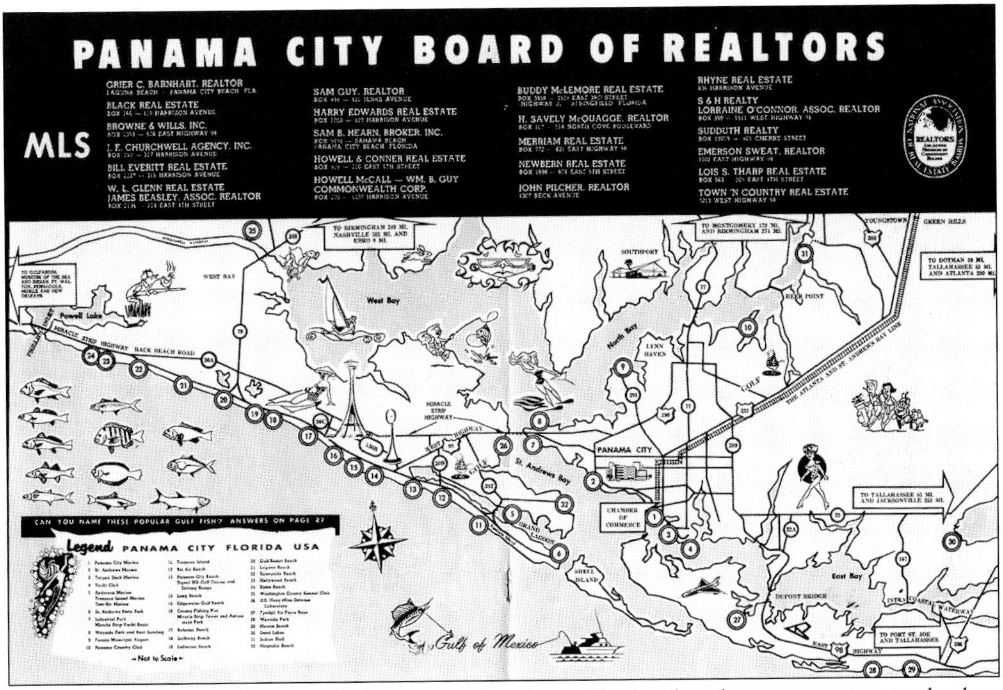

This whimsical map of the Gulf Coast was distributed by local realtors to tourists in the late 1960s. It highlights many of the Panama City beaches and local attractions, including the Observation Tower. (Courtesy Bay County Library.)

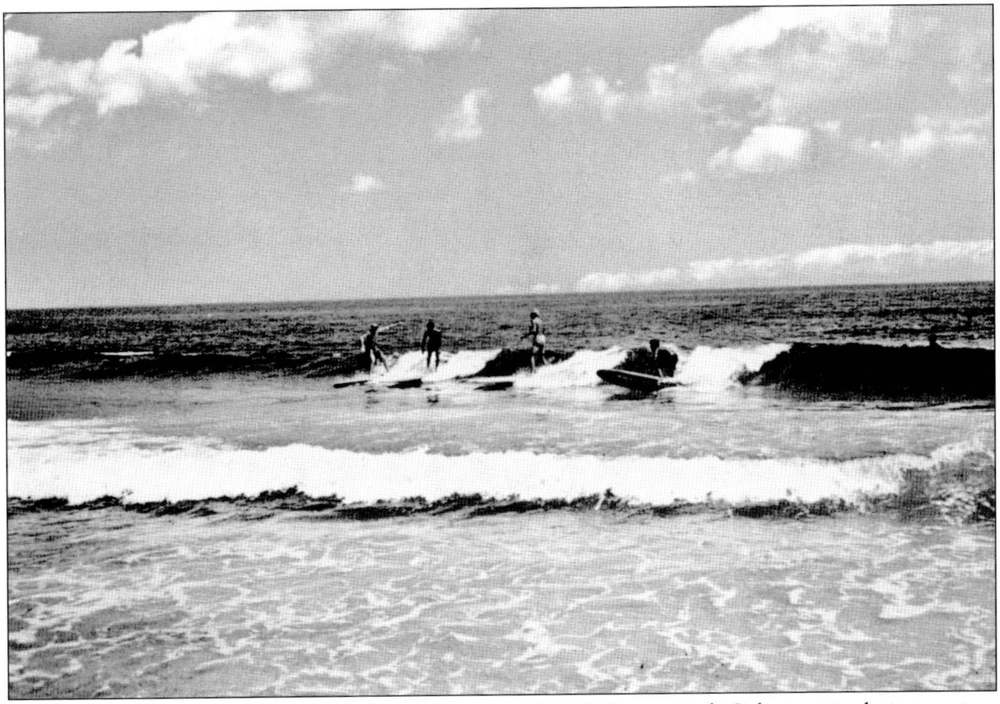

Four surfers are pictured here riding the waves on this 1960 postcard. Others wait their turn just beyond the swell, at right. (Courtesy Bay County Library.)

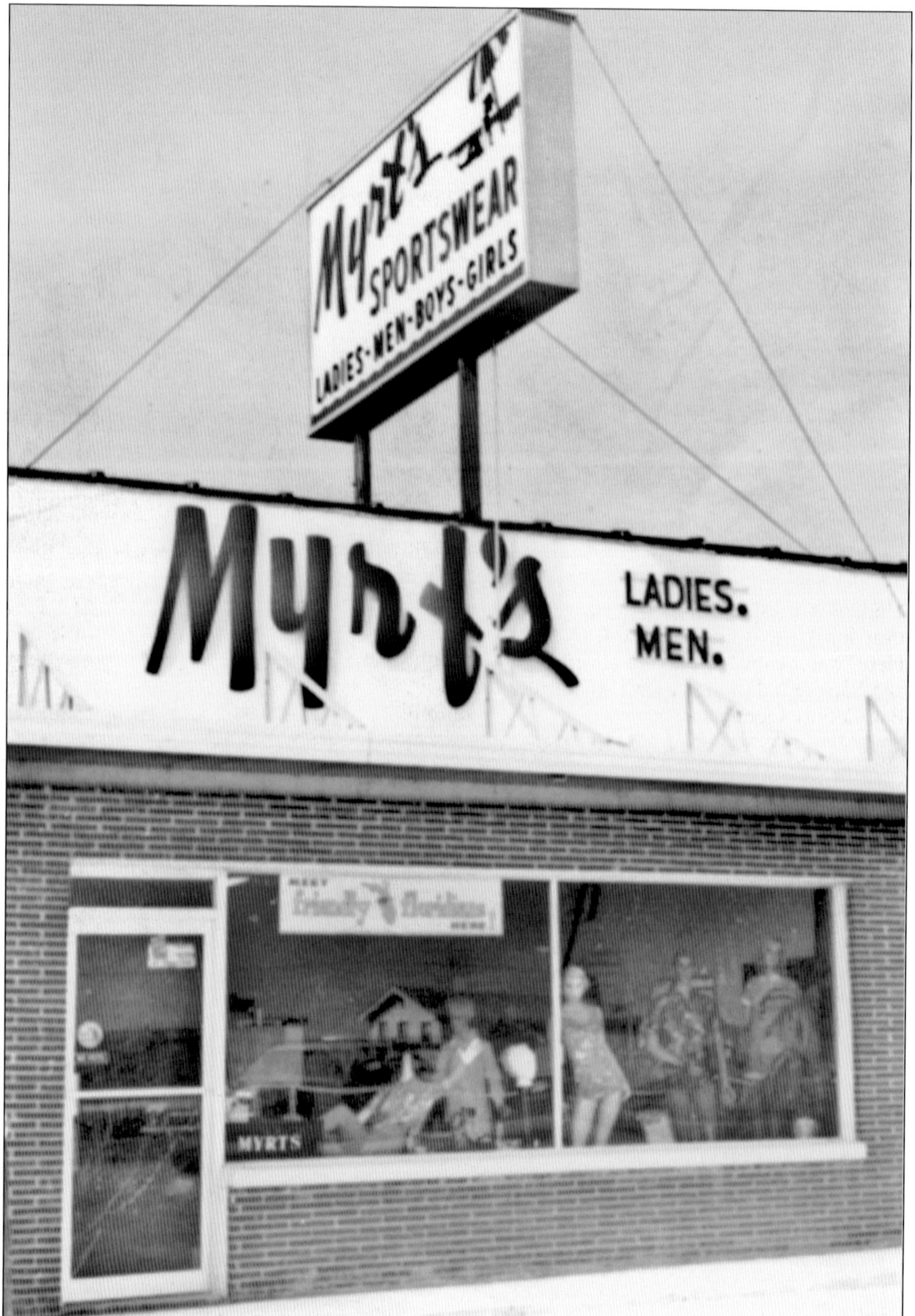

As it looked in the 1970s, Myrt's Sportswear was owned by Mrs. Myrtle Hatcher, who clothed generations of Panama City Beach residents and visitors. Located on Highway 98 in Bahama Beach, Myrt's stocked fashionable swimwear. (Courtesy Bay County Library.)

This is the second Hathaway Bridge, built in 1959. Age and increased usage made the old bridge (at far right) obsolete. (Courtesy Bay County Library.)

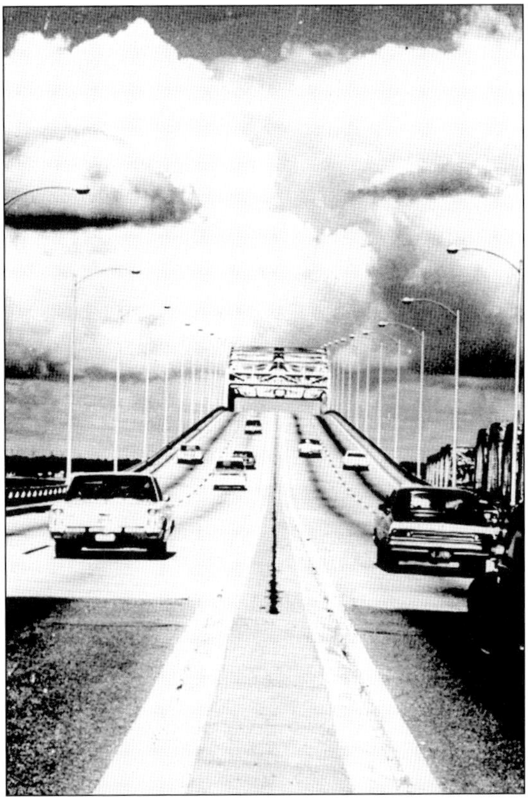

Underwater diving equipment was available for rent at a reasonable rate. Here "water baby" rentals are advertised at $2.50 per half hour. . . for 2! (Courtesy Bay County Library.)

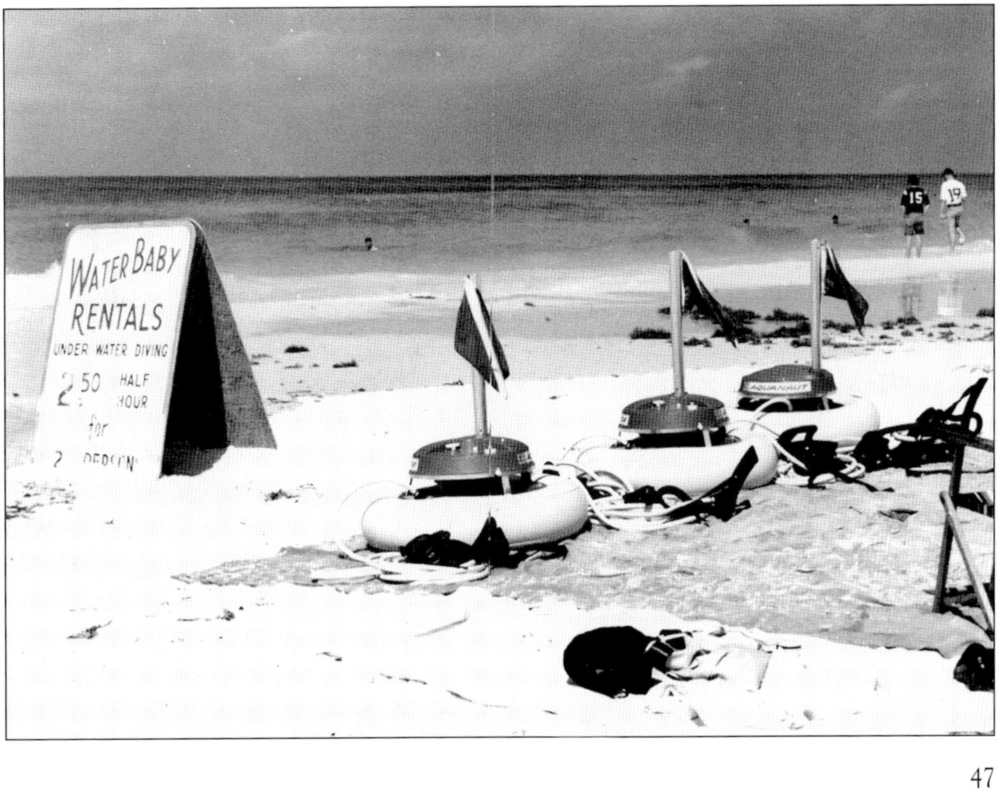

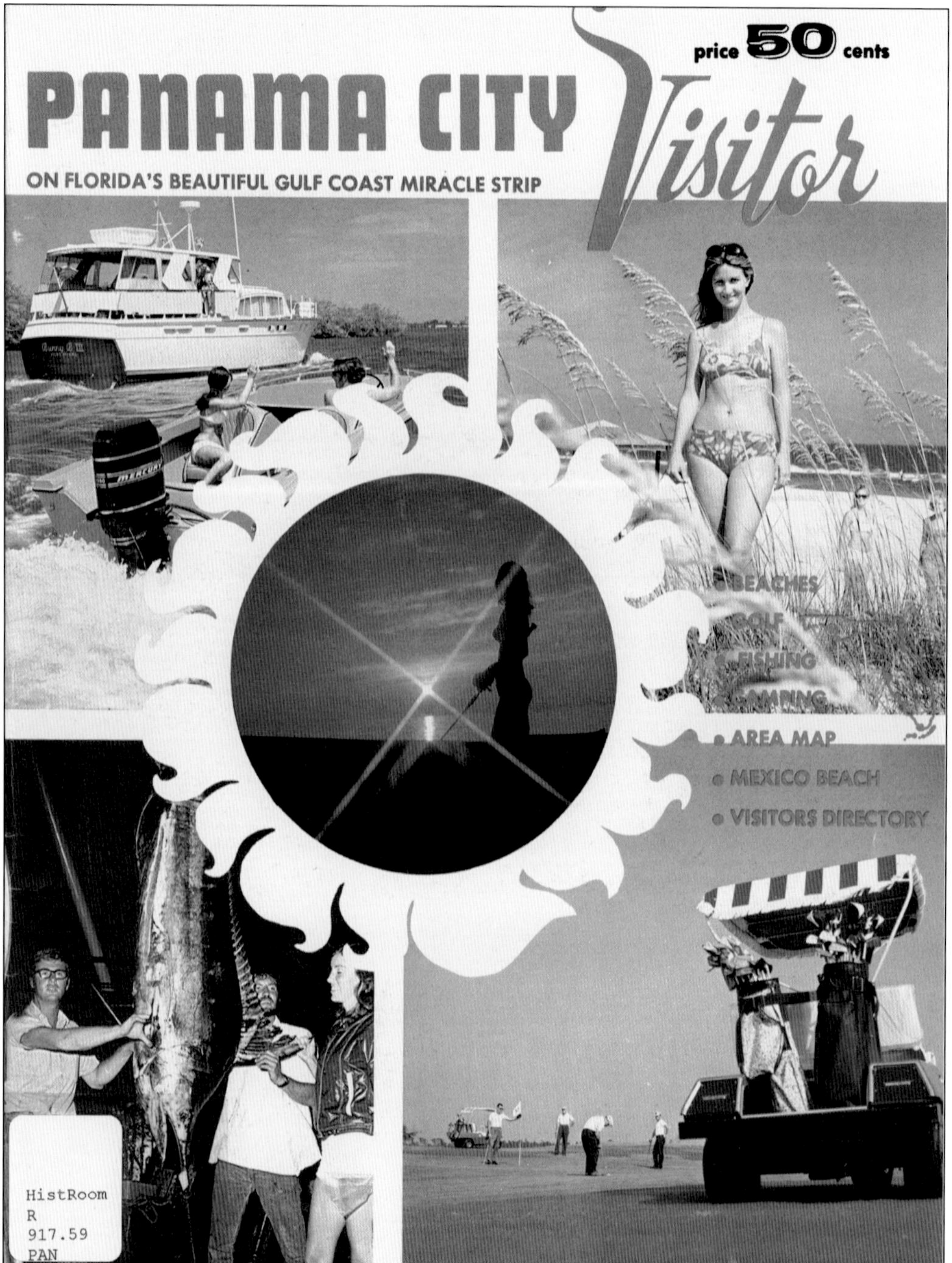

The front cover of *Panama City Visitor* magazine boasts of the many activities that one might find along "Florida's Beautiful Gulf Coast Miracle Strip" (Courtesy Bay County Library.)

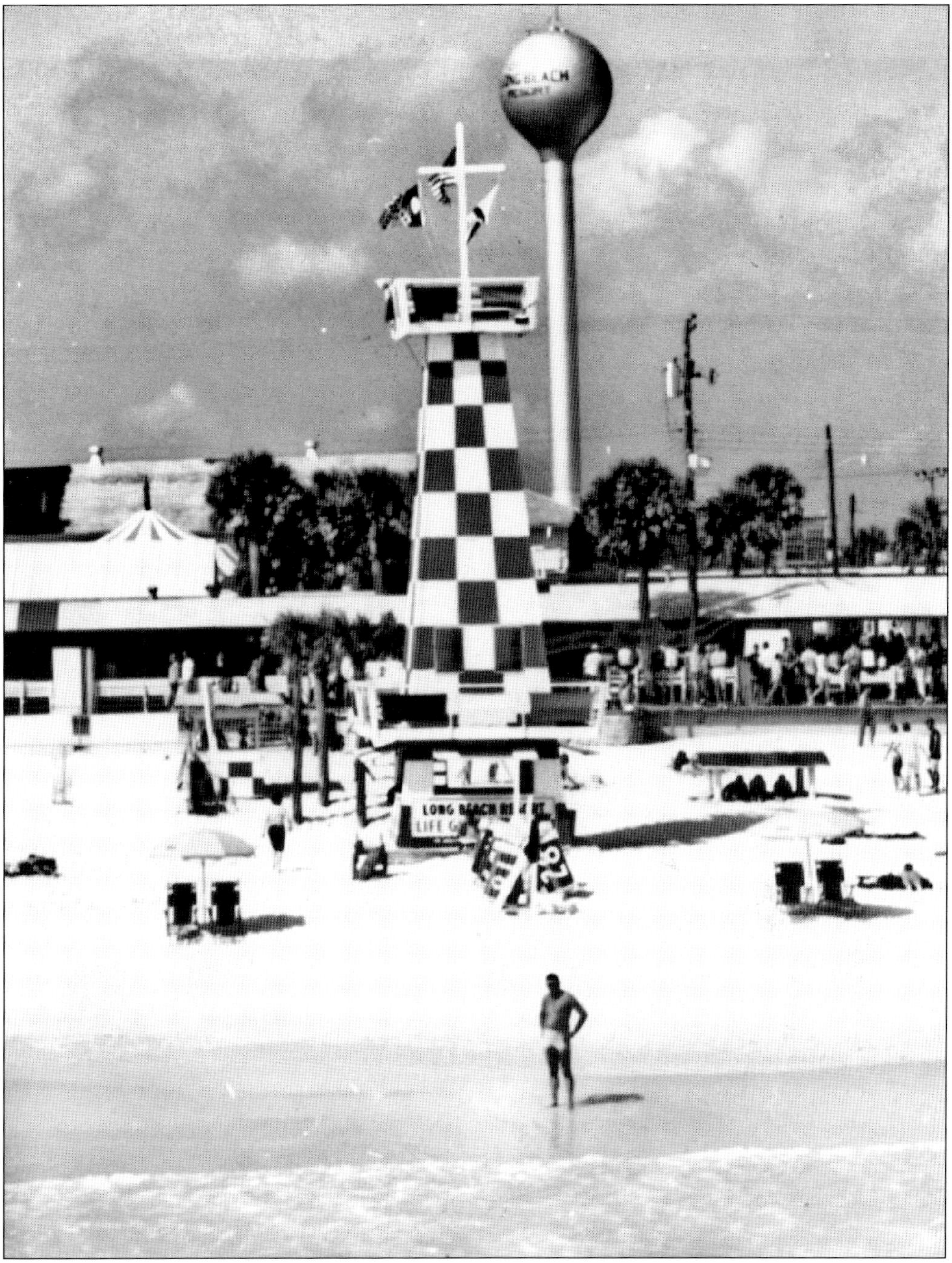

A longtime landmark, the checkered Long Beach lifeguard station could be seen from miles away. It stood like a sentry at the beach. The Long Beach Resort water tower is in the background. (Courtesy Bay County Library.)

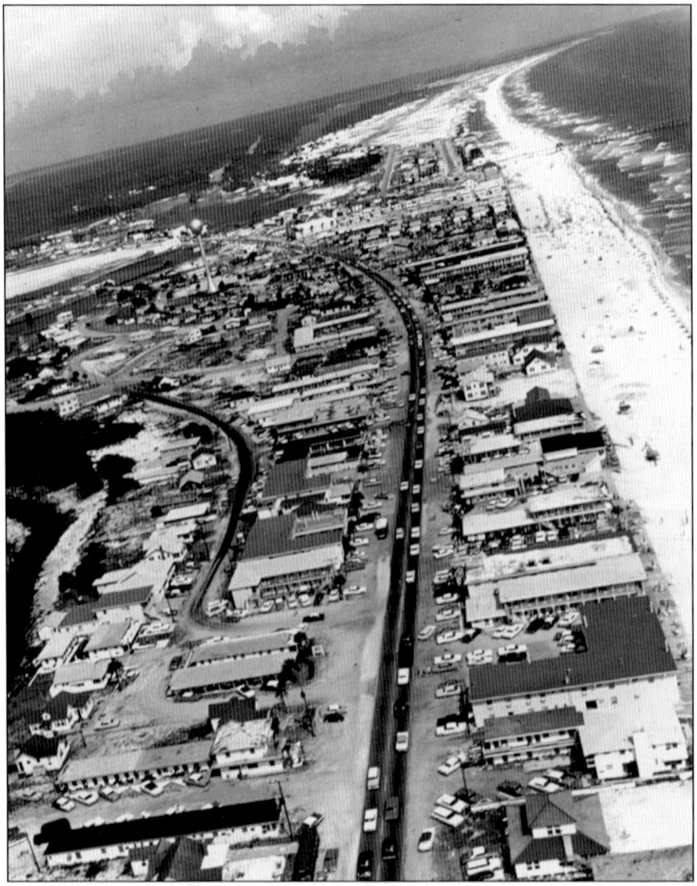

This 1970s aerial view of Long Beach shows the Pier and the then-undeveloped Thomas Drive area at the top of picture. (Courtesy Bay County Library.)

Located at 16022 W. Highway 98 in Panama City Beach, the Wayside Shopping Center was one of the first strip malls in the area. (Courtesy Bay County Library.)

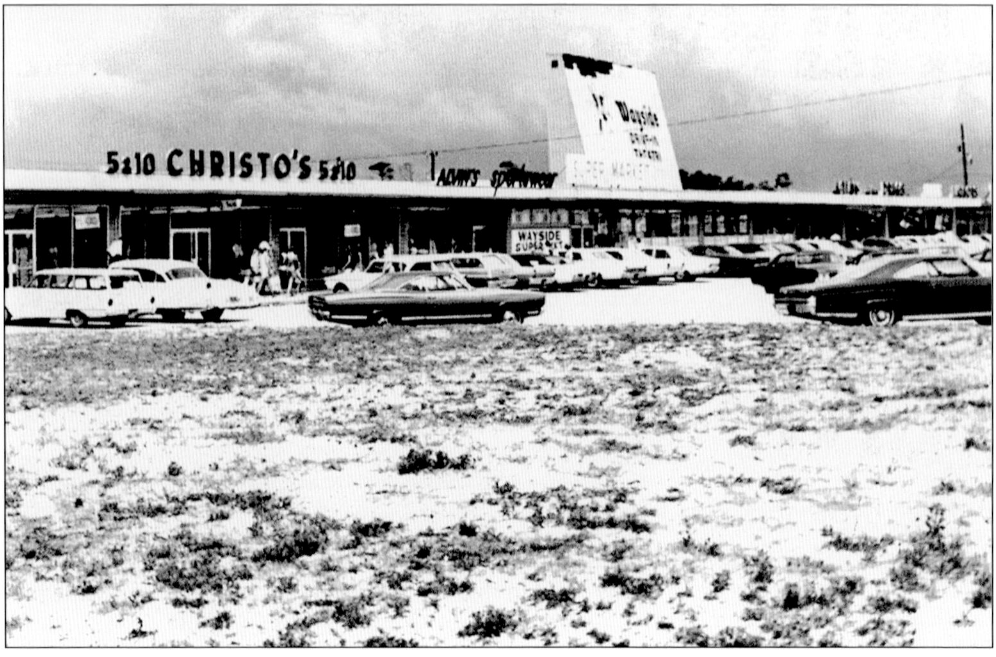

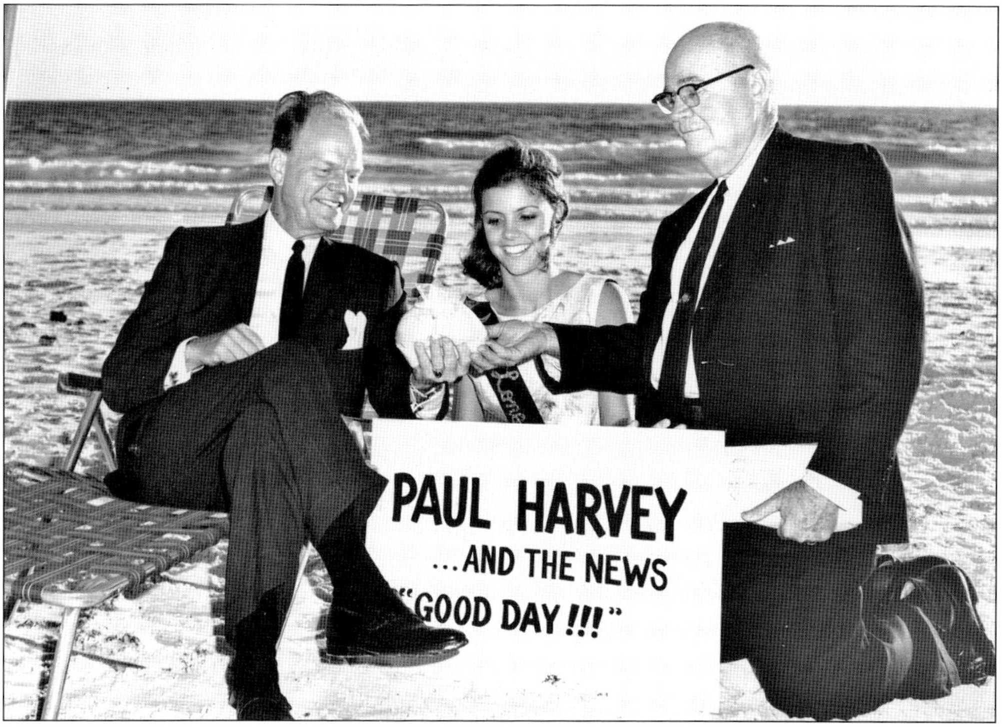

J.E. Churchwell presents beach sand to Paul Harvey on his 1970s visit to Panama City Beach as Miss Long Beach Marie Savage looks on. A beloved newscaster and radio personality, Harvey's sign-off "Good Day" has become his trademark. (Courtesy Bay County Library.)

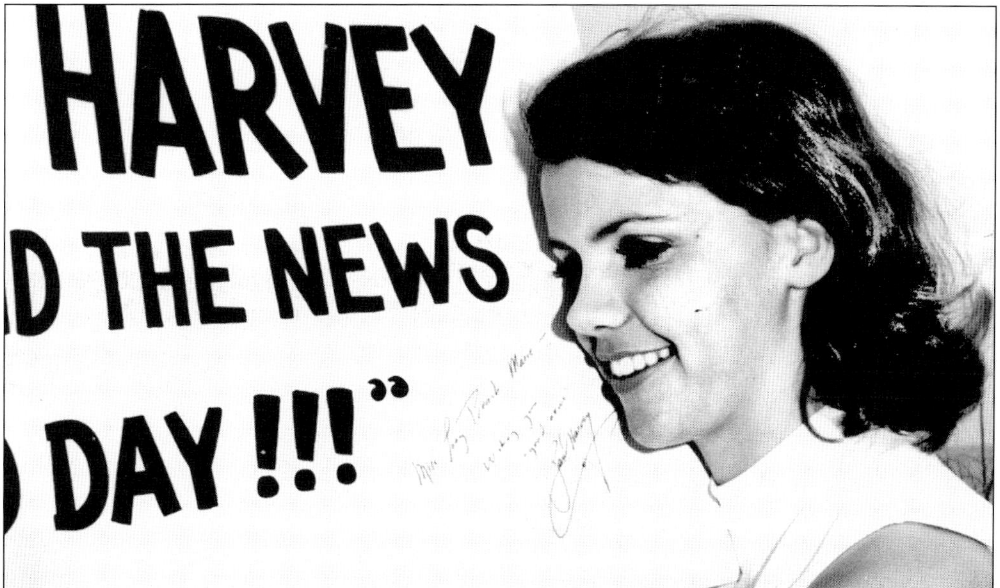

Marie Savage, Miss Long Beach, is pictured in this 1970s photo holding a sign autographed for her by Paul Harvey. The message from Harvey reads, "Miss Long Beach, Marie. . . wishing you good news." (Photography by Bob Hargis.)

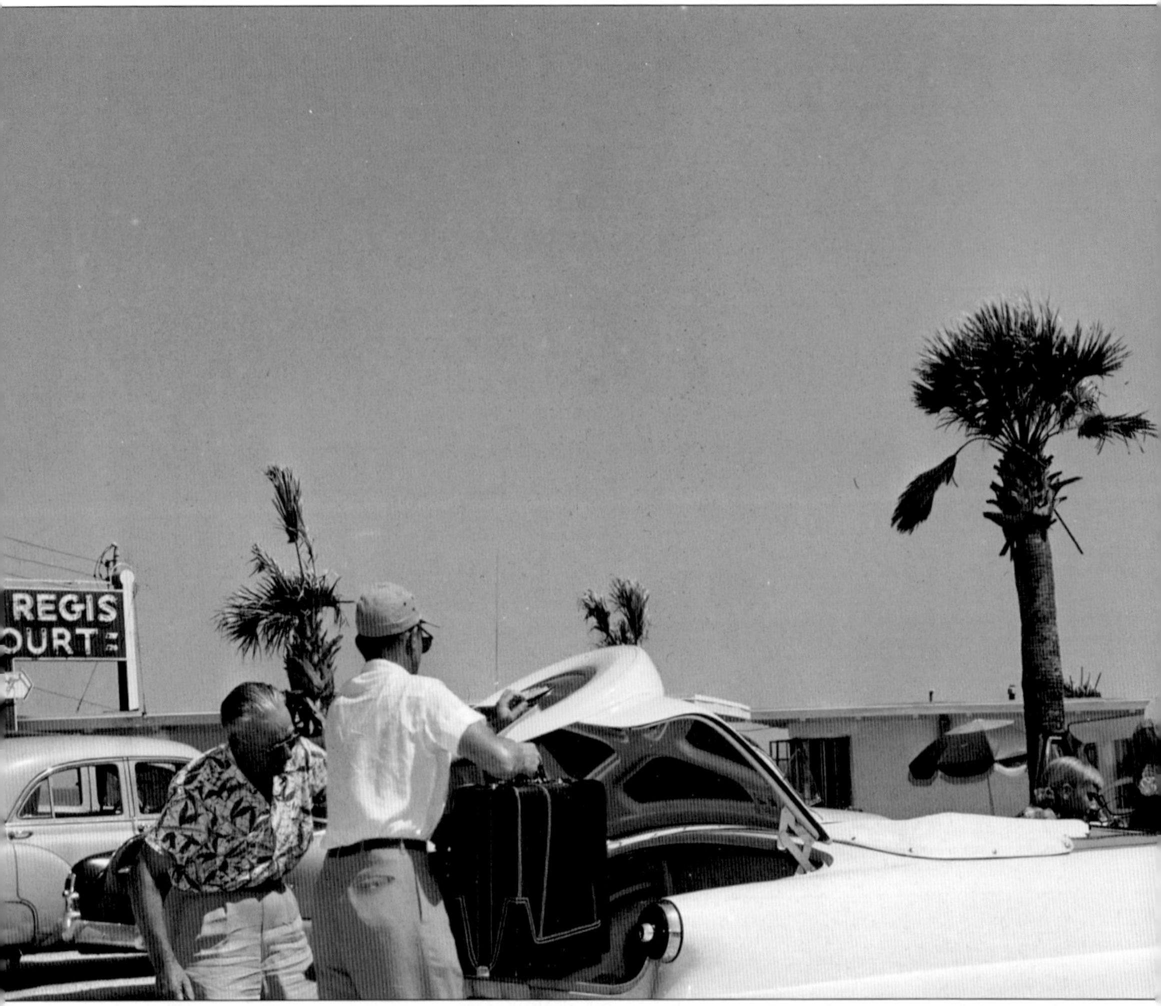

Francis Johnson took this 1955 photograph of a family unloading their automobile at the St. Regis Court motel in Panama City Beach. (Courtesy Florida State Archives.)

Five

Miracle Strip

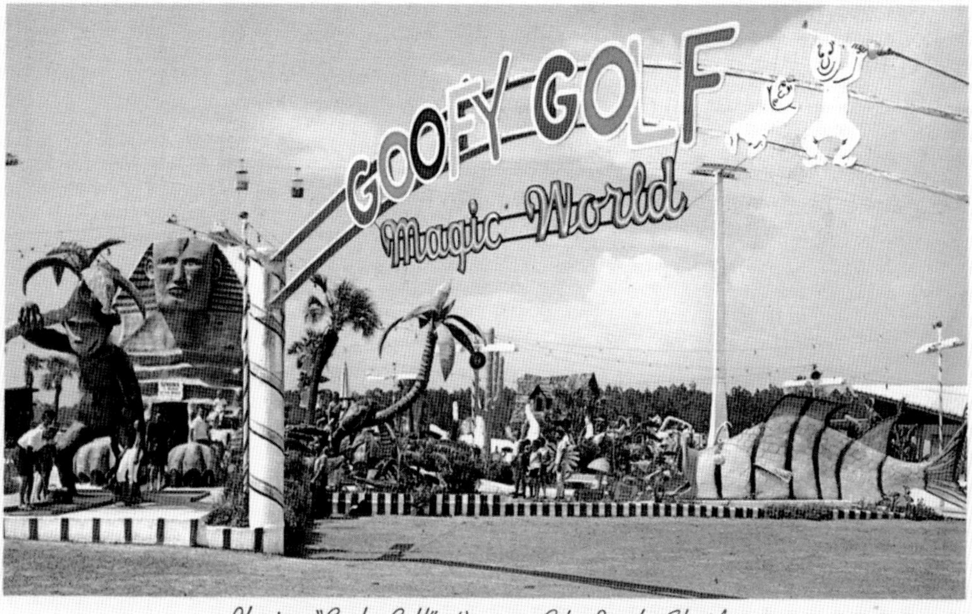

Playing "Goofy Golf", Panama City Beach, Florida

The 1960s saw a whole different kind of amusement-type business open at Panama City Beach. Children, influenced by television, wanted bigger and better attractions at the beach. Entrepreneurs like Leo Koplin and Jimmy Lark saw an opportunity to put some of their ideas to work and the Miracle Strip was born. (Courtesy Goofy Golf.)

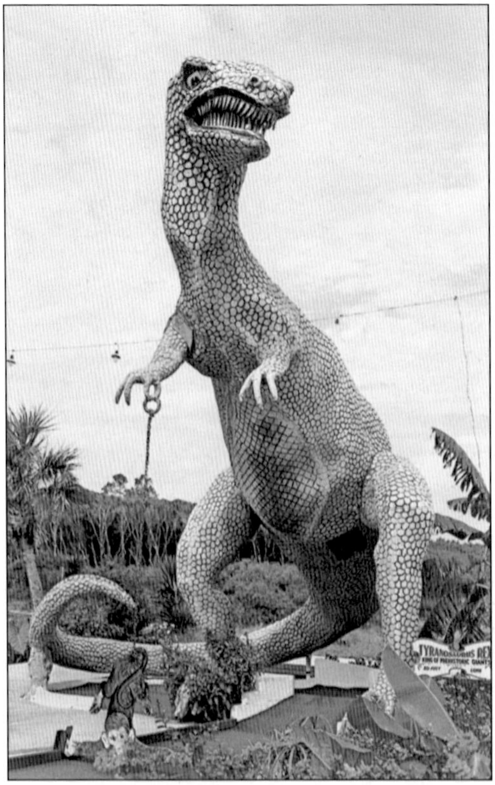

Leo Koplin opened the first Goofy Golf in Panama City Beach in 1958. Oversize creatures like this giant dinosaur added a whole new dimension to the game of miniature golf. (Courtesy Goofy Golf.)

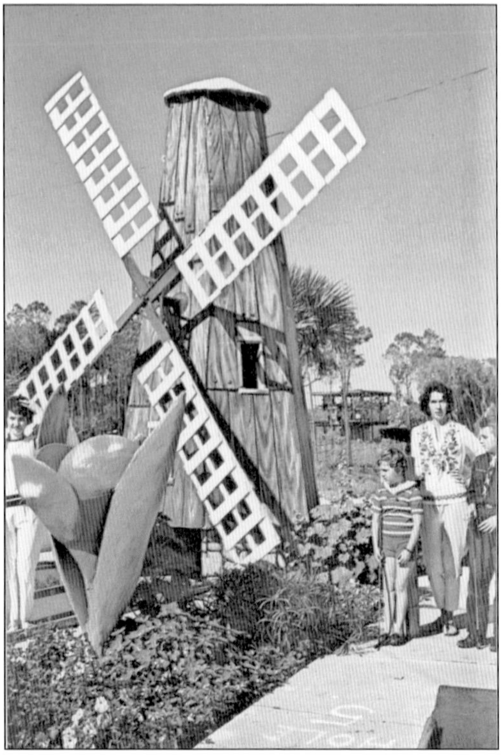

Goofy Golf served as the model for amusement-type miniature golf courses around the country. Although Leo Koplin died in 1988, his son continues the business with many franchises throughout the United States. (Courtesy Goofy Golf.)

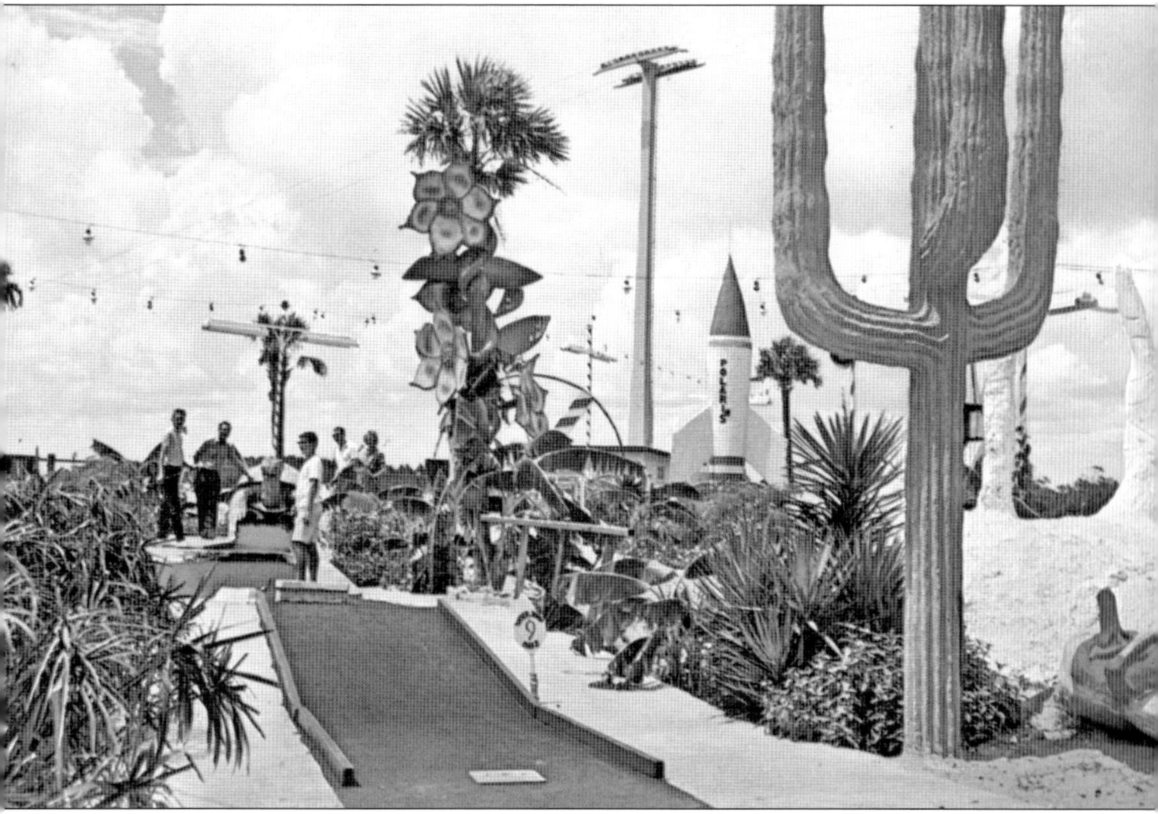

Whacky sculptures tower over the putting greens at Goofy Golf. The original course is still operating and remains much the same as when it first opened in the late 1950s. (Courtesy Goofy Golf.)

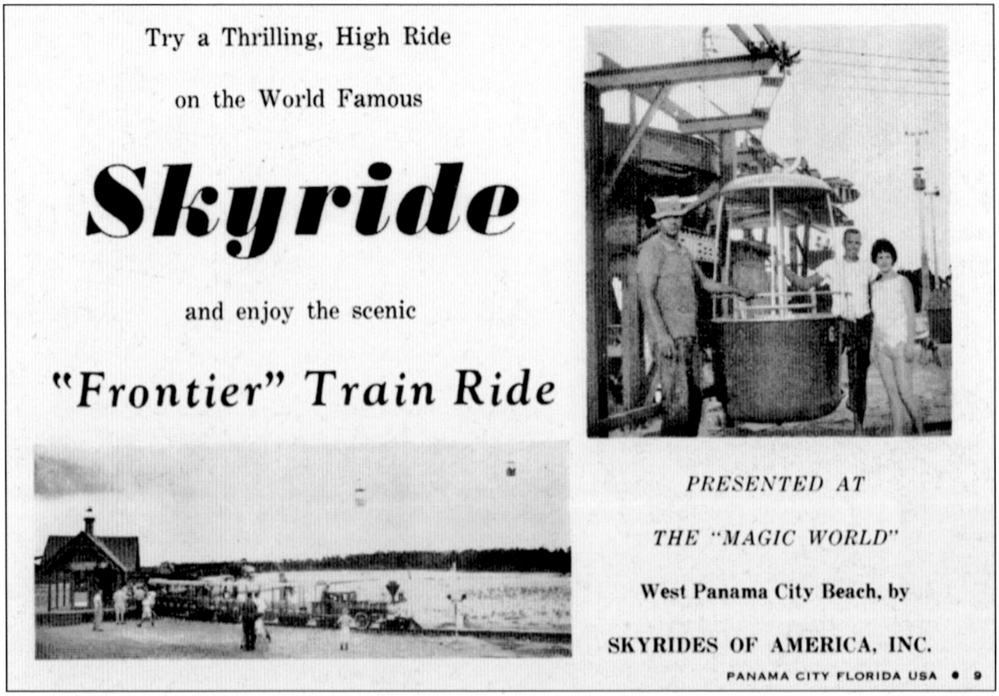

In 1960, Goofy Golf creator Leo Koplin leased property adjoining his miniature golf facility to a concessionaire who constructed a Skyride. In an era when beach structures over two stories were non-existent, the Skyride was an instant hit. Suspended 100 feet above ground, visitors had a bird's-eye view of the beach and its surrounds. (Courtesy Bay County Library.)

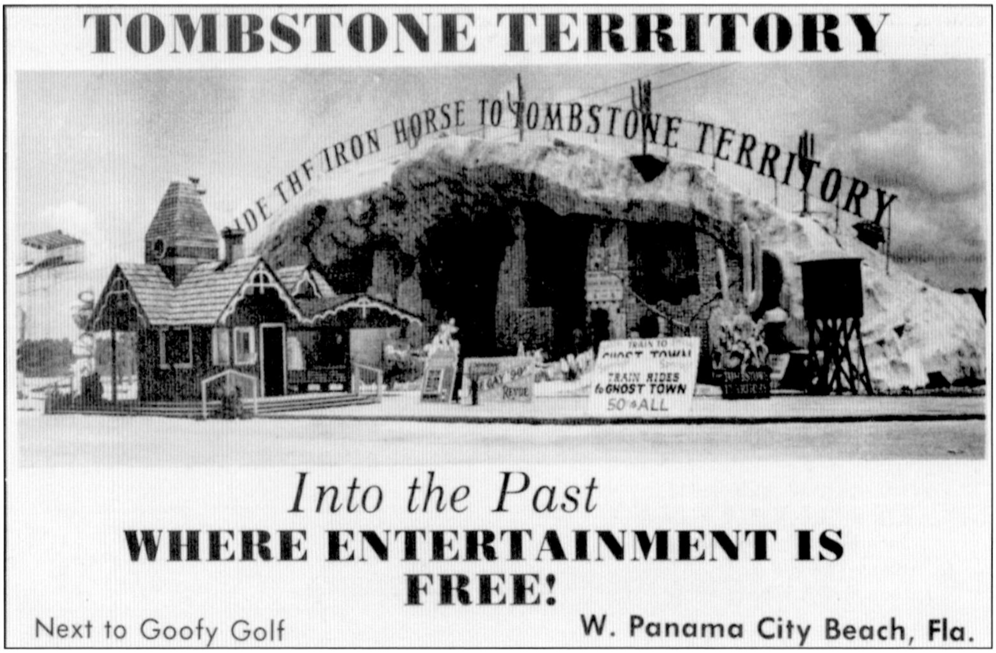

This 1960s advertisement for Tombstone Territory invites visitors to step "into the past." (Courtesy Bay County Library.)

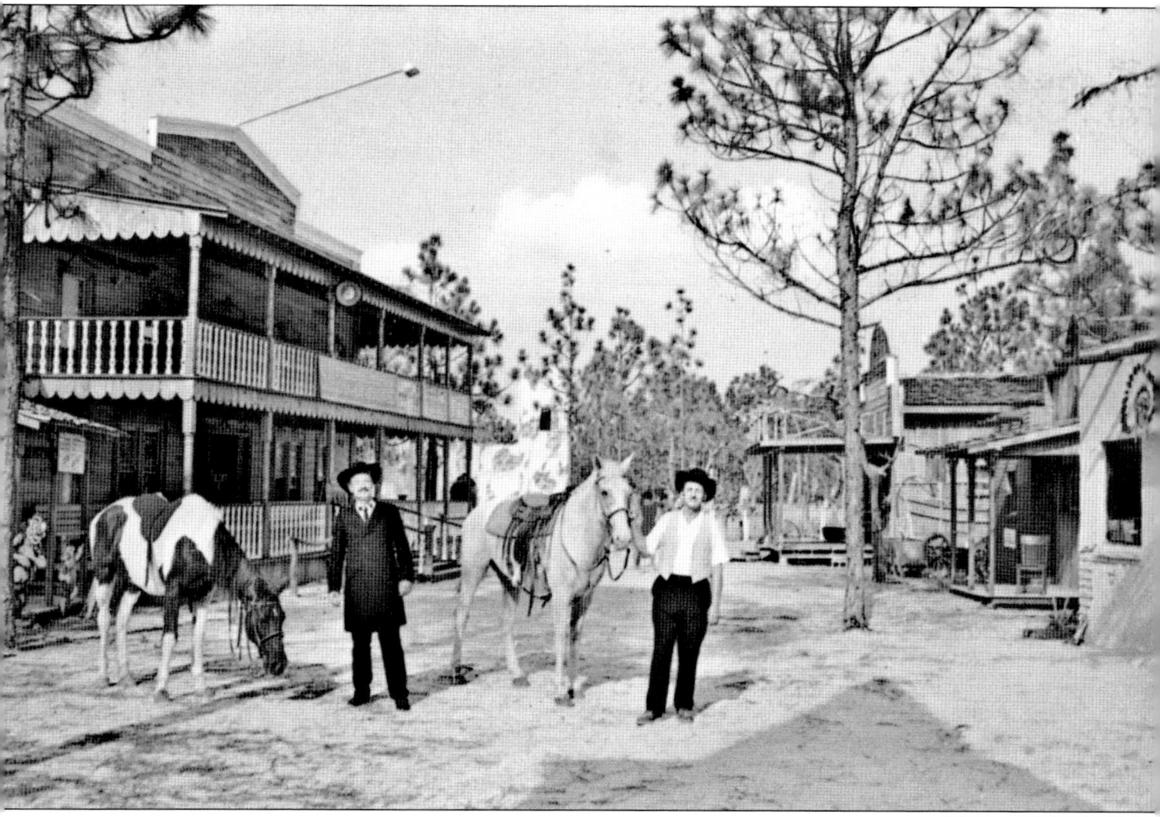

By 1963, TV westerns were all the rage, and Koplin capitalized on their popularity by creating his Tombstone Territory theme park. Authentic-looking buildings, period sculptures, and an-honest-to-goodness frontier train ride added to the appeal. Here "townsfolk" pose with horses for a 1960s promotional postcard. (Courtesy Goofy Golf.)

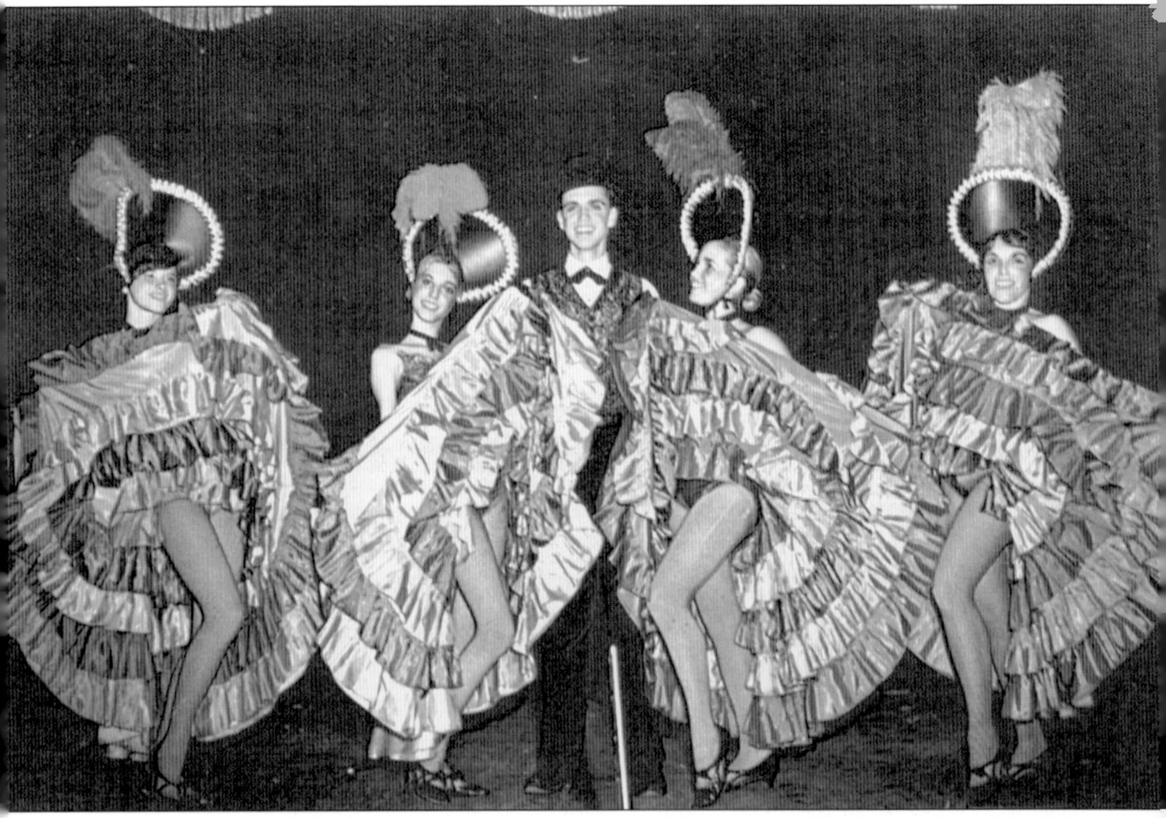

What little girl hasn't dreamed of becoming a can-can dancer? Dancers pictured on this 1960s postcard may have just completed a performance at the Tombstone Territory dancehall. (Courtesy Goofy Golf.)

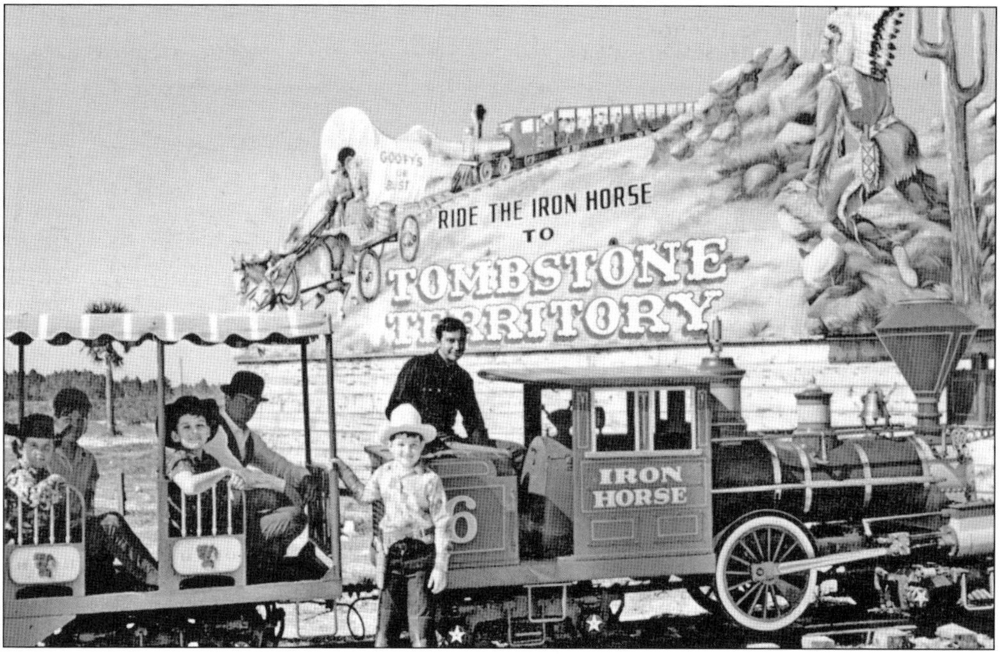

Known as the "Iron Horse," this miniature train captured the imagination of young and old alike as it ambled through Tombstone Territory. Appropriately outfitted in cowboy duds, youngsters pose for a 1960s postcard. (Courtesy Goofy Golf.)

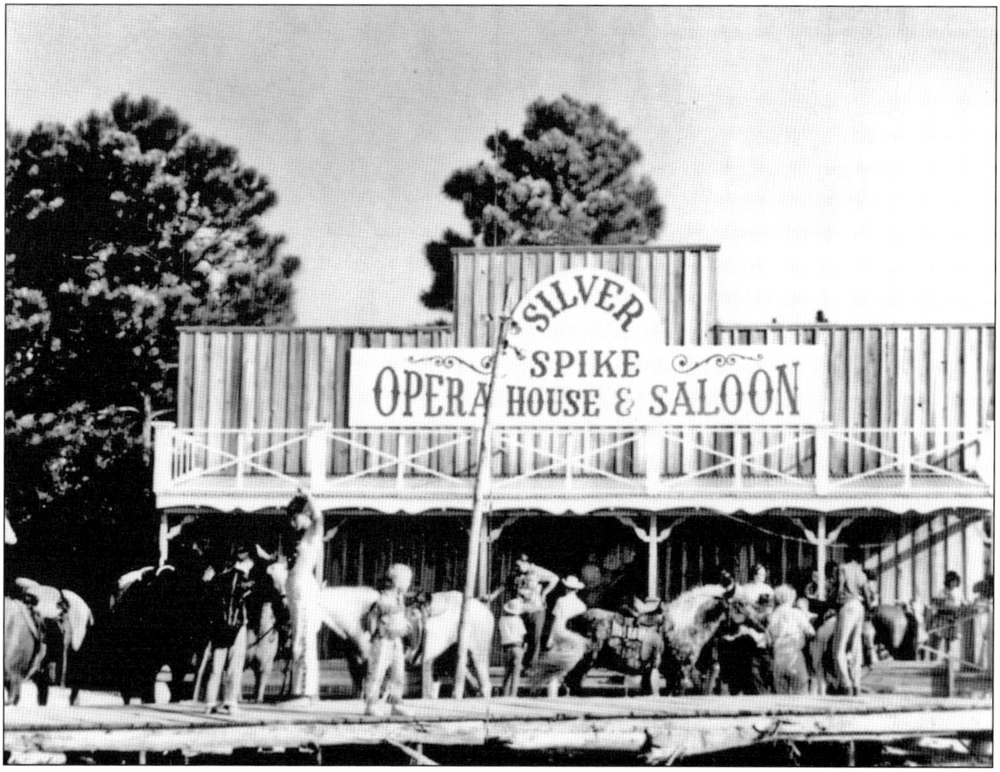

The Silver Spike Opera House and Saloon is seen in the 1960s. (Courtesy Bay County Library.)

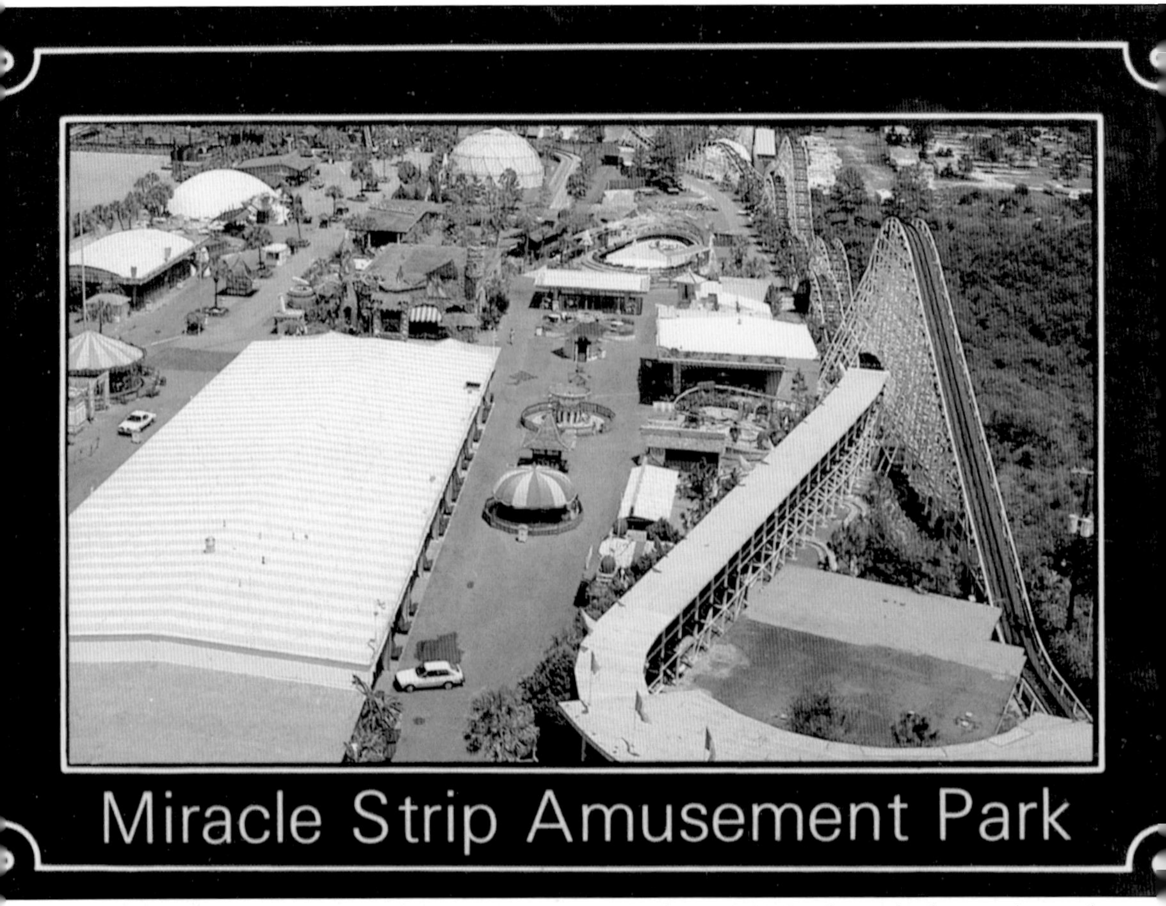

Jimmy Lark built the Miracle Strip Amusement Park in 1963. In the early days, it featured midway-style rides, or "metal monsters" as they were called. This postcard shows an aerial view of the park.

The Miracle Strip Tower was a famous beach landmark and allowed visitors to view the beaches for miles around, seen from above in this postcard from the 1960s.

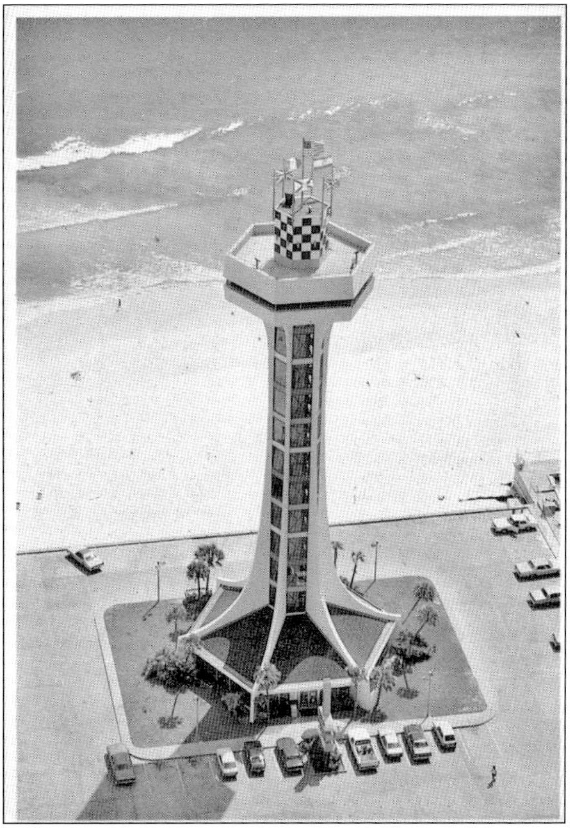

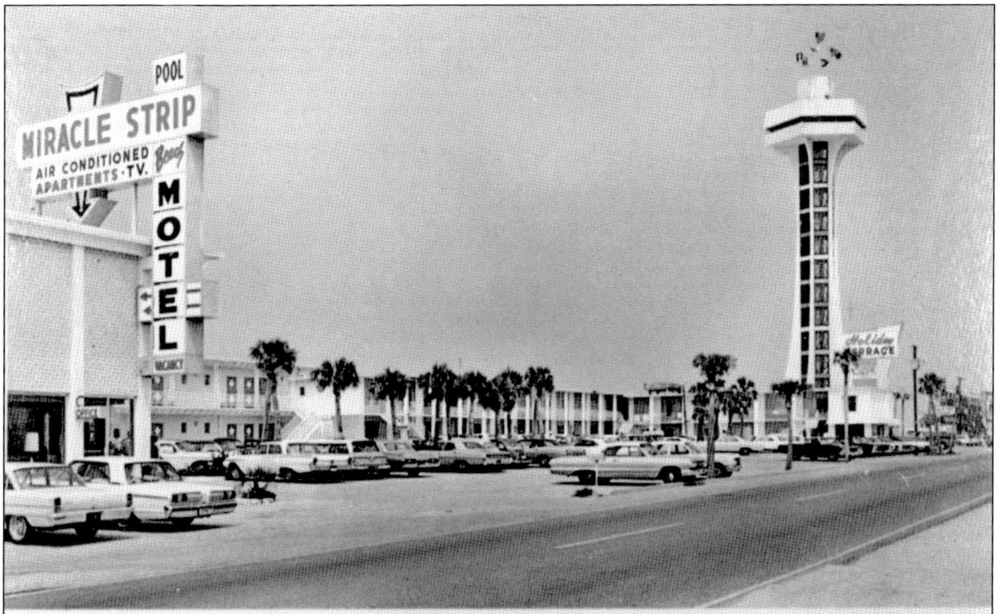

Along Miracle Strip Amusement Park, West Panama City Beach, Florida

This 1970s Bob Hargis photograph shows the Miracle Strip, looking west past the observation tower. Note the vintage signs at left advertising the many amenities of the Miracle Strip motel.

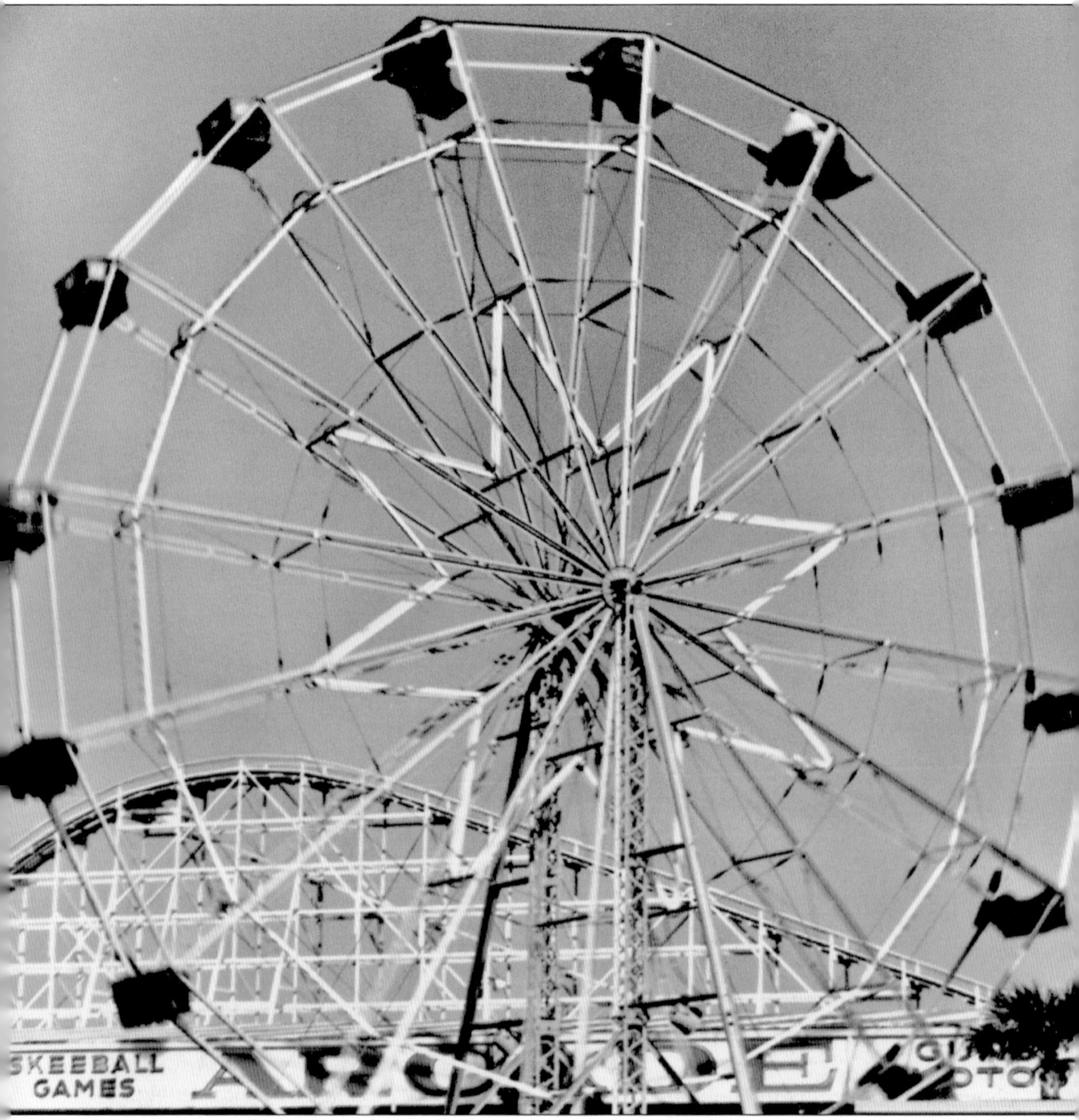

This 1970s photo shows the Ferris wheel at Miracle Strip Amusement Park. Although the park closed its doors for good in September 2004, it will long be remembered by many as an integral part of their Panama City Beach experience. (Courtesy Bay County Library.)

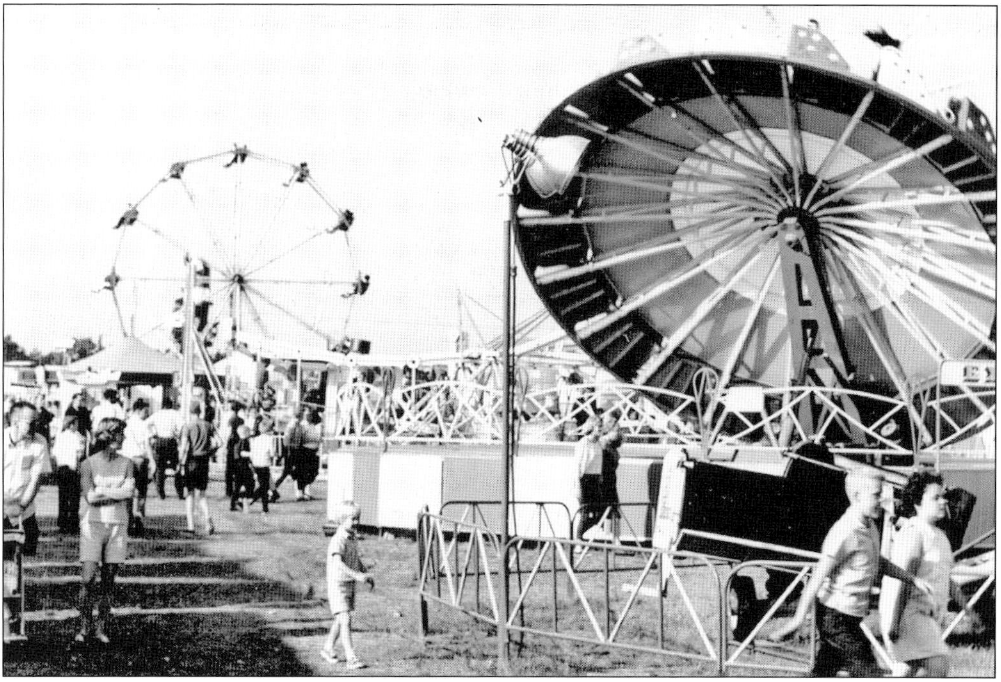

Youngsters rush to get on the rides as their parents stroll alongside (far left) at Miracle Strip Amusement Park. The Ferris wheel is in background. (Courtesy Bay County Library.)

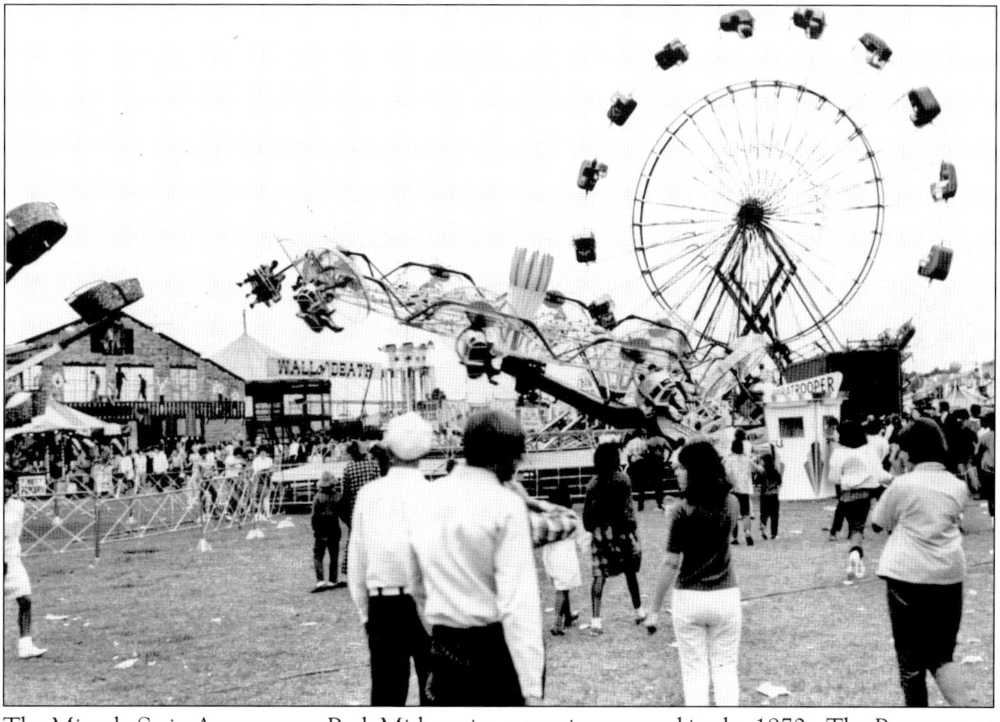

The Miracle Strip Amusement Park Midway is seen as it appeared in the 1970s. The Paratrooper is in mid-ground, the Ferris wheel in the background. The Wall of Death can be seen at left. (Courtesy Bay County Library.)

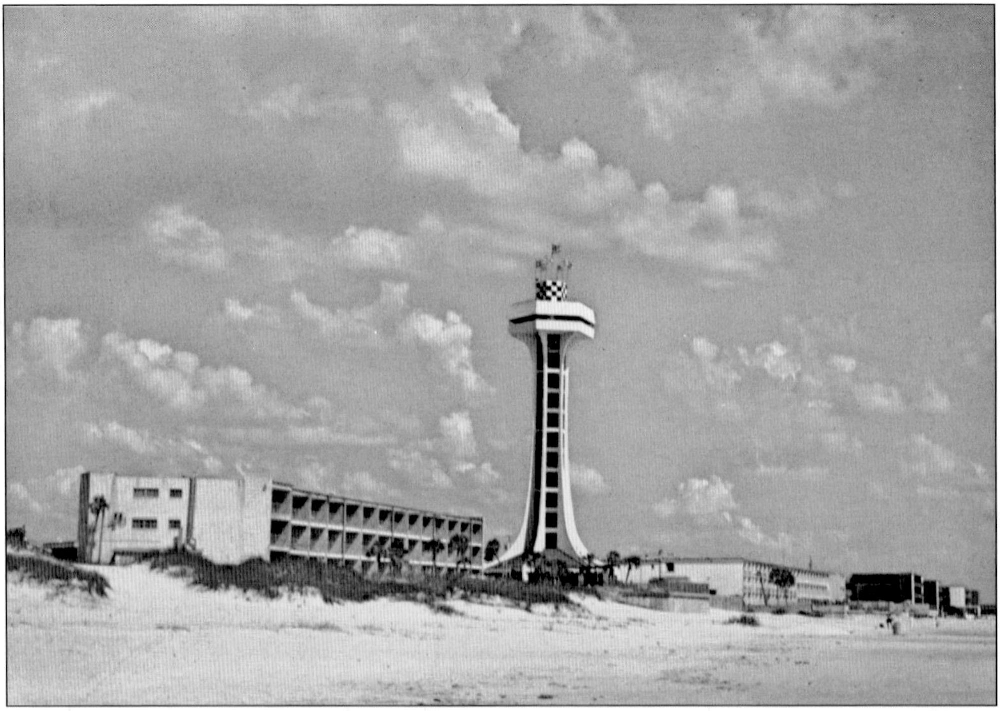

This 1960s postcard invites tourists to "have fun in the sun" while enjoying white sandy beaches and the Miracle Strip Observation Tower. Jimmy Lark built the Miracle Strip Amusement Park's companion Ship-Wreck Island Water Park in 1982.

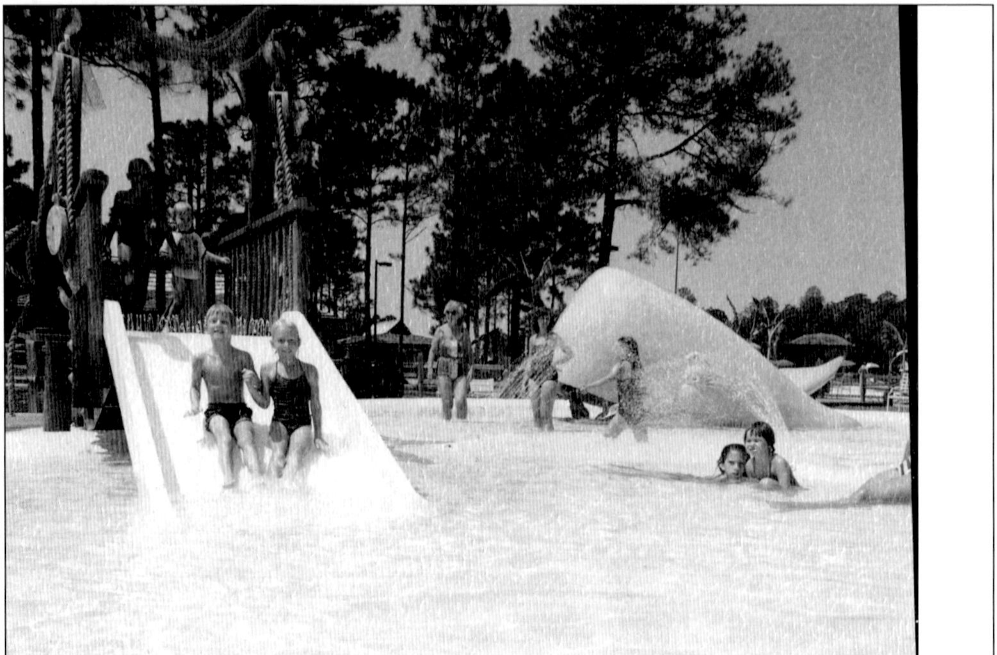

Children enjoy the water slide at Ship Wreck Island Water Park. This photo was taken by Barry Gross in 1983. (Courtesy Florida State Archives.)

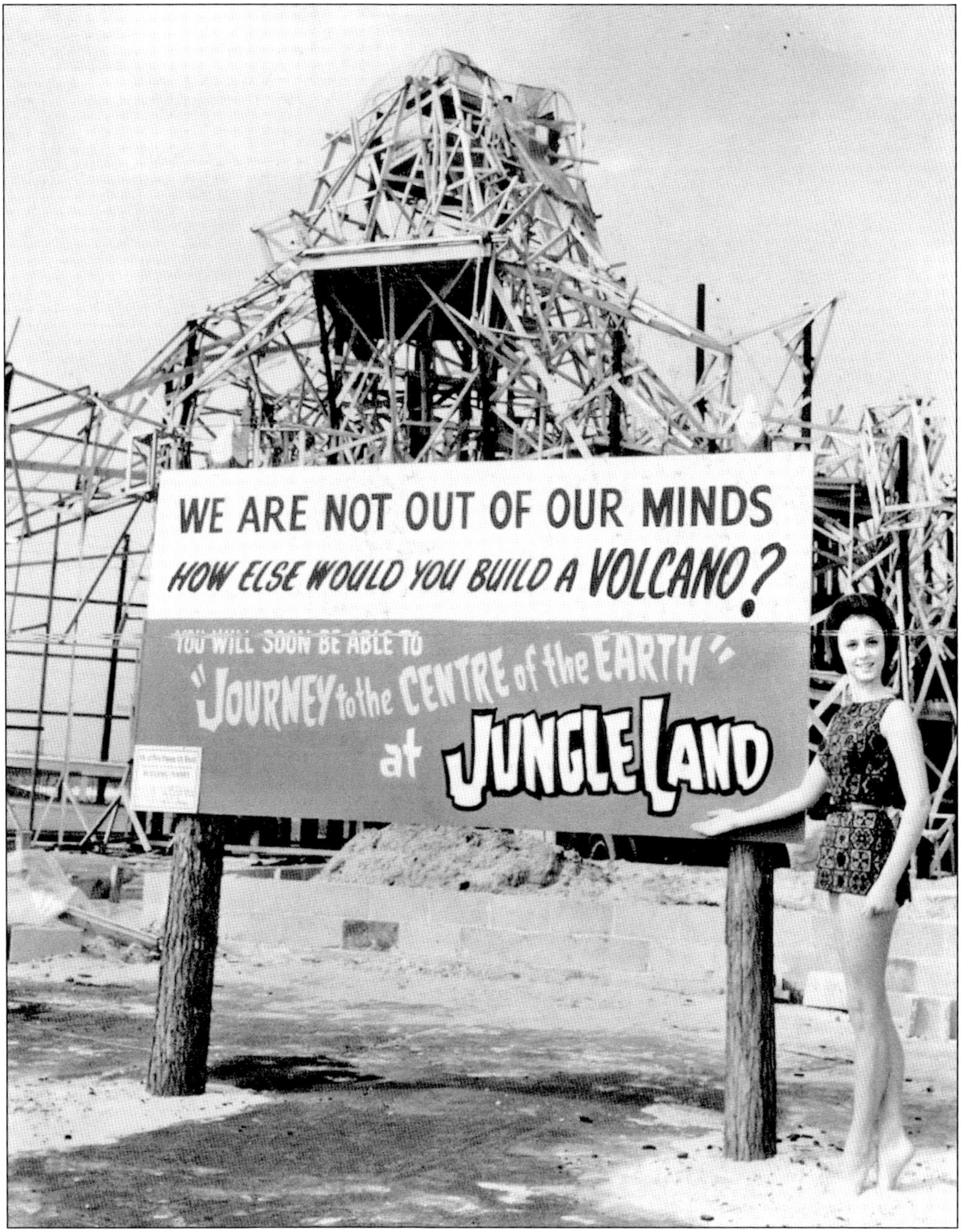

This photo of the 1970s construction site for Jungle Land shows a young lady standing next to a sign that reads, "We are not out of our minds. How else would you build a volcano?" (Courtesy Bay County Library.)

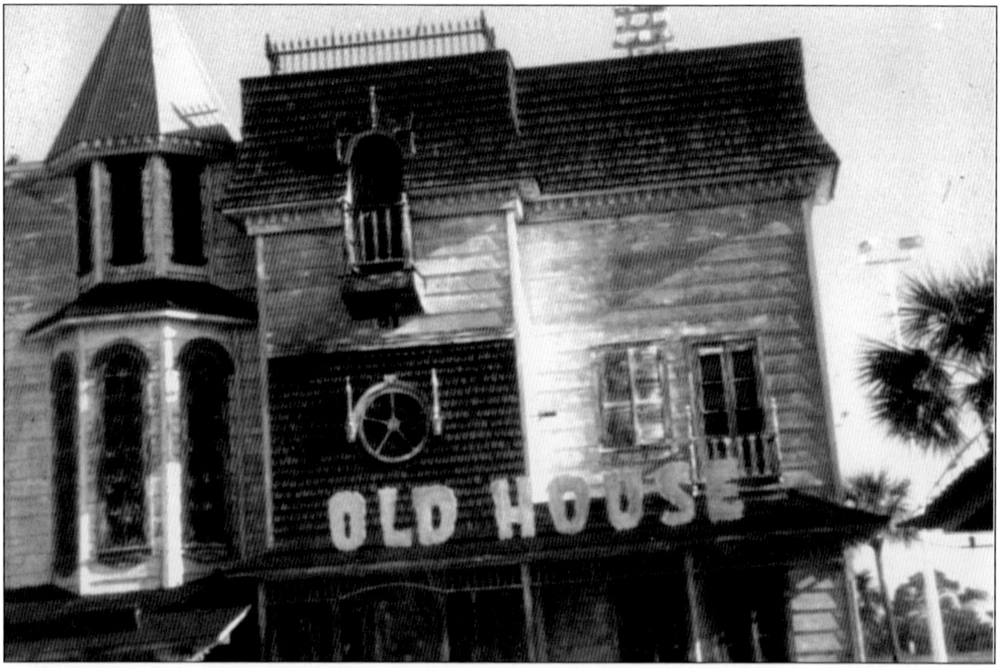

One of three haunted houses at Miracle Strip Amusement Park, the Old House featured a ghost that traversed its roofline from time to time. The Hurricane House and a medieval castle made up the rest of the trio. (Courtesy Bay County Library.)

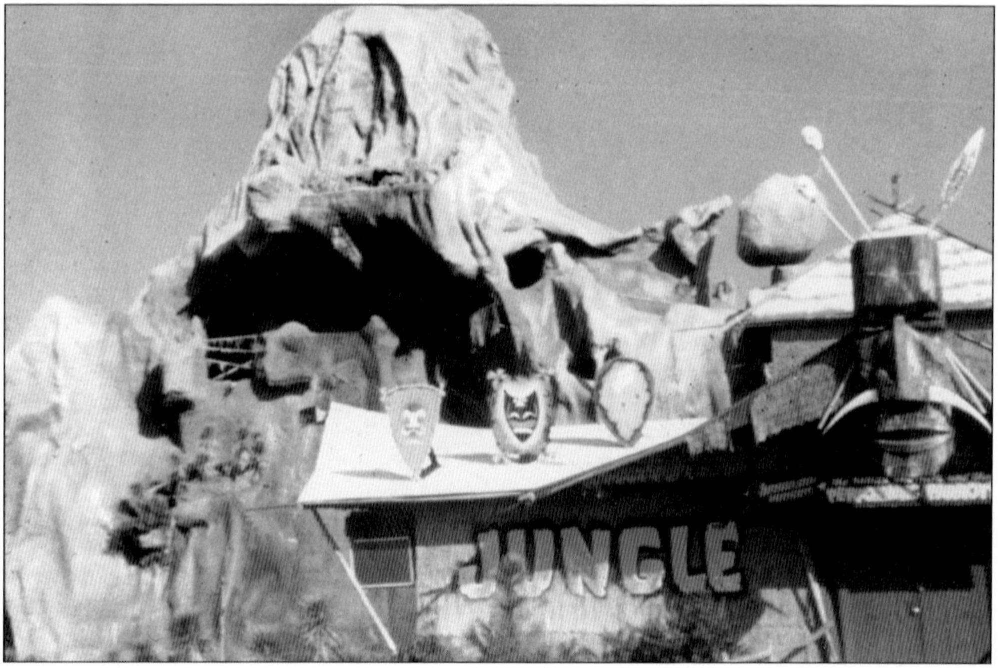

The Jungle Land "volcano" was built by Vincent Valentine to attract visitors to his small zoo near the Miracle Strip Amusement Park. His volcanic creation successfully lured folks to the site, where they could watch the "volcano" belch fire and smoke from its center. It is currently the focal point of Alvin's Island at the Magic Mount Mall. (Courtesy Bay County Library.)

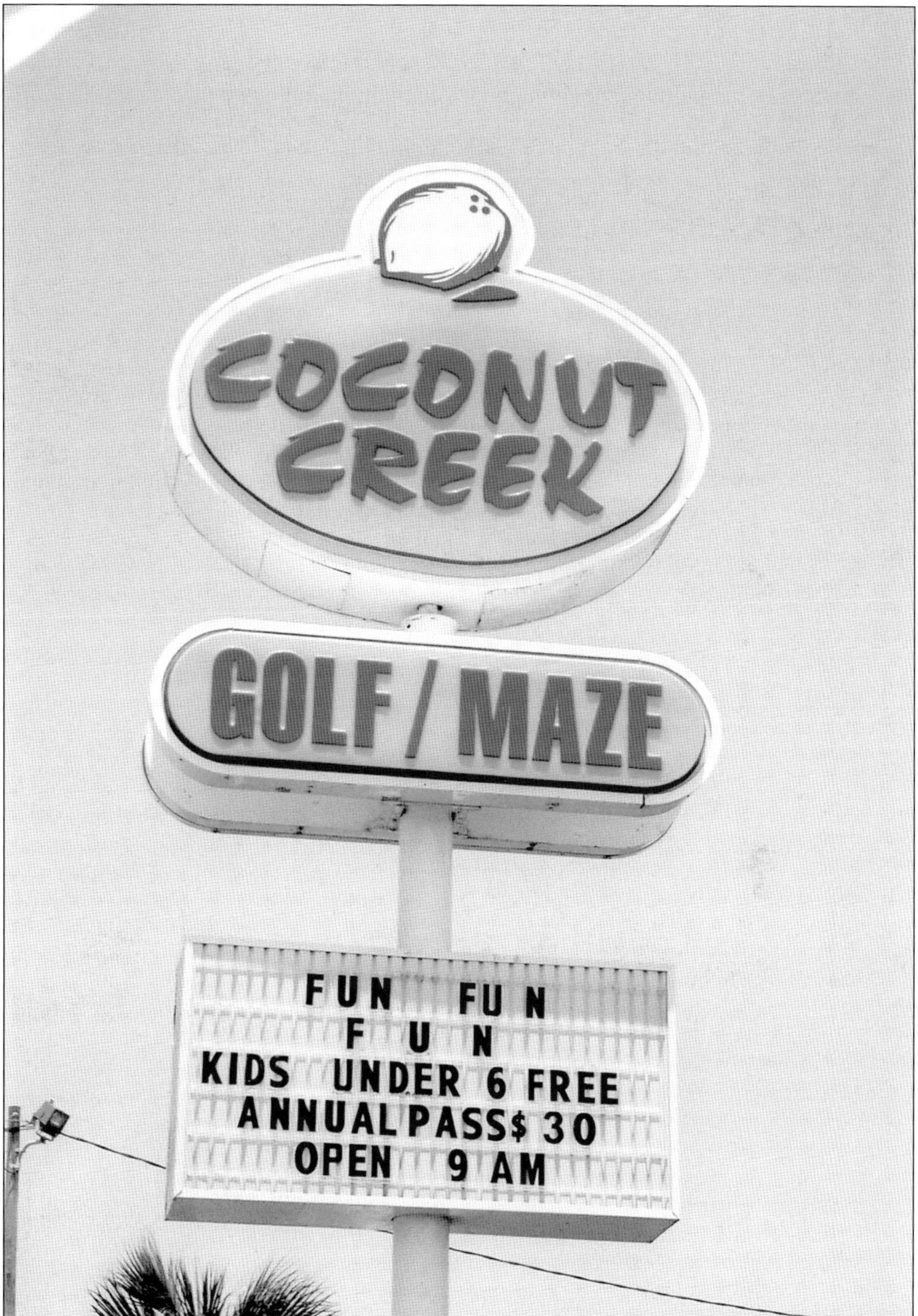

Opened in the spring of 1984, Coconut Creek features a whimsical miniature golf course and intricate Gran Maze. The family fun park is located on Front Beach Road and is owned by the Weber family. (Courtesy Carolyn Insley.)

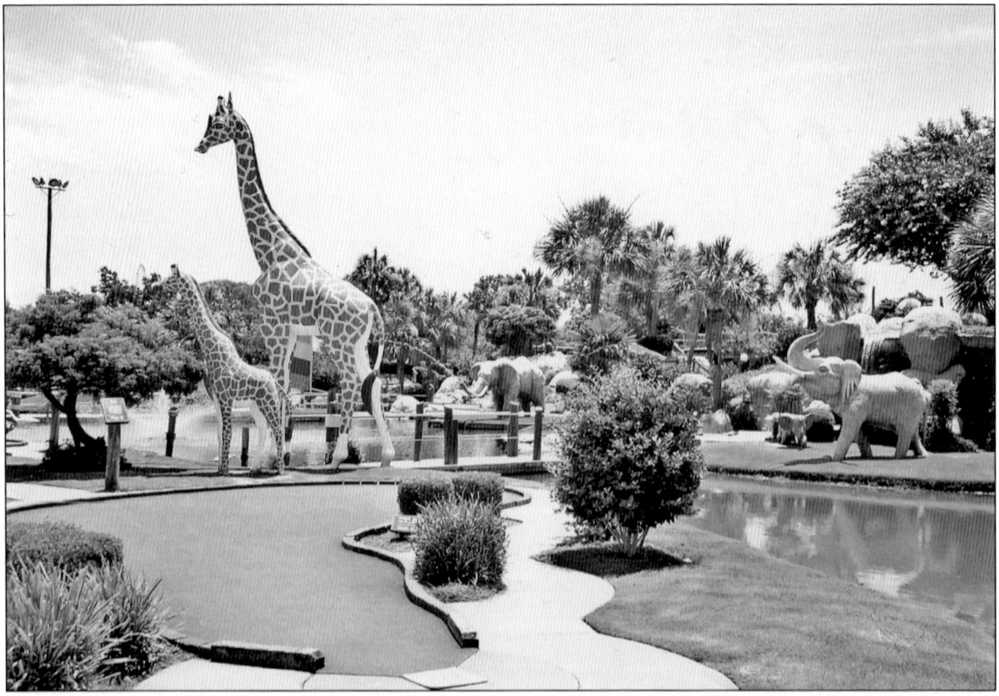

Lifelike elephants and leggy giraffes dwarf the putting greens at the Coconut Creek Golf and Gran Maze Park. (Courtesy Carolyn Insley.)

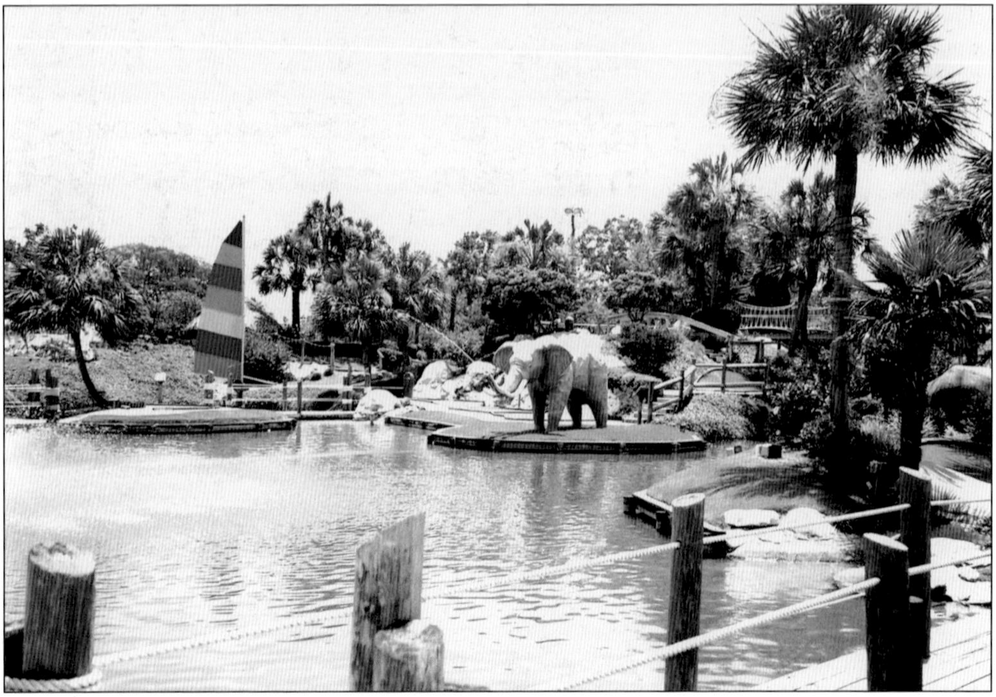

Jungle sounds are just part of the adventure at this safari-themed miniature golf course. (Courtesy Carolyn Insley.)

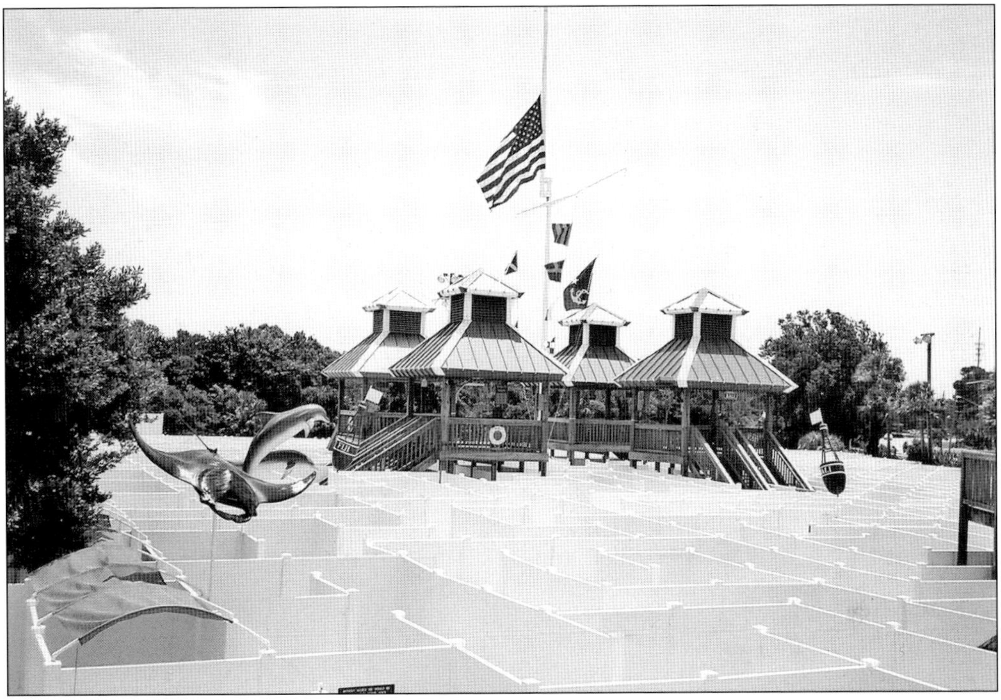

The Gran Maze at Coconut Creek offers vacationers a chance to test their directional skills. Note the watchtowers located at the center of this picture. They contain guides who help those who become lost in the maze find their way out. (Courtesy Carolyn Insley.)

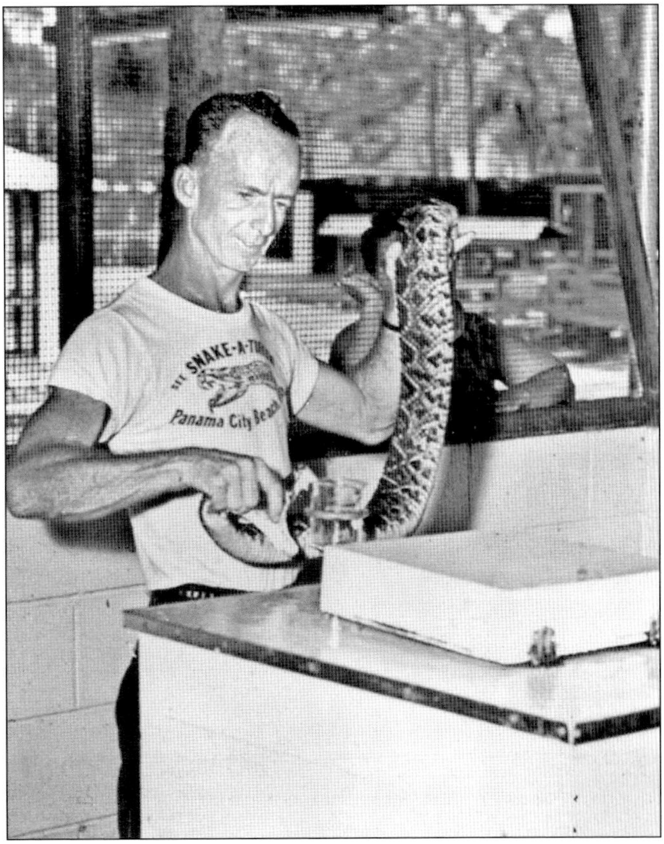

The Snake-A-Torium housed all types of snakes from boa constrictors to common garter snakes at its location on Highway 98. It has since been replaced by a petting zoo. (Courtesy Bay County Library.)

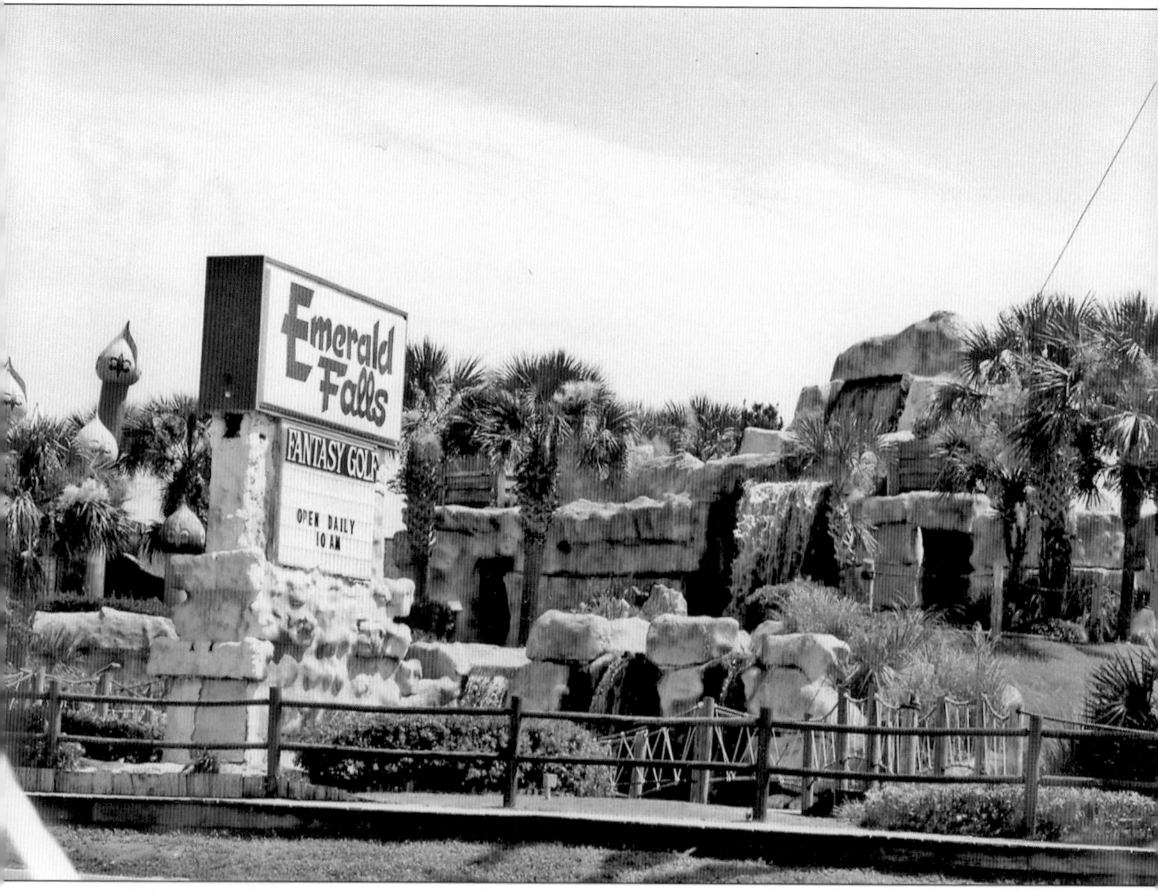

Noted for its gigantic "green water" waterfall, the Emerald Falls Family Center opened in 1986. According to Johnny Reynolds, general manager and partner of the facility, the site was originally part of the St. Thomas complex until purchased by the Emerald Falls Company. Over the years the golf course has expanded to incorporate a go-kart track, bungee bounce, arcade, and snack bar. (Courtesy Carolyn Insley.)

Six

The Lifeguards

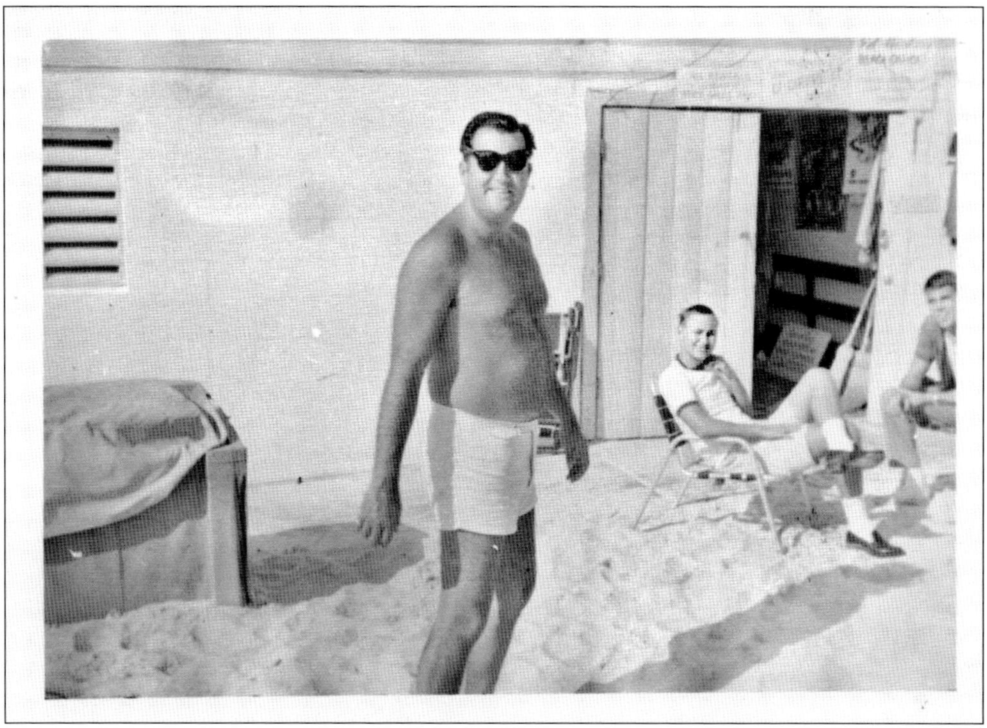

Ed Hickey (pictured in this 1960s photo) started Ed's Beach Service (E.B.S.) in the early 1950s. For many years, E.B.S. supplied lifeguards free of charge to Panama City beaches in exchange for being its sole beach equipment rental concessionaire. Having recently celebrated their 52nd year of business, E.B.S. continues to be a recognizable presence on the beach. (Courtesy Dick Doerr.)

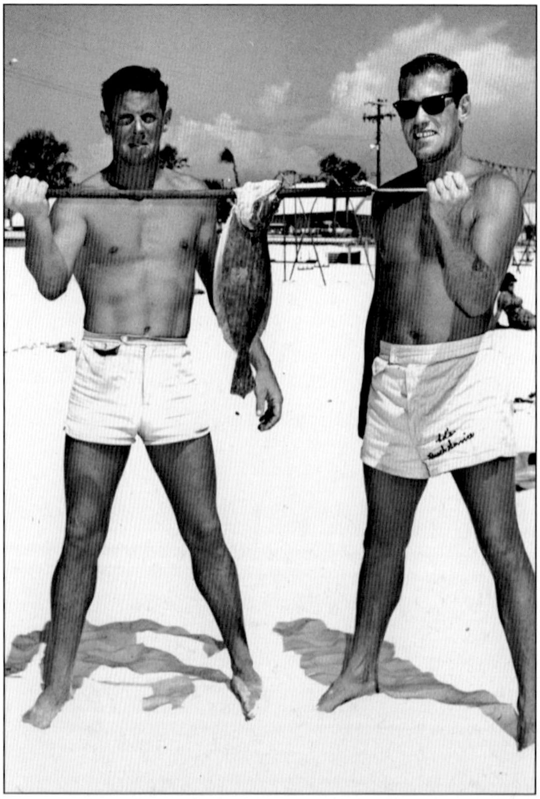

Lifeguard Leo Tober and an unidentified colleague proudly display a fish caught in the Gulf of Mexico just off Panama City Beach. The two worked as lifeguards for E.B.S. in the early 1960s. (Courtesy Dick Doerr.)

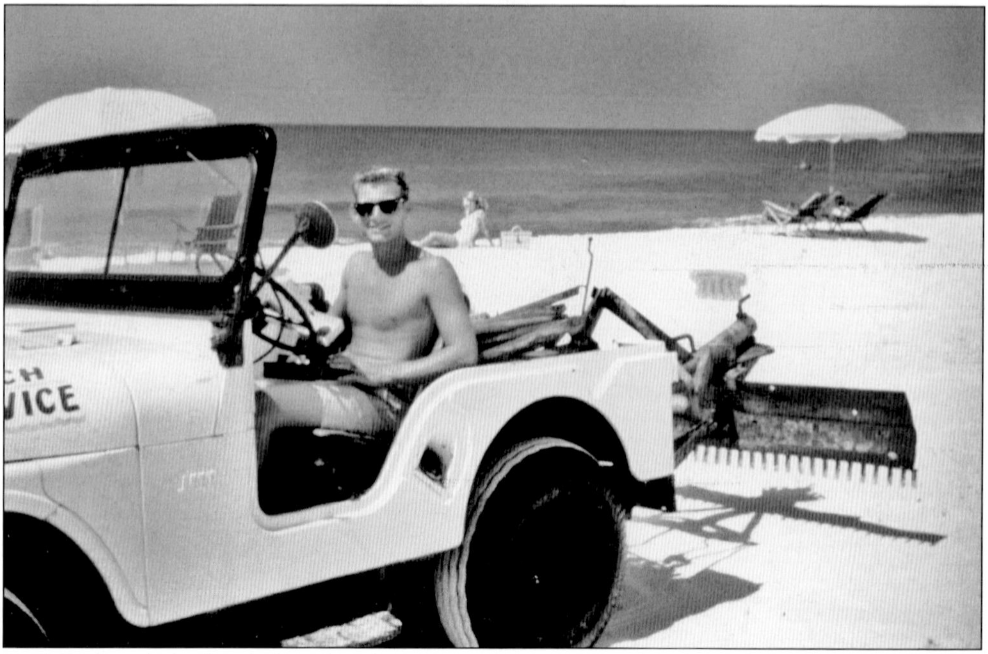

Dick Doerr takes a break from his duties. His jeep is outfitted with a rake to keep the beaches clean of driftwood and debris. Yellow E.B.S. umbrellas can be seen in background. (Courtesy Dick Doerr.)

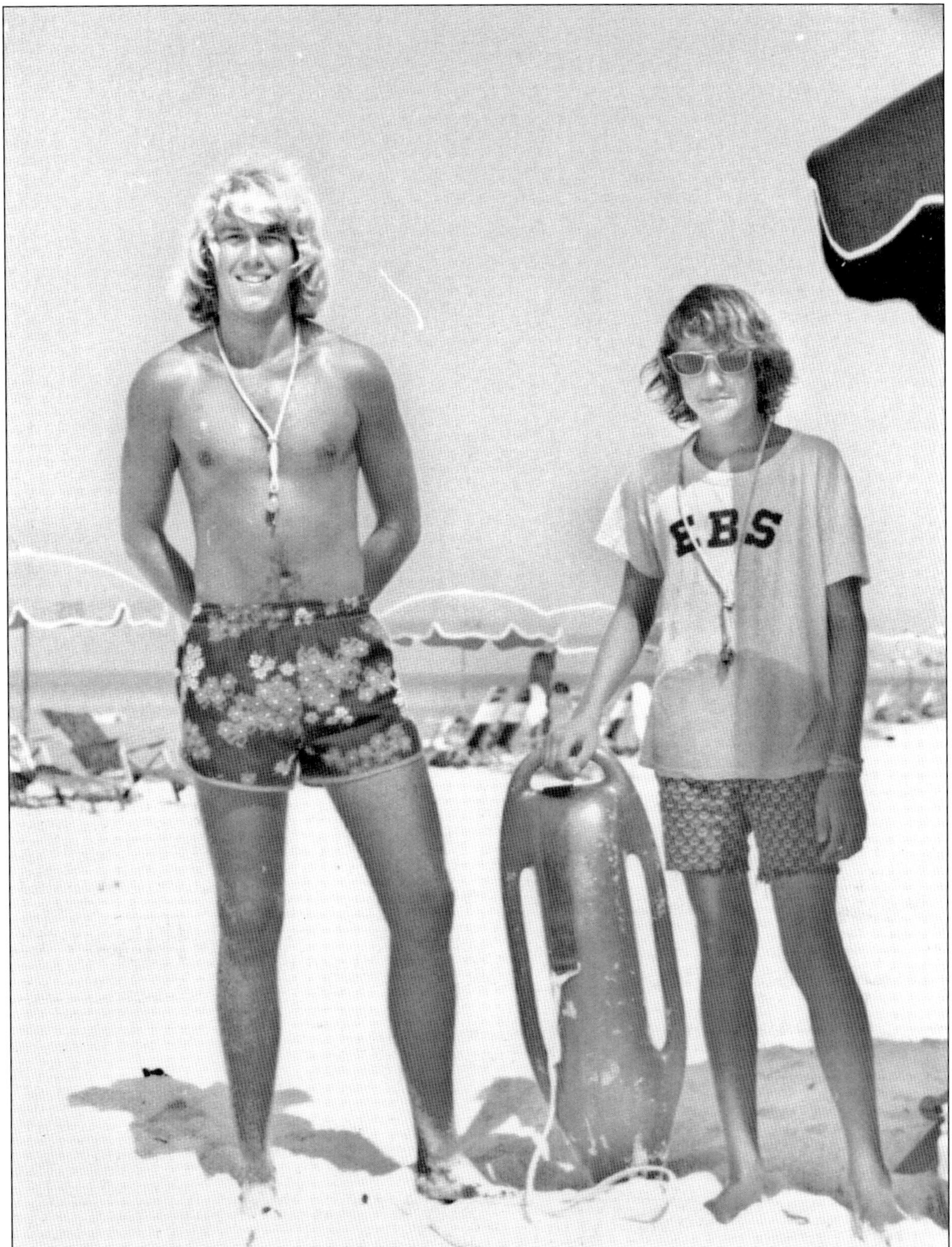

Johnny Ray, from Birmingham, Alabama, is pictured in front of the Chateau Motel with an unidentified helper in 1971. Johnny was a lifeguard on Panama City beaches from 1970 to 1972. (Courtesy James Stevenson.)

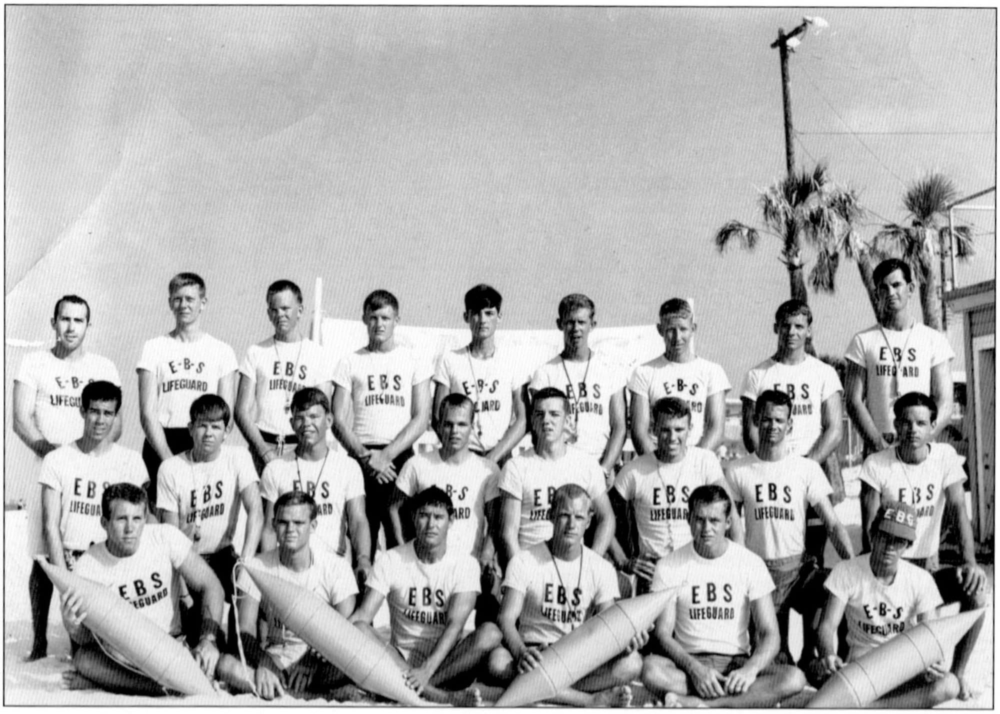

This late 1960s photo of E.B.S. lifeguards features manager Dean Williams in the back row at left, the "Kid," Al Fisher, Jimmy Lubnow, Tuffy Adams, and Chuck Buckley. (Courtesy James Stevenson.)

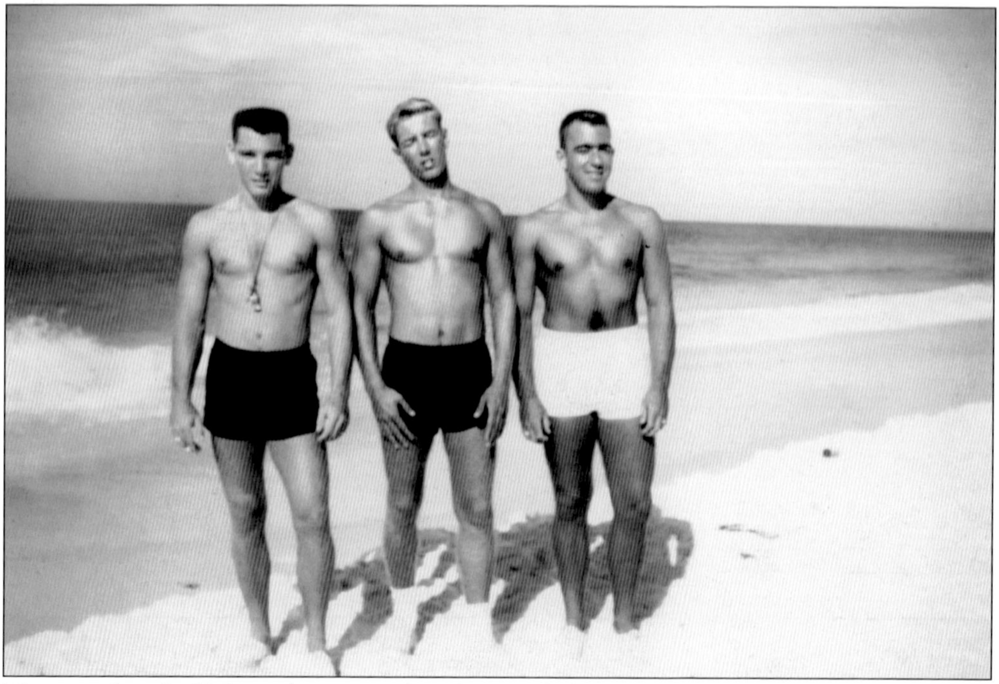

Three unidentified lifeguards pose on the white sandy beaches of Panama City Beach *c.* 1960s. (Courtesy Dick Doerr.)

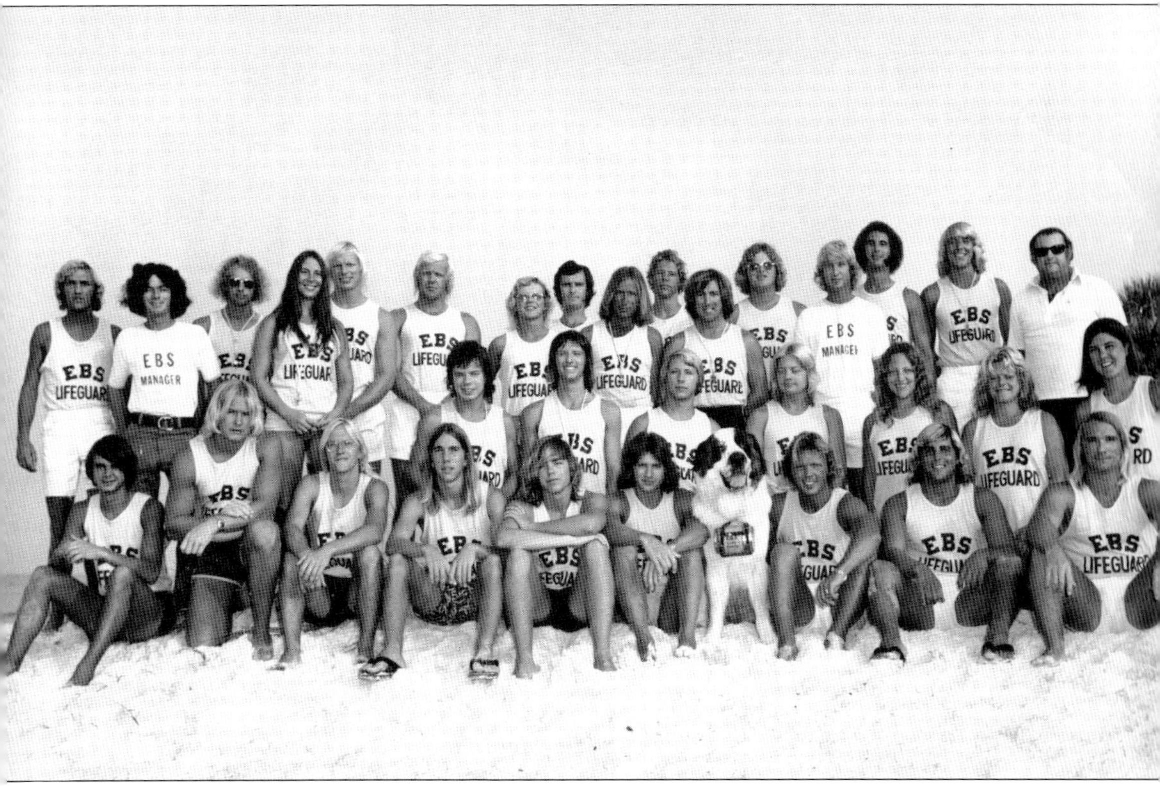

This group photo of E.B.S. lifeguards was taken *c.* 1970. Some of the lifeguards in the picture are Larry Pierce, manager Chuck Buckley, Chris Timm, James Stevenson, Dusty, manager Rudy Valle, Johnny Ray, John Barkley, Jerry Bryant, and B.J. Matthews. "Sebastian," the group's mascot, is in the front row, fourth from right. Ed Hickey, the owner of E.B.S., is standing in the last row at right. Note that female lifeguards are starting to become more prevalent. (Courtesy James Stevenson.)

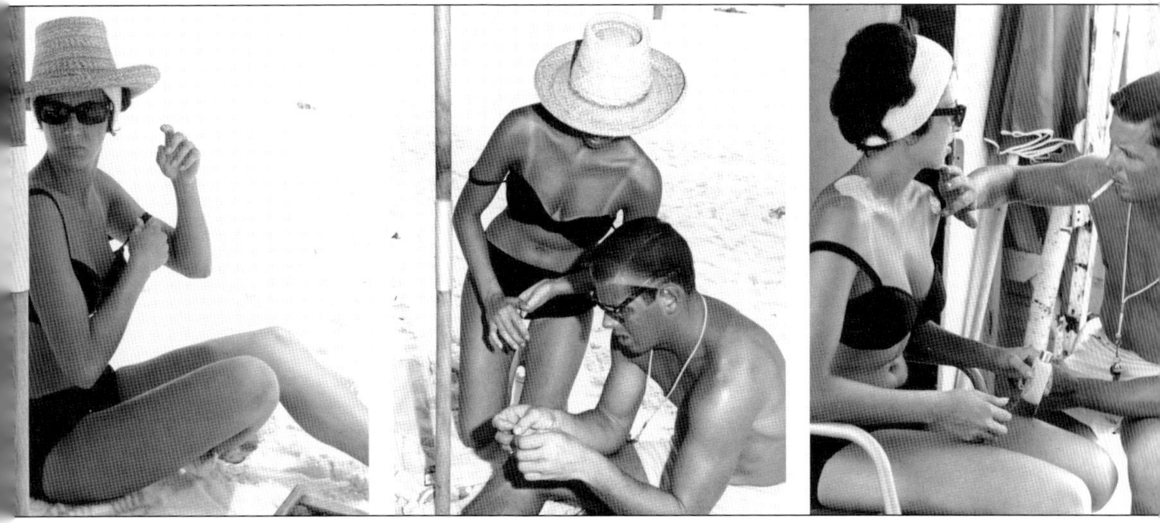

This is just one of the perks of being a lifeguard in Panama City Beach! Here Leo Tober helps an unidentified vacationer apply suntan lotion *c.* 1960. (Courtesy Dick Doerr.)

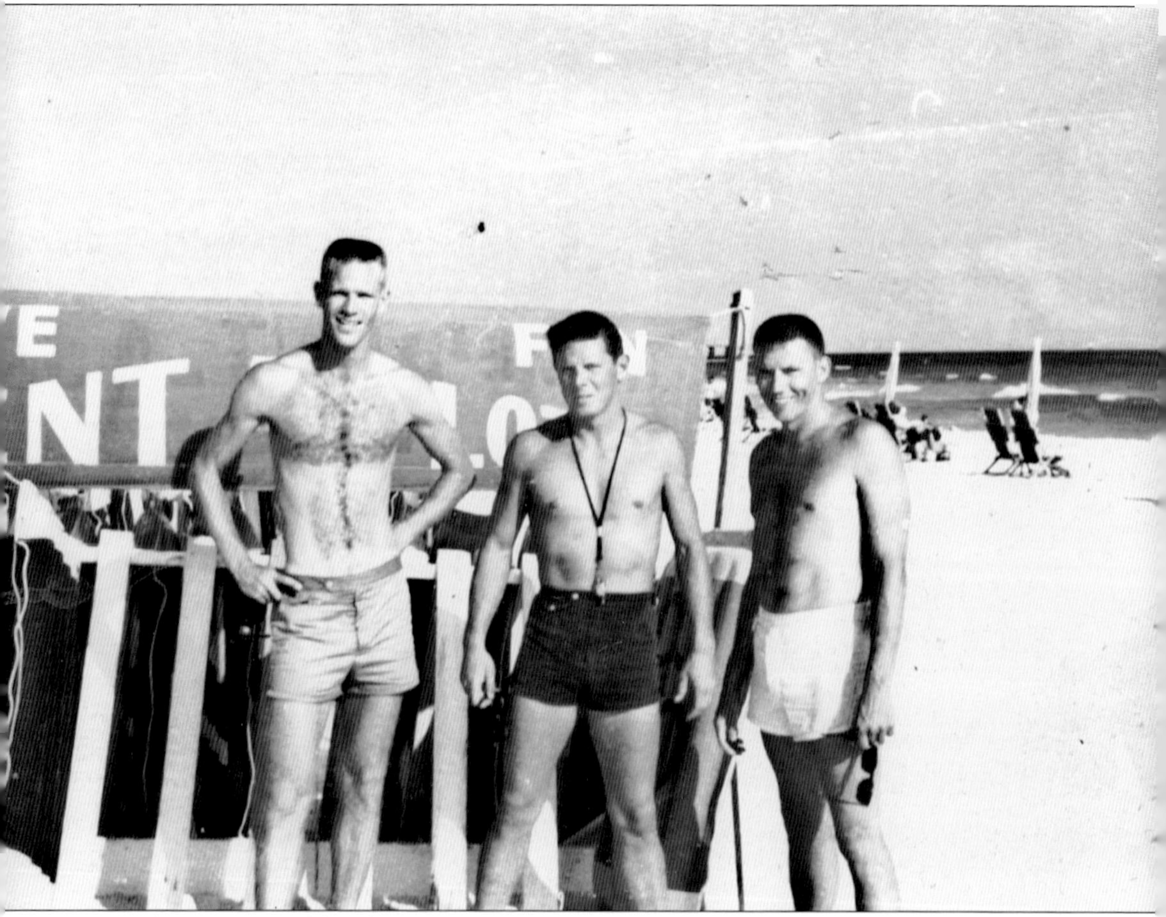

Years before *Baywatch* hit the airwaves, lifeguards Arlen "Butter" Fulwiler (left) and Leo Tober (center), pictured in this late 1950s photo with Fred Phagen, always thought that a television show about lifeguards would be a big hit. (Courtesy Dick Doerr.)

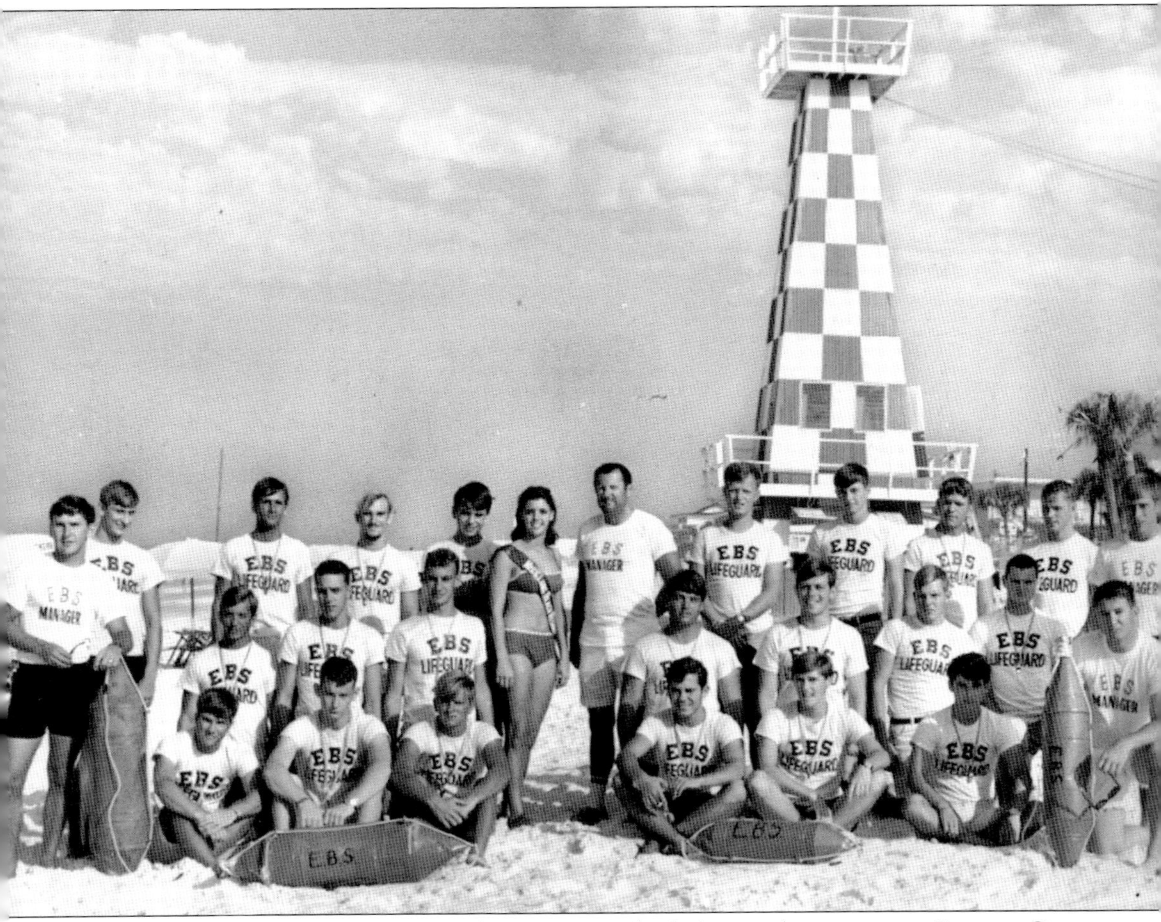

Miss Long Beach, Marie Savage, welcomes E.B.S. back for another season at Panama City Beach. Dean Williams and his brother Glen are pictured in this Bob Hargis photo. (Courtesy Bay C ounty Library.)

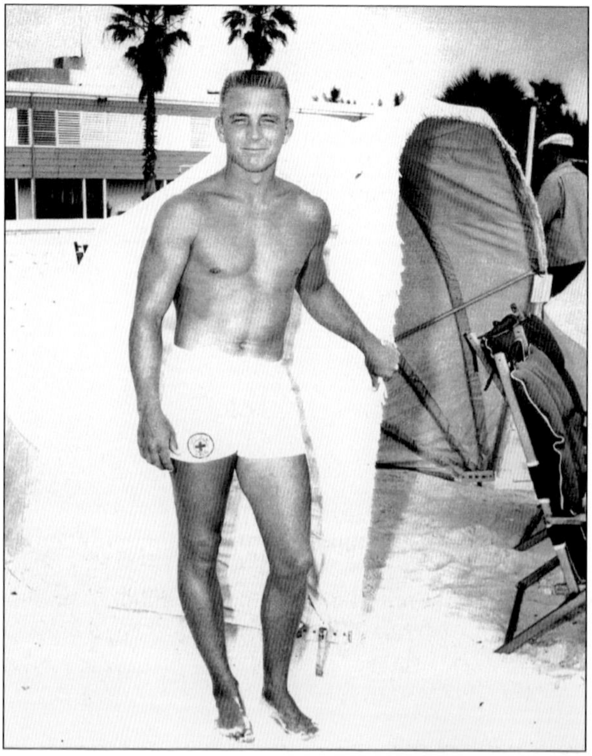

A noted wrestler in his own right, lifeguard John Wallace, pictured here in the 1960s at Panama City Beach, came from a family of wrestling enthusiasts. Brother James, also a lifeguard, was a world champion arm wrestler and runner-up for the Mr. World competition in Europe. (Courtesy Dick Doerr.)

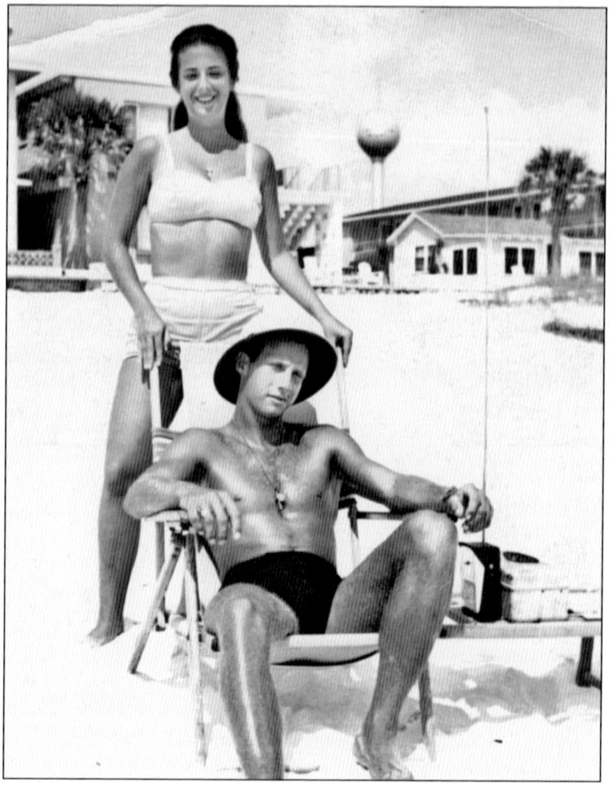

Jim Miller was a Panama City Beach lifeguard in the summer of 1962. He is pictured here with woman about whom little is known, except that she had red hair and hailed from Chicago. (Courtesy Jim Miller.)

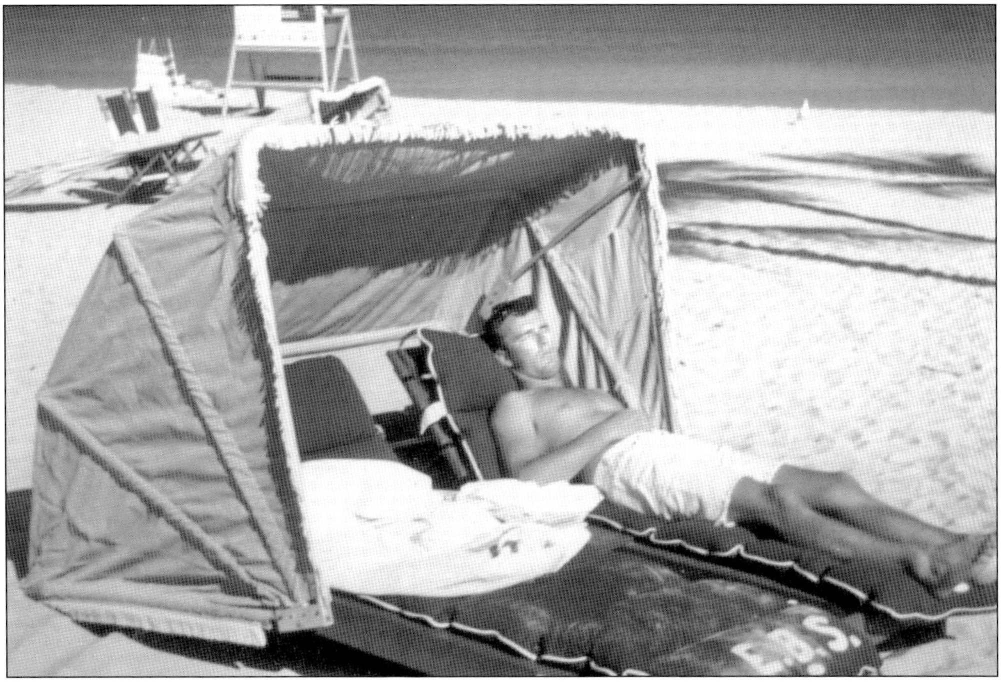

Fred Phagen was a lifeguard for E.B.S. in the 1960s. Here he takes a snooze after a day on the beach.

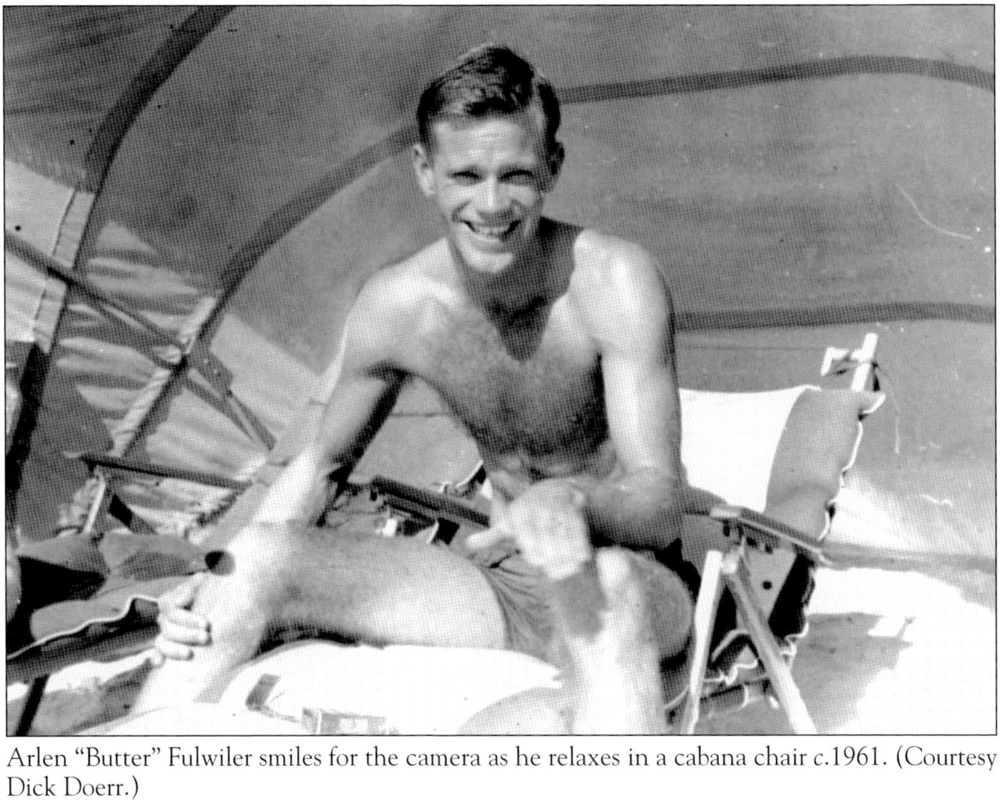

Arlen "Butter" Fulwiler smiles for the camera as he relaxes in a cabana chair c.1961. (Courtesy Dick Doerr.)

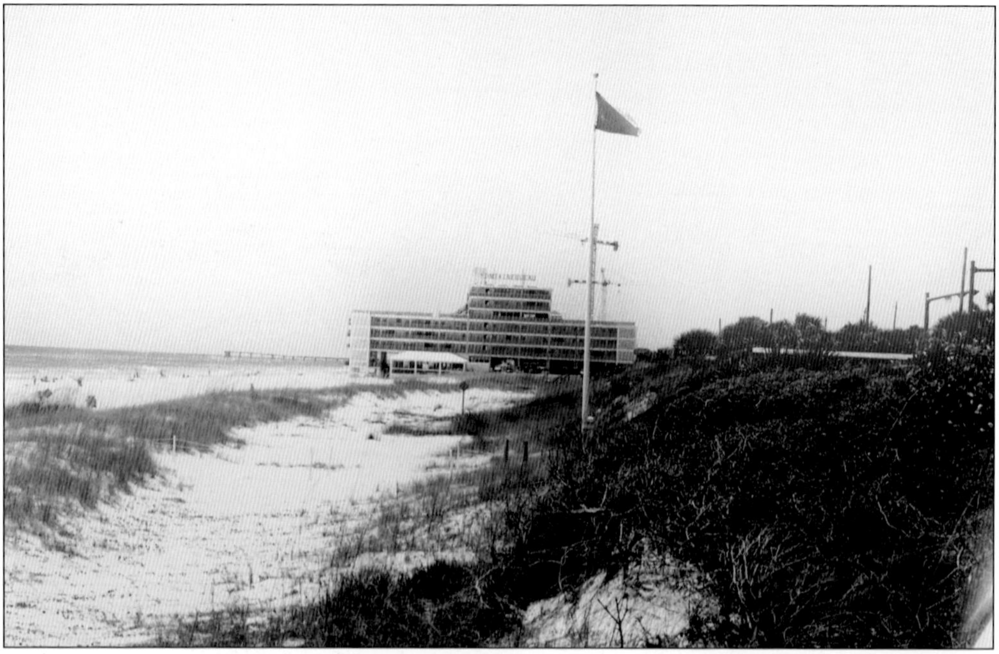

Pictured here in 2004 is the Fountainbleu Terrace Motel. For years, Labor Day marked the end of the tourist season, as vacationers from Alabama, Georgia, and Tennessee returned home to jobs and school. In the late 1970s, merchants began to realize that their temperate climate would appeal to Northerners looking for relief from winter weather. Marketing efforts met with great success, and many "snowbirds" return yearly to winter in Panama City Beach. Note the color-coded flag at center, which warns swimmers of surf conditions. (Courtesy Carolyn Insley.)

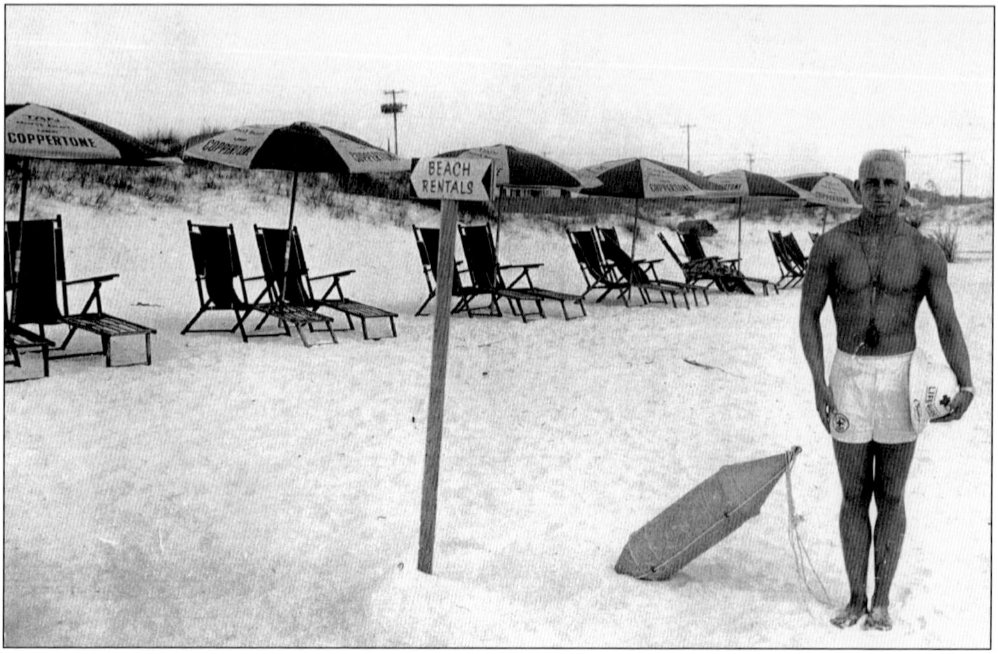

Lifeguard John Wallace is pictured here in the early 1960s. Note his bleached blonde hair. John went on to start his own beach service in the Destin–Fort Walton area. (Courtesy Dick Doerr.)

John Wallace stands beside his beach service truck. John passed away in the spring of 2004 and will be missed by those who knew him.

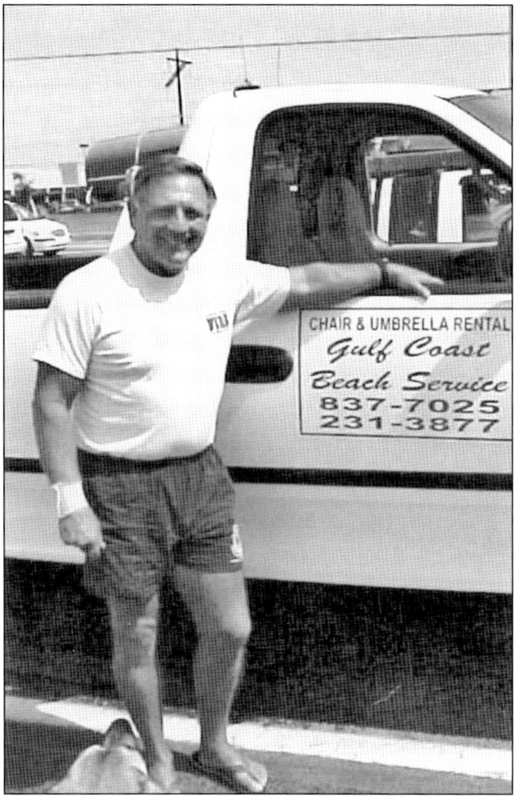

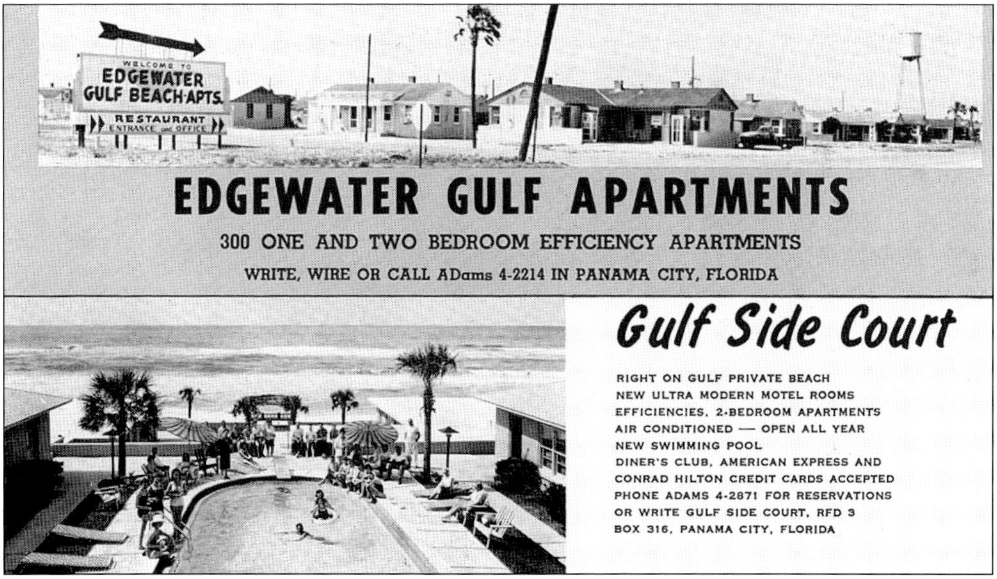

Most of the lifeguards stayed the summer at the Edgewater Gulf Apartments, pictured here in a 1958 advertisement. At season's end, they packed all the beach rental equipment—umbrellas, chairs, and rafts—into U-Hauls and transported it back to E.B.S. headquarters in St. Petersburg, Florida, for winter storage. (Courtesy Bay County Library.)

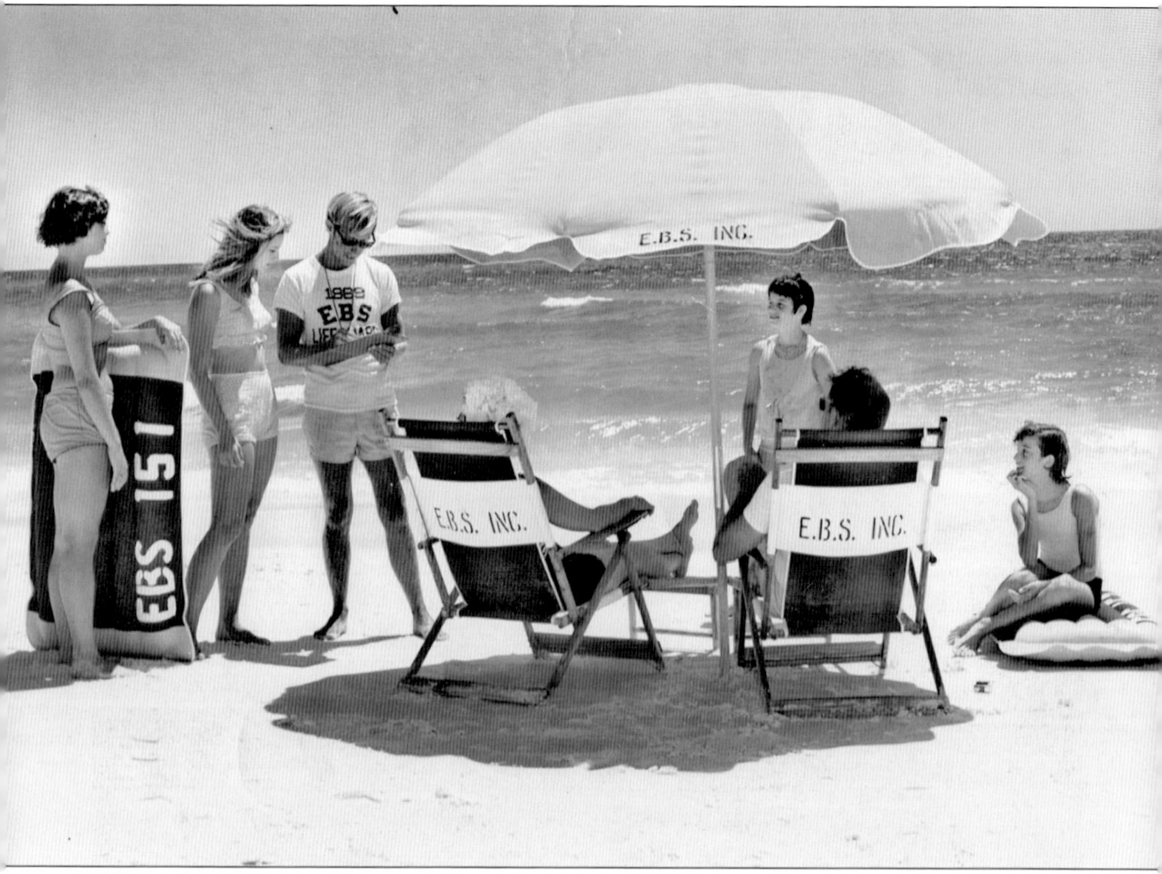

E.B.S. lifeguard James Stevenson is seen here renting beach equipment to a family in 1969. This photograph graced the cover of *Beachweek*, a weekly magazine devoted to Panama City Beach life edited by Bob Hargis. (Courtesy James Stevenson.)

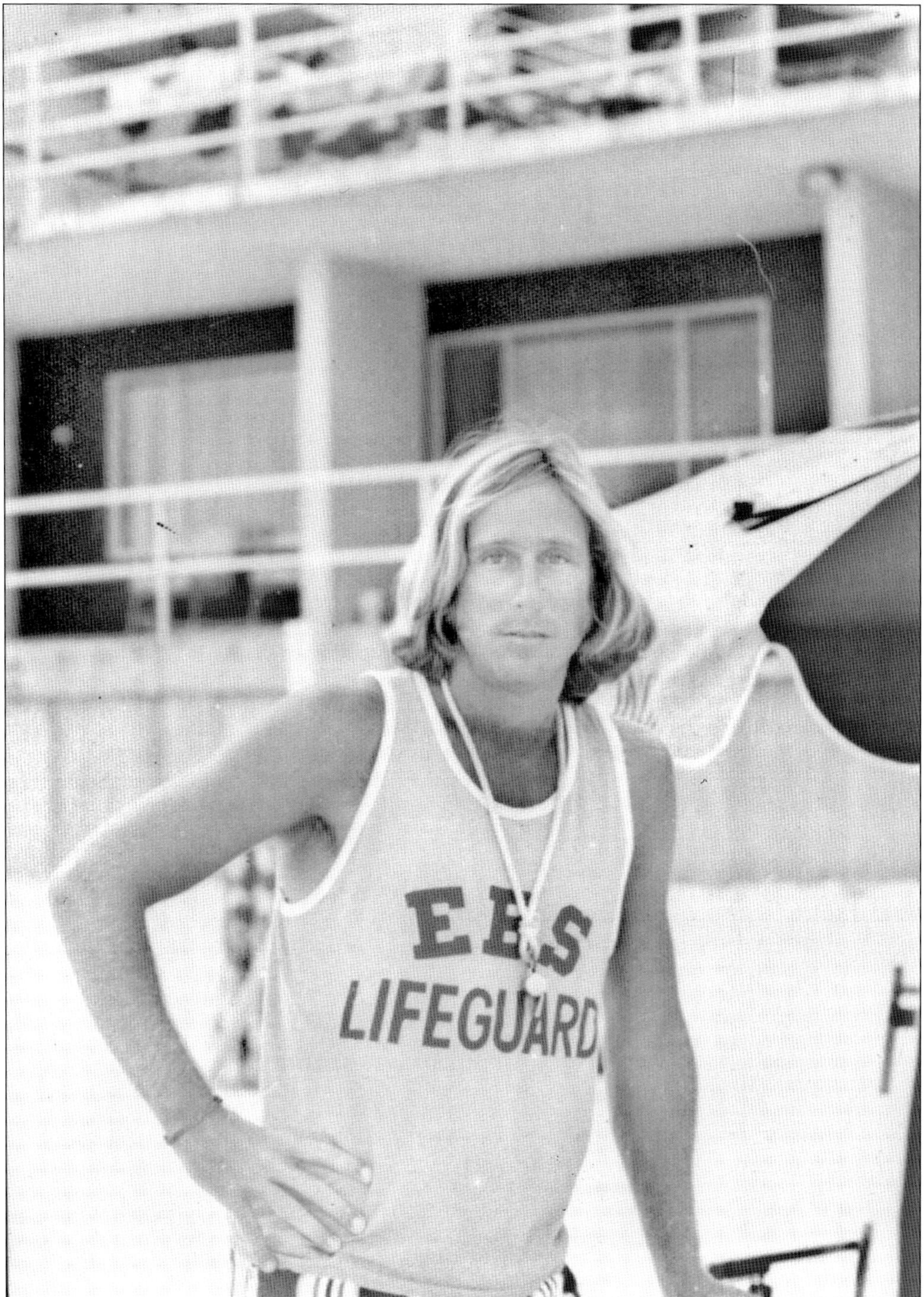

James Stevenson was a lifeguard in Panama City Beach during the late 1960s and early 1970s. He is pictured here in front of the Chateau Motel in 1969. (Courtesy James Stevenson.)

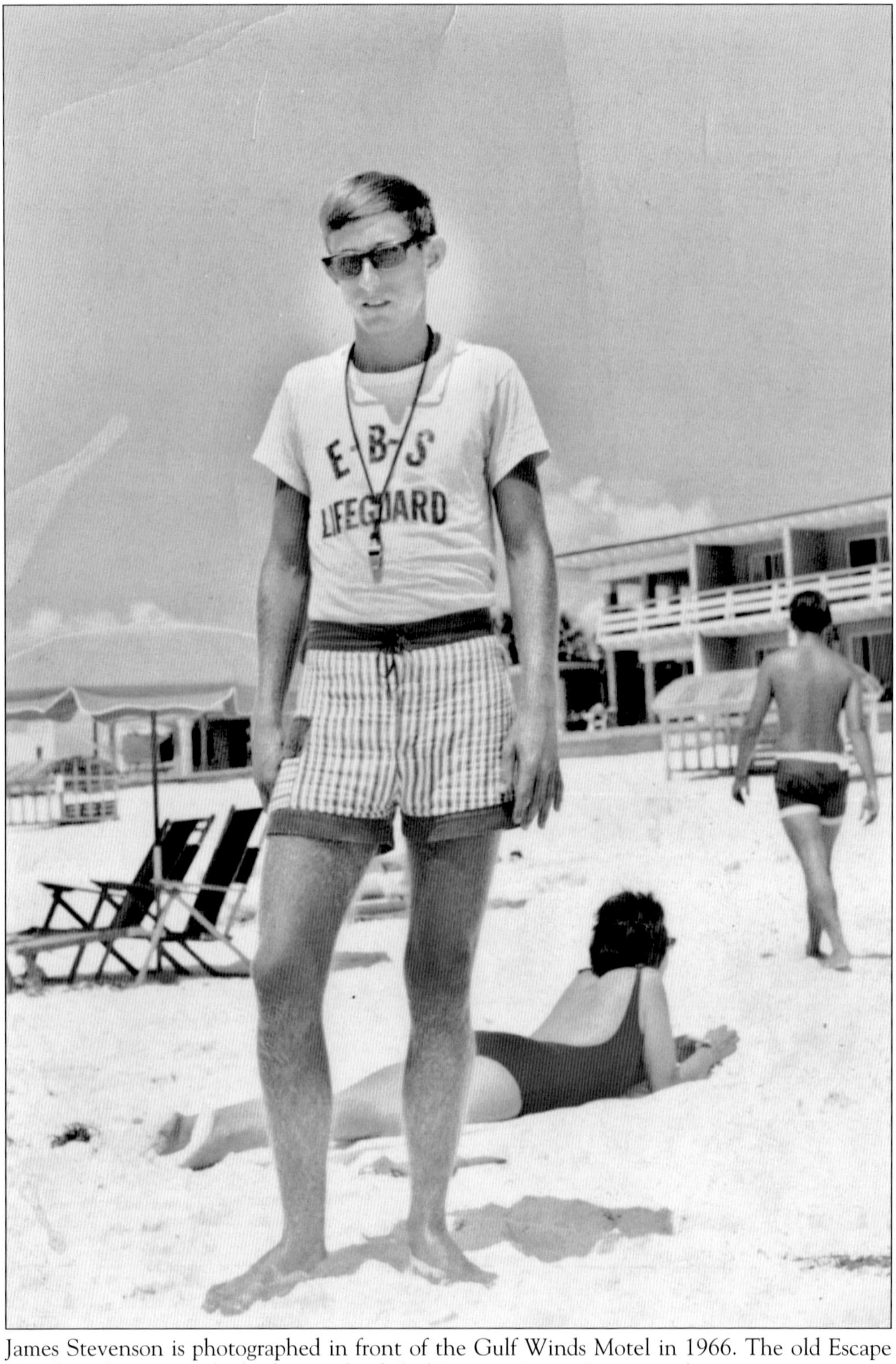

James Stevenson is photographed in front of the Gulf Winds Motel in 1966. The old Escape Motel can be seen in the background at left. (Courtesy James Stevenson.)

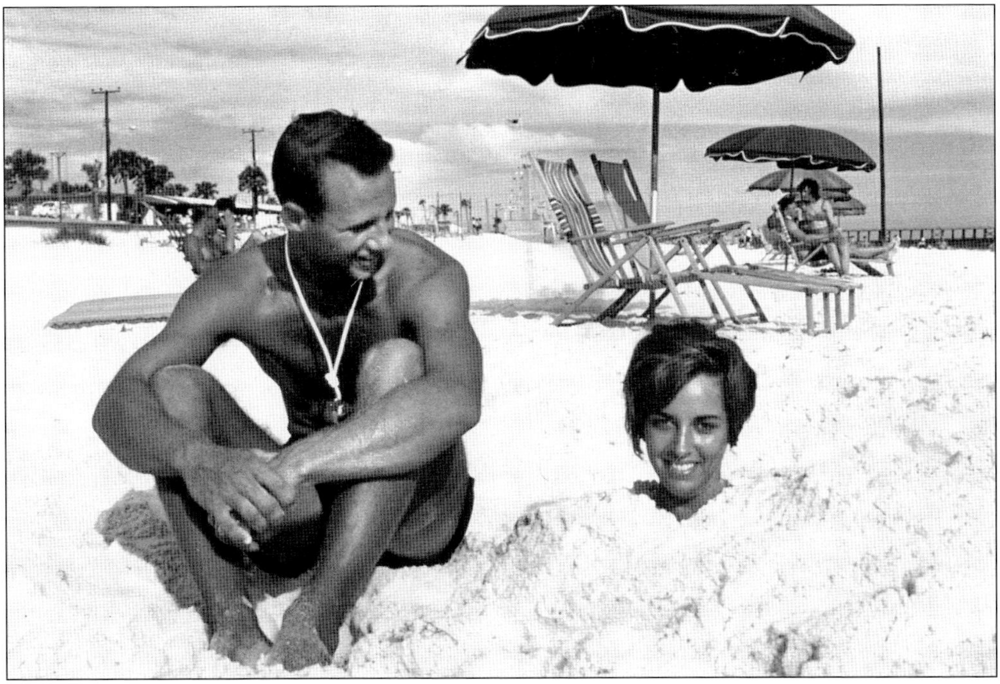

Panama City Beach lifeguard Jim Miller seems amused by Brenda Cheek's predicament, as evidenced by this 1961 photograph. Ironically, Jim had to rescue the woman in the background under the umbrella several days later when she grew fatigued while swimming in the Gulf of Mexico. (Courtesy Jim Miller.)

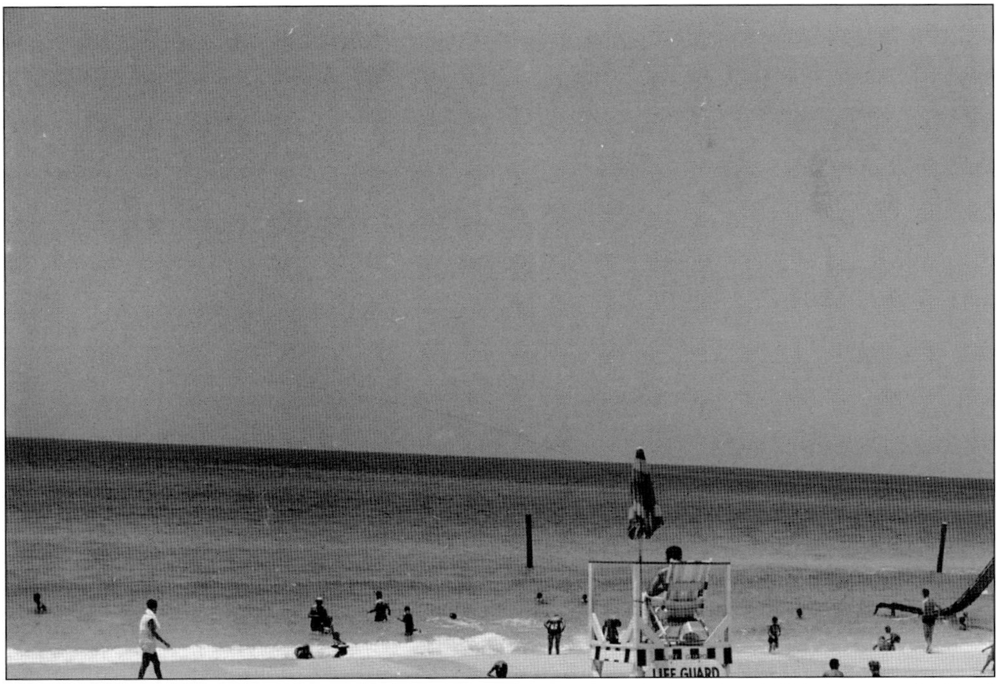

The Long Beach Resort lifeguard stand can be seen at center left in this 1954 photograph. Sand chairs weren't yet in vogue with this "beach blanket" crowd. (Courtesy Florida State Archives.)

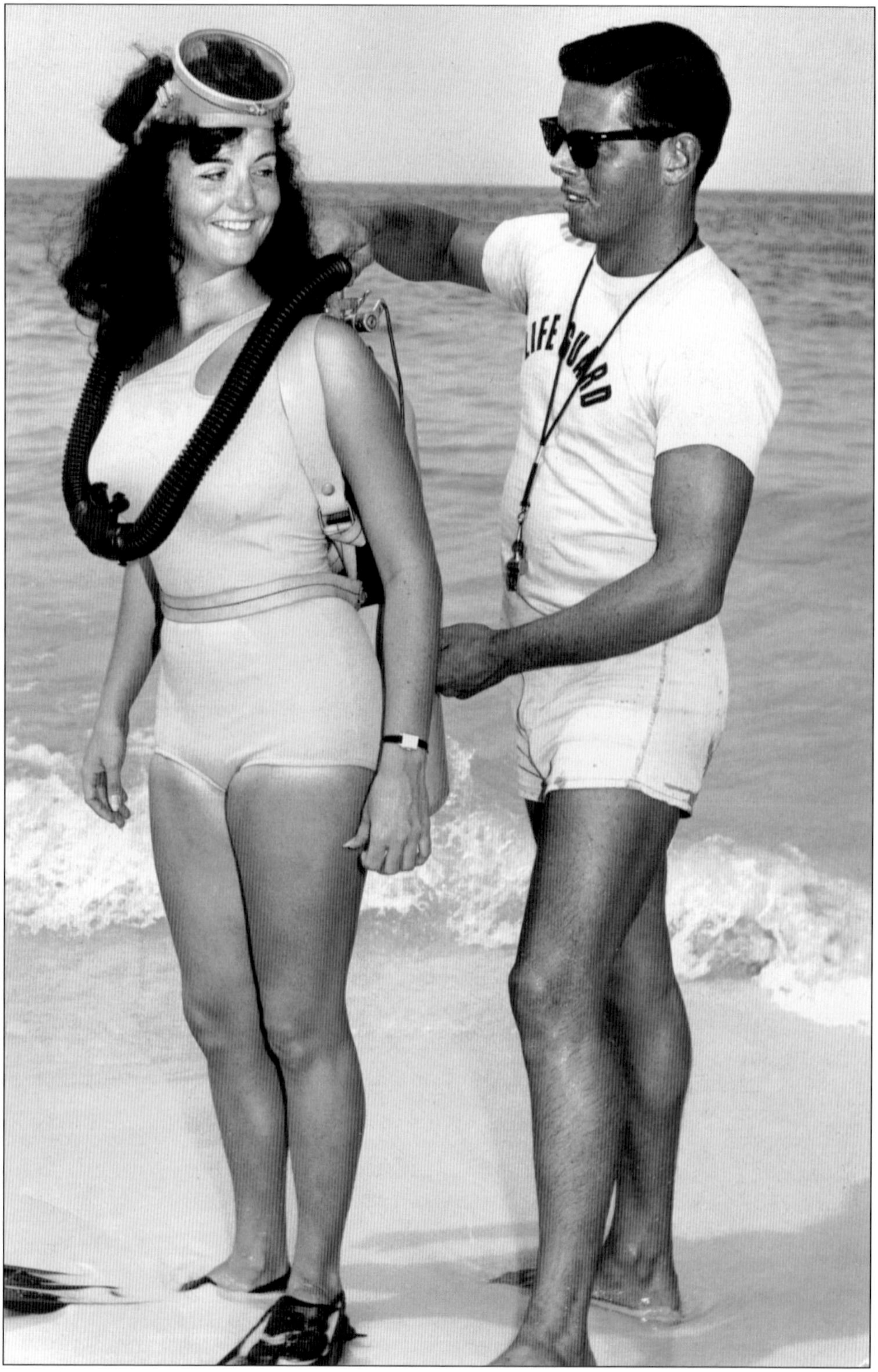

Leo Tober helps an unidentified vacationer with scuba gear, *c.* 1960s. (Courtesy Dick Doerr.)

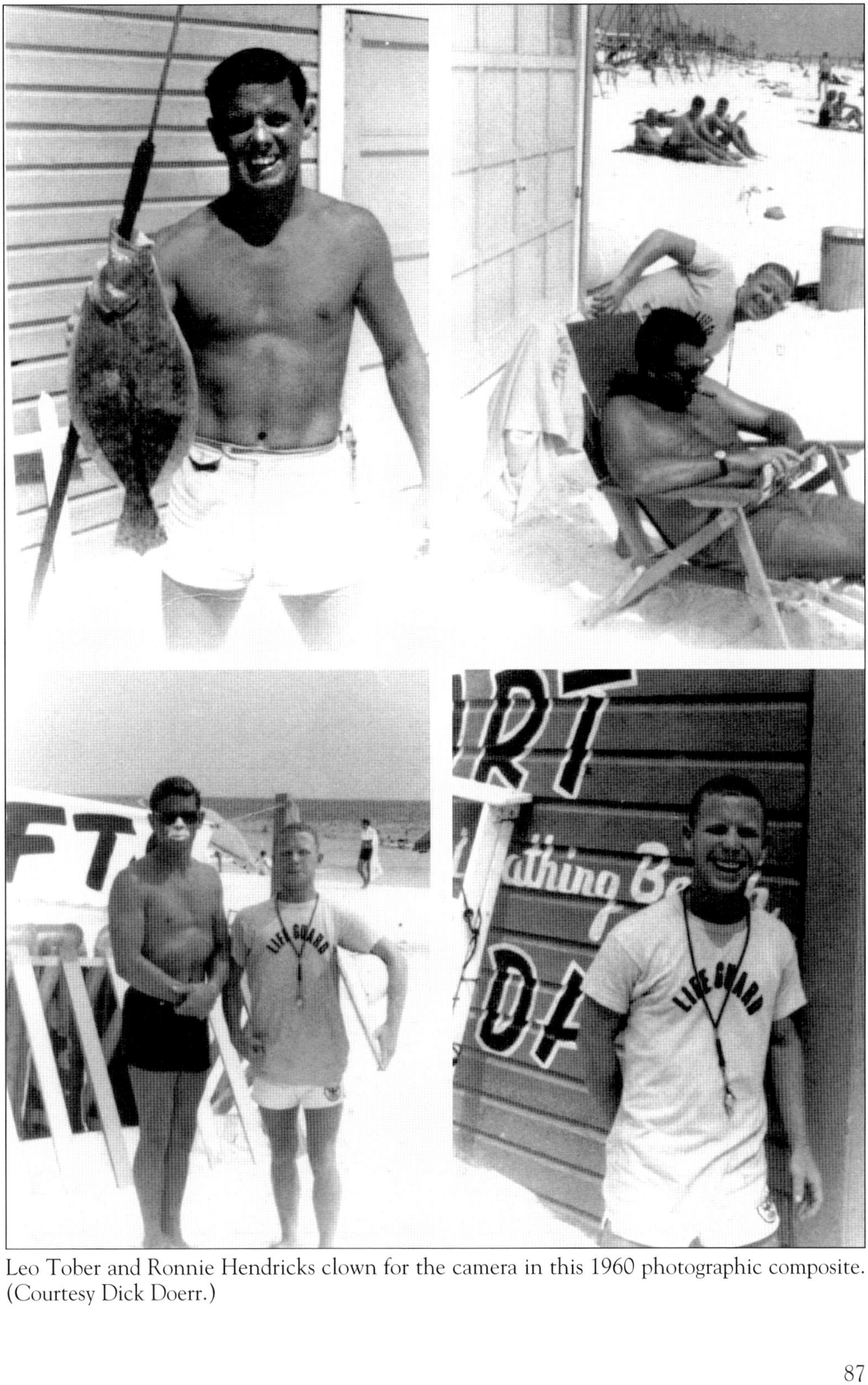

Leo Tober and Ronnie Hendricks clown for the camera in this 1960 photographic composite. (Courtesy Dick Doerr.)

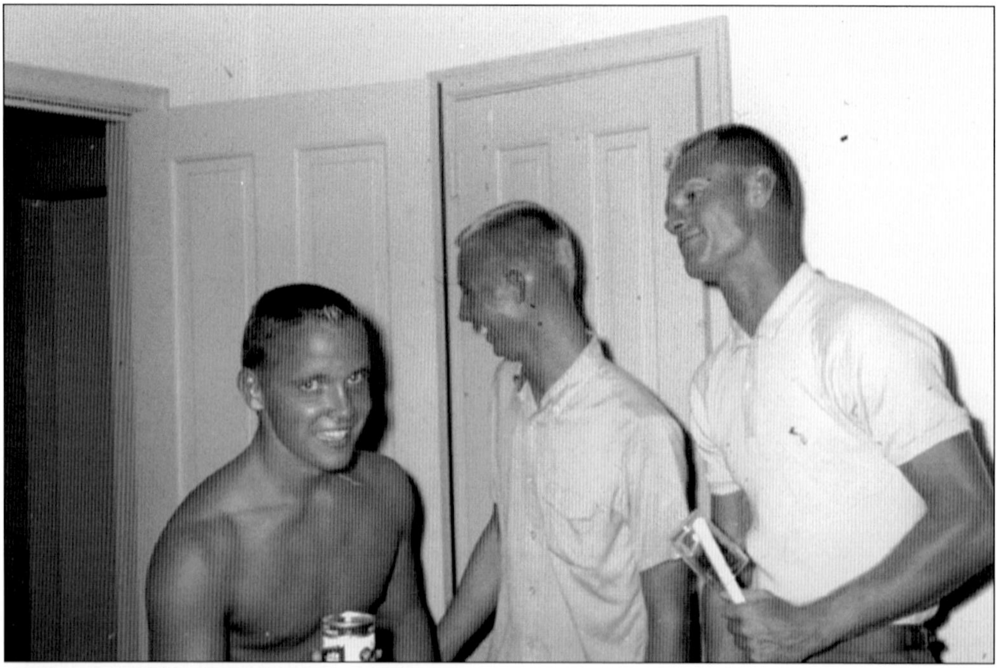

At the end of the day, lifeguards Jim Horton, "Germ," and Arlen Fulwiler are getting ready to head to the Hang Out. (Courtesy Dick Doerr.)

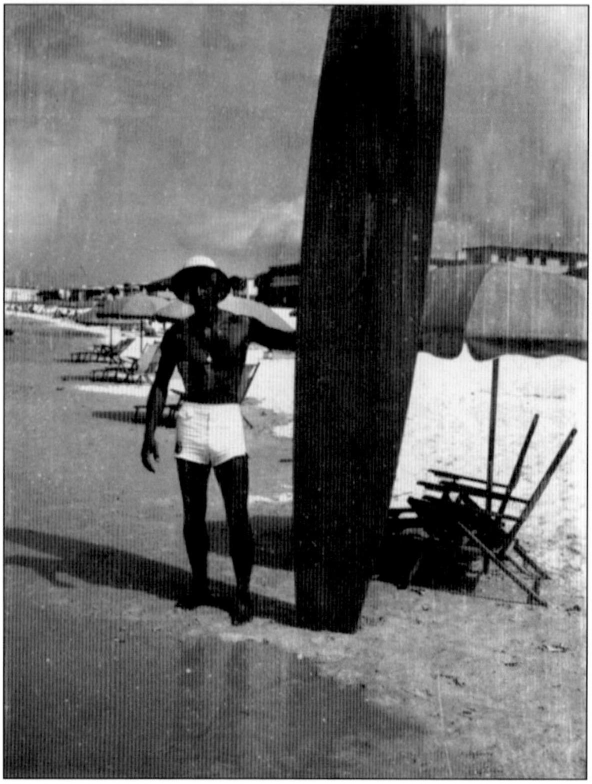

Jim Miller is seen on the last day of the 1962 summer season with a rescue board. Built in the winter of 1961 and constructed of marine wood with pine struts, the hollow rescue board could support up to three adults. (Courtesy Jim Miller.)

Seven

HURRICANES

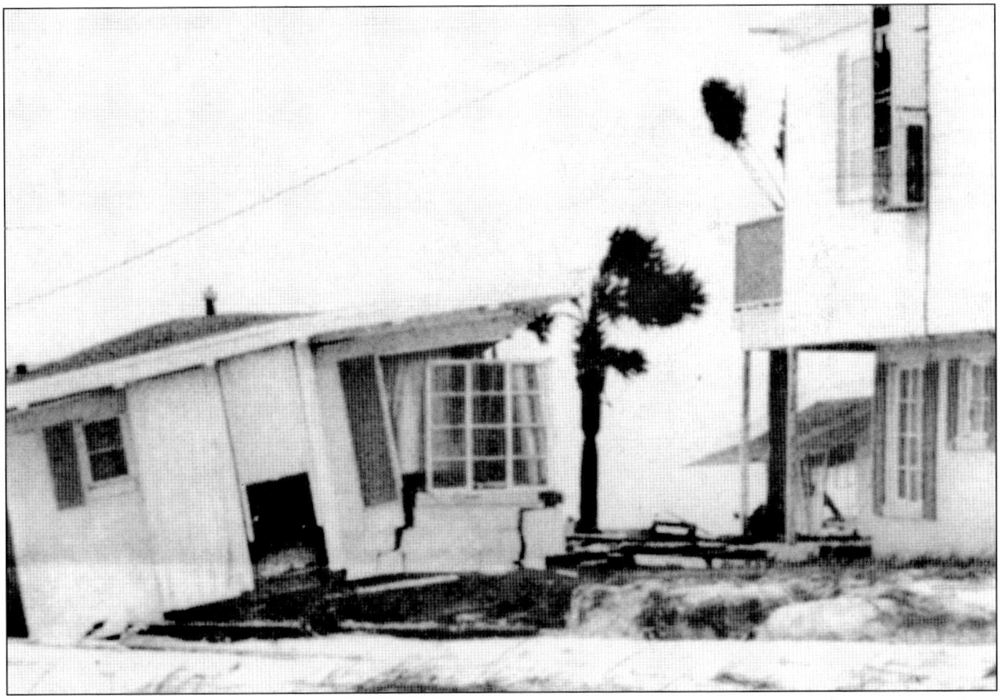

"The task of rebuilding Panama City Beach will be a formidable one," reports the Panama City *New-Herald* on Thursday, September 25, 1975, just two days after Hurricane Eloise struck the community, "but the beach colony has already started digging out from the debris and is not discouraged." (Courtesy *News-Herald.)*

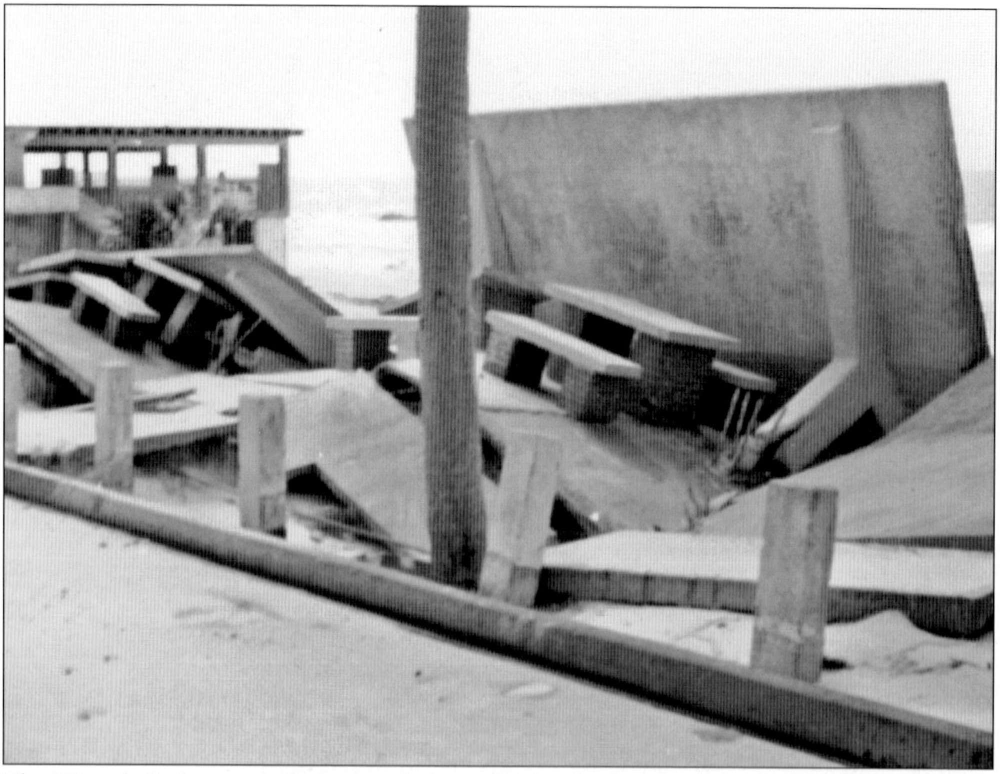

The Wayside Park area along the beach shows the harsh effects of Hurricane Eloise. The storm hit Panama City Beach in September 1975. This photo was taken on September 23, 1975.

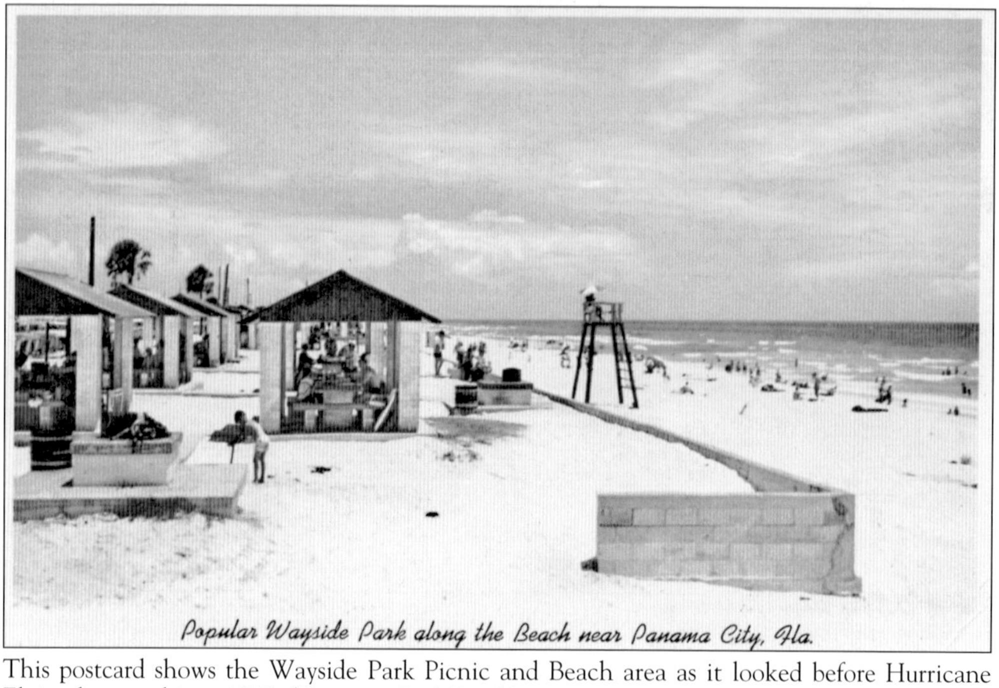

This postcard shows the Wayside Park Picnic and Beach area as it looked before Hurricane Eloise destroyed it in 1975. (Courtesy Bud Creel.)

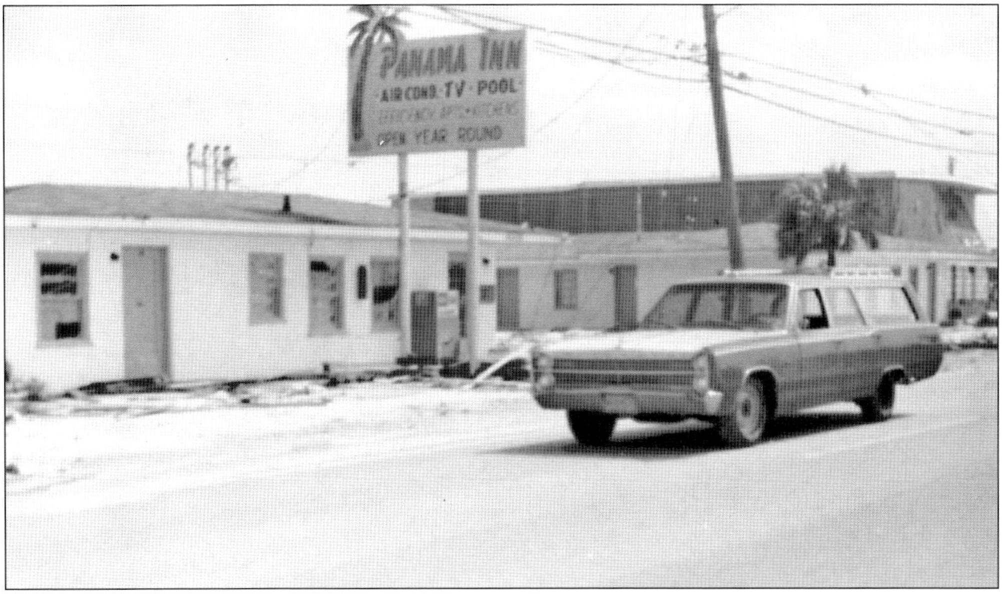

This photo was taken on September 23, 1975, after Hurricane Eloise struck Panama City Beach. Note that the sign in front of the Panama Inn on Highway 98 seems to have suffered little damage.

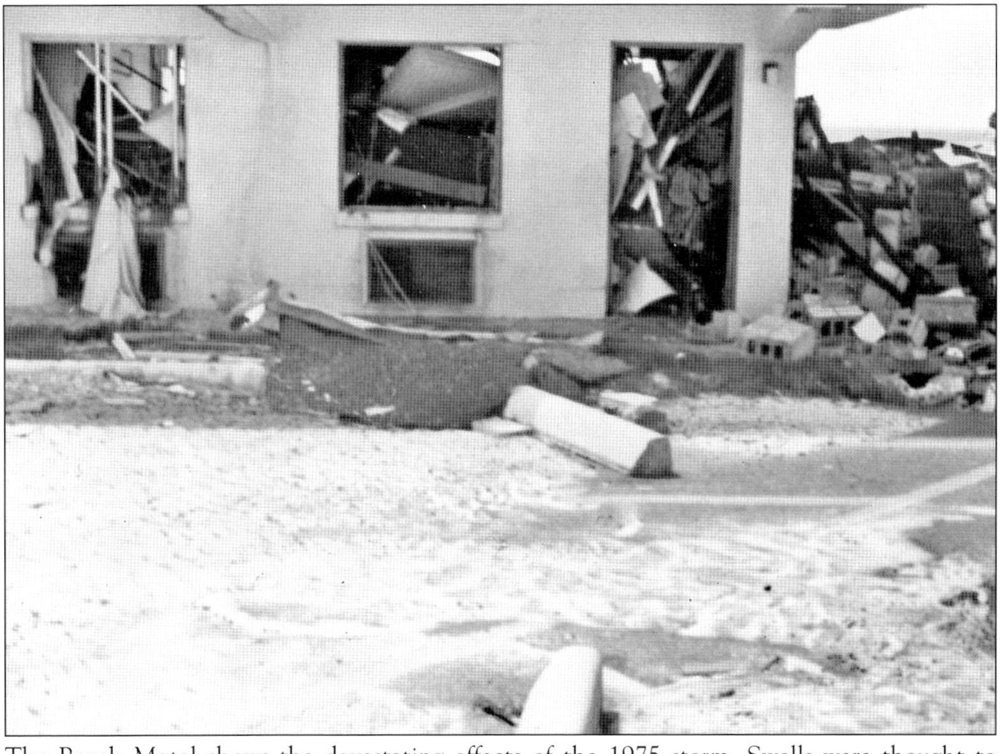

The Beach Motel shows the devastating effects of the 1975 storm. Swells were thought to have been as high as 16 feet at the height of the hurricane. Several days later, the Panama City *News-Herald* quoted property owners as saying that Panama City Beach would emerge "brighter than ever."

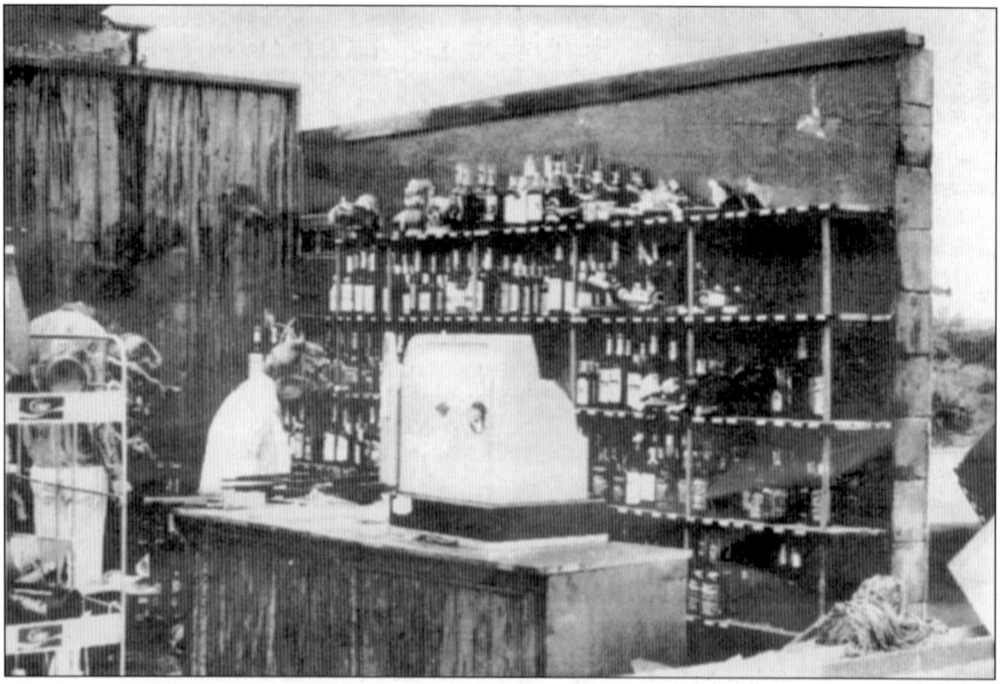

This Panama City *News-Herald* photograph captures the spirit of Panama City Beach business owners after Hurricane Eloise hit in 1975. "Open for Business," the caption reads and further describes how a local liquor store owner "lost her roof but not her bottles." (Courtesy *News-Herald*.)

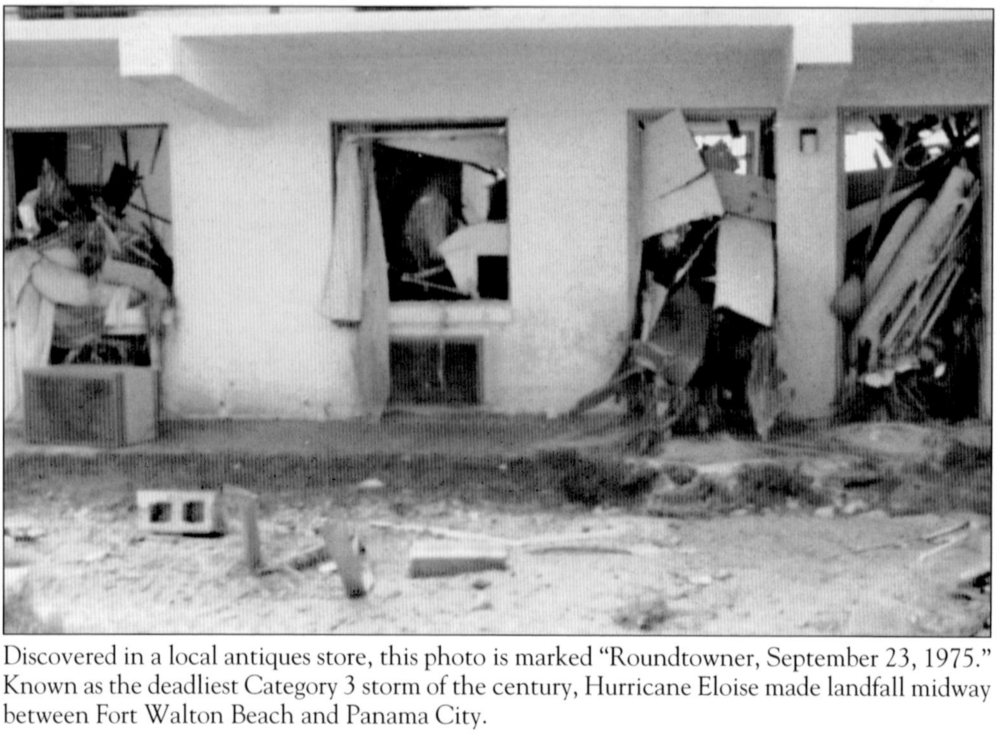

Discovered in a local antiques store, this photo is marked "Roundtowner, September 23, 1975." Known as the deadliest Category 3 storm of the century, Hurricane Eloise made landfall midway between Fort Walton Beach and Panama City.

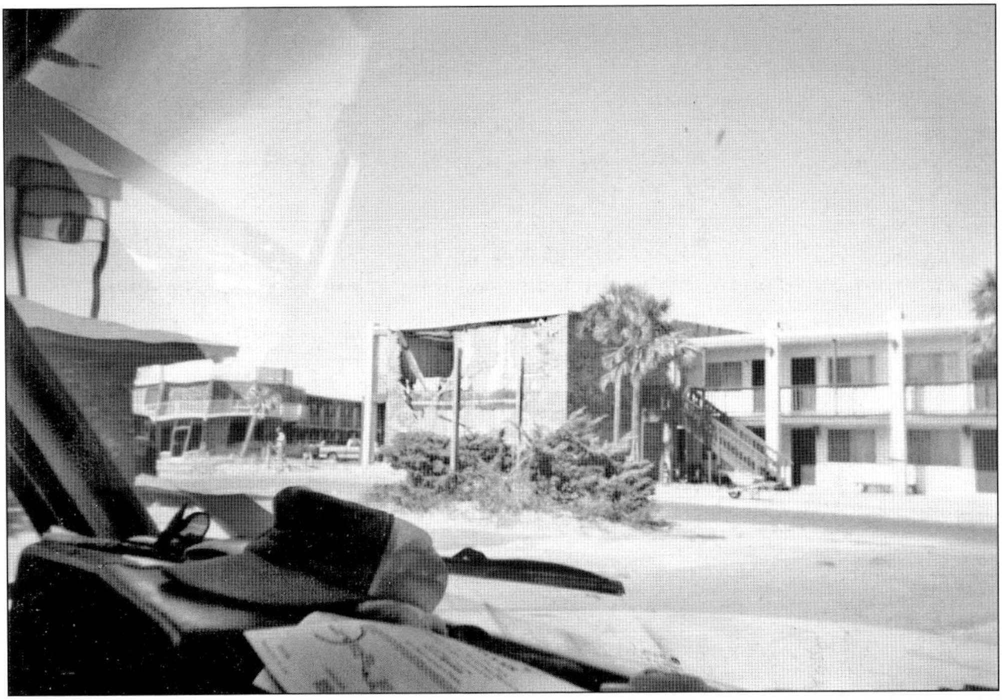

Hurricane Opal, at times classified as a Category 4 storm, hit landfall at Pensacola, Florida, in 1995. The effects of this storm were widespread and strongly felt by property owners in Panama City Beach. The Spyglass Inn, pictured here, was severely damaged. (Courtesy Shannon Knight.)

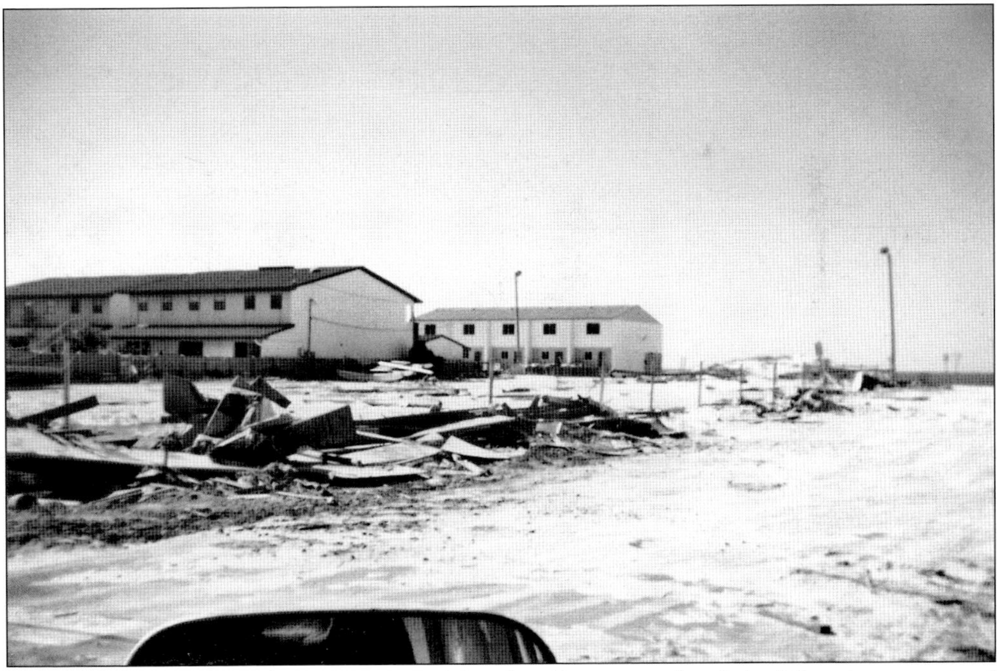

It's a mystery to many why some parts of Spyglass Drive were leveled while others remained unscathed when Hurricane Opal hit the Panhandle in 1995. (Courtesy Shannon Knight.)

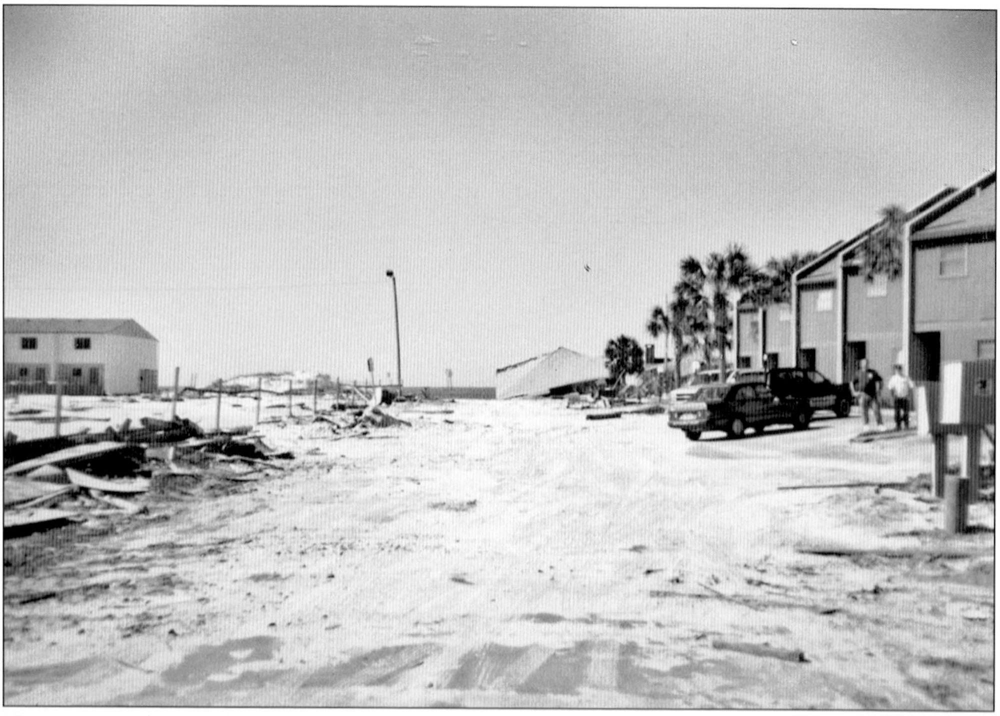

Here two unidentified men survey the damage wrought by Hurricane Opal on Spyglass Drive in Panama City Beach. (Courtesy Shannon Knight.)

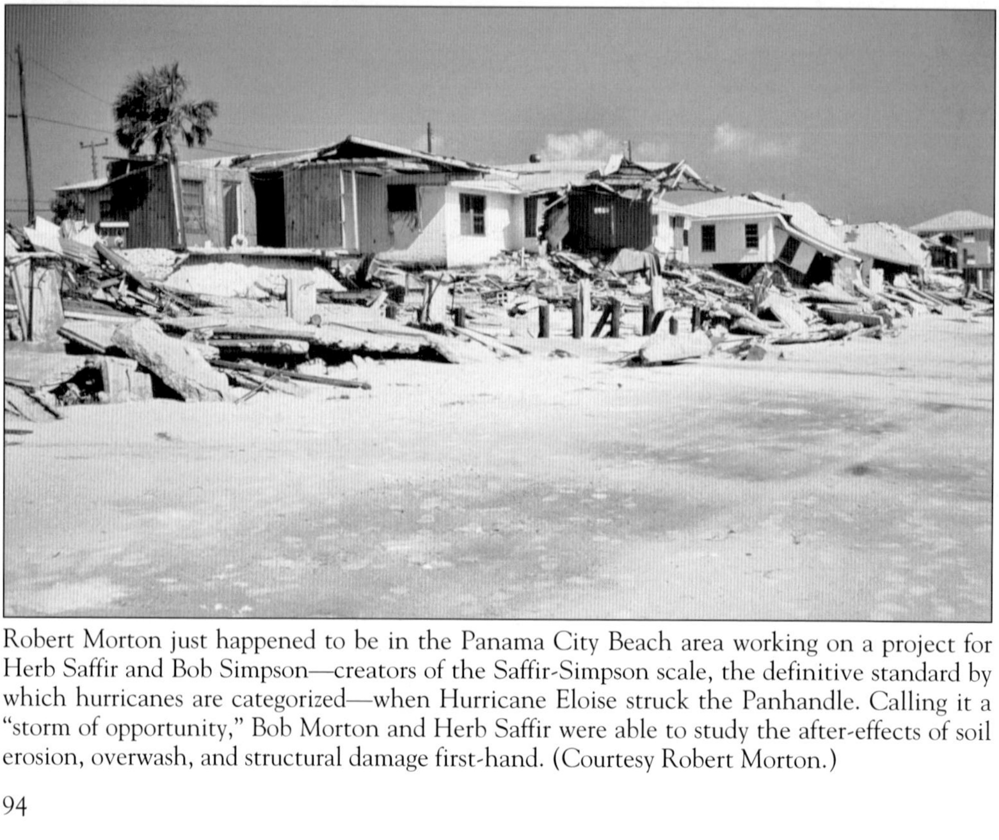

Robert Morton just happened to be in the Panama City Beach area working on a project for Herb Saffir and Bob Simpson—creators of the Saffir-Simpson scale, the definitive standard by which hurricanes are categorized—when Hurricane Eloise struck the Panhandle. Calling it a "storm of opportunity," Bob Morton and Herb Saffir were able to study the after-effects of soil erosion, overwash, and structural damage first-hand. (Courtesy Robert Morton.)

Eight

Events and Happenings

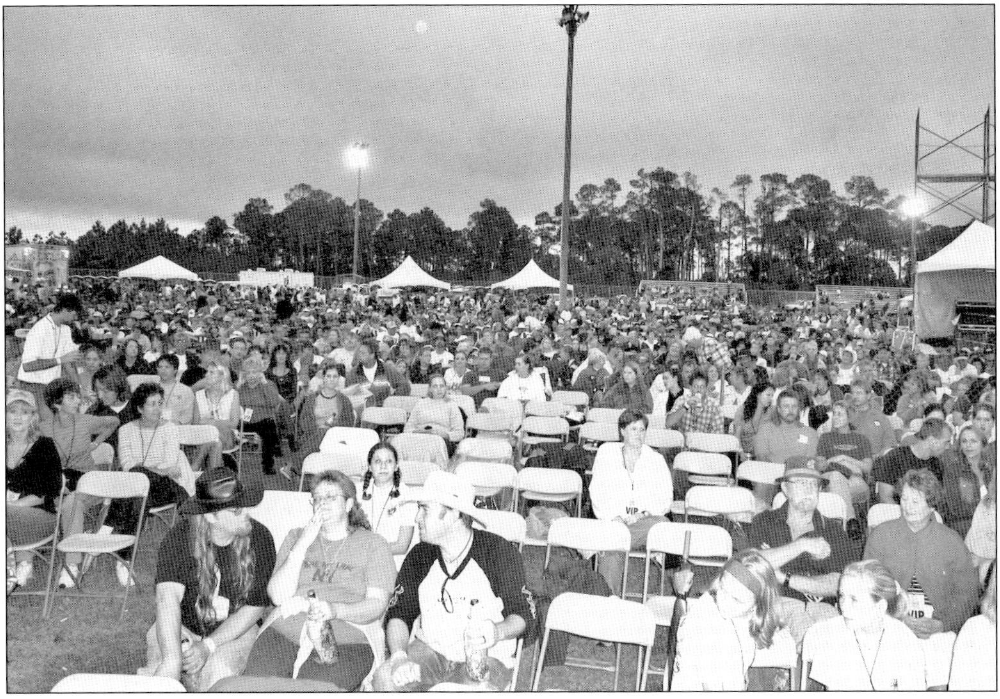

Panama City Beach folks have always been fond of parties, and the annual Indian Summer Festival held each fall is one of the biggest and best around. The people pictured here in 2003 await the start of a live performance at Pier Park. (Courtesy Panama City Beach Visitors and Convention Center.)

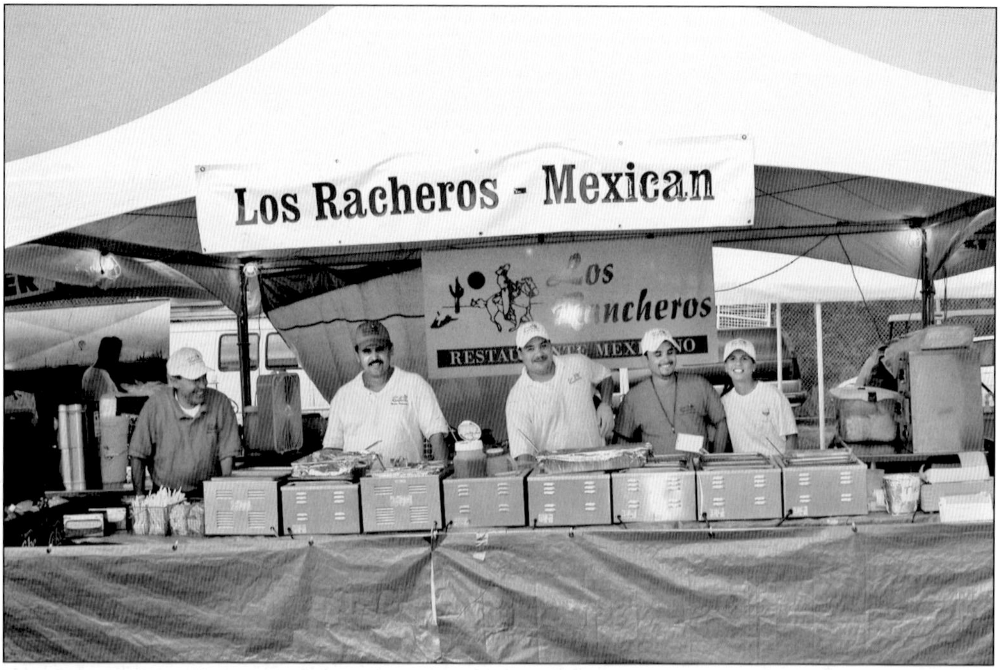

Restaurants from all over the area tempt festivalgoers with their tasty and diverse food offerings. Here members of the Los Racheros restaurant team prepare to serve up some Mexican cuisine. (Courtesy Panama City Beach Convention and Visitors Bureau.)

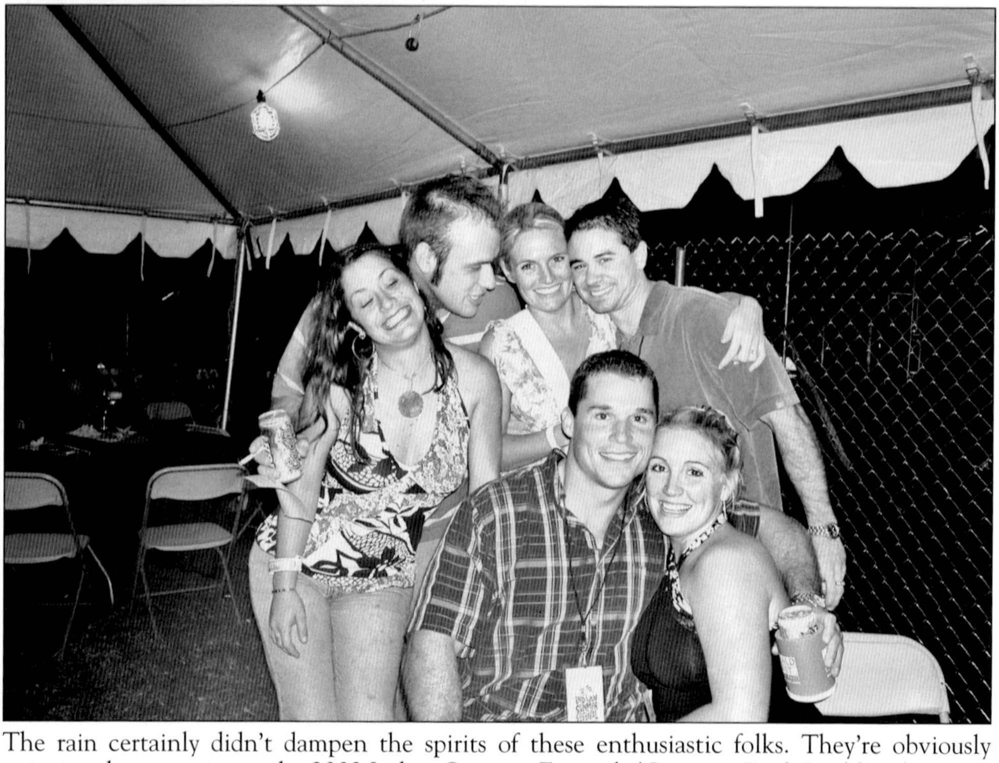

The rain certainly didn't dampen the spirits of these enthusiastic folks. They're obviously enjoying their evening at the 2003 Indian Summer Festival. (Courtesy Paul Goulding.)

The young man looks pretty pleased by the prospect of receiving a doggy kiss. The Humane Society of Bay County sold canine kisses for $1 as part of its annual fund-raising effort. (Courtesy Panama City Beach Convention and Visitors Bureau.)

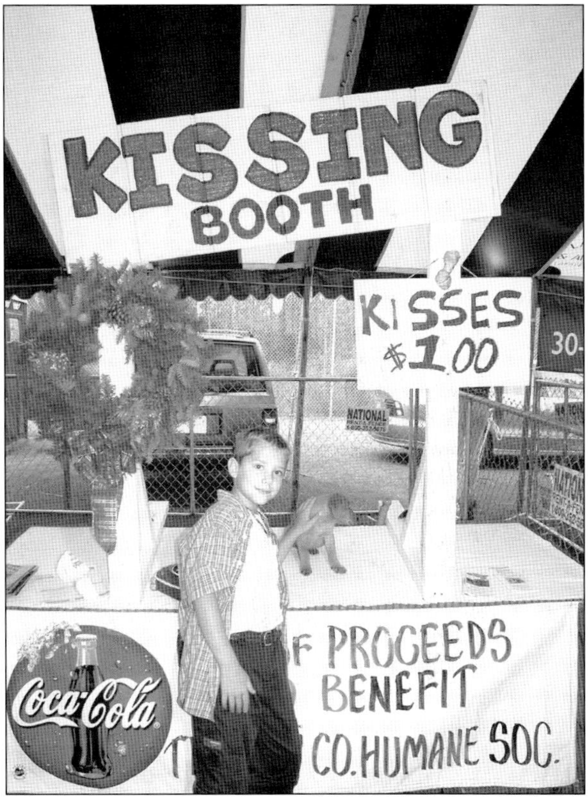

Performers at the Indian Summer Festival in 2003 are seen here. (Courtesy Panama City Beach Convention and Visitors Bureau.)

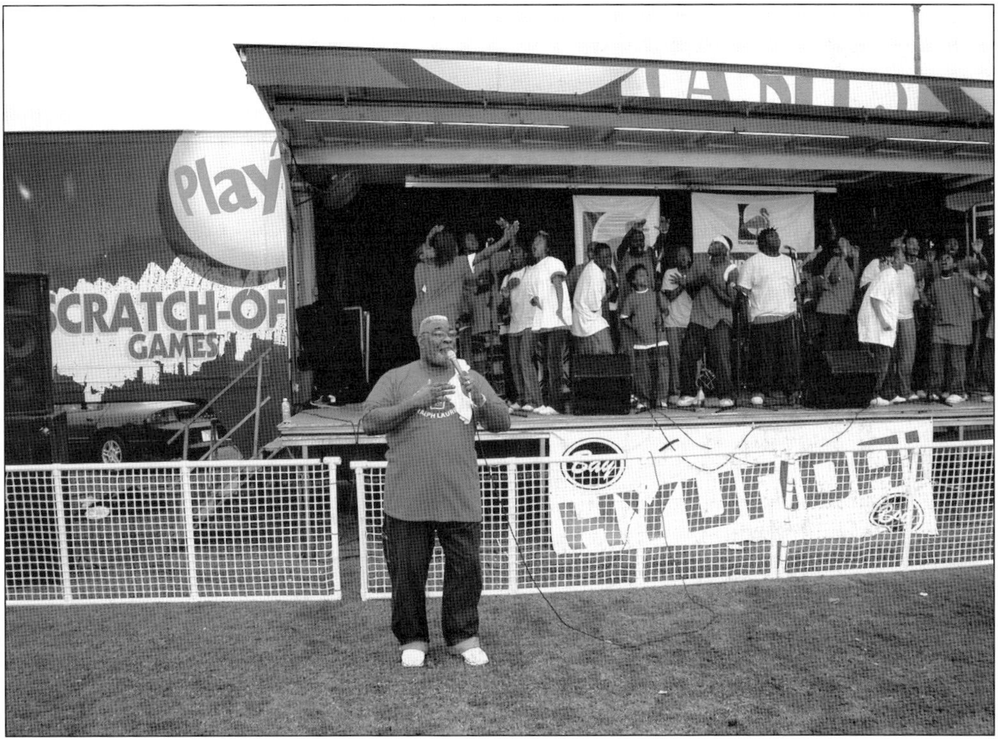

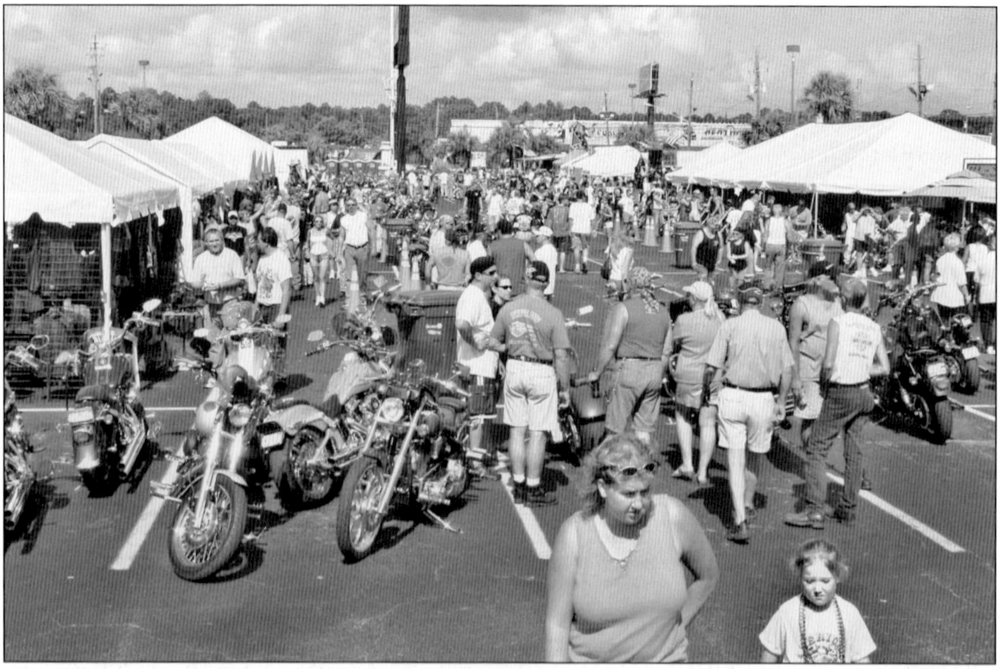

The Thunder Beach Motorcycle Rally is held each spring in Panama City Beach. Motorcycle enthusiasts from all over the country get together to show off their bikes, swap stories, and check out the vendor merchandise. (Courtesy Walt Lumpkin.)

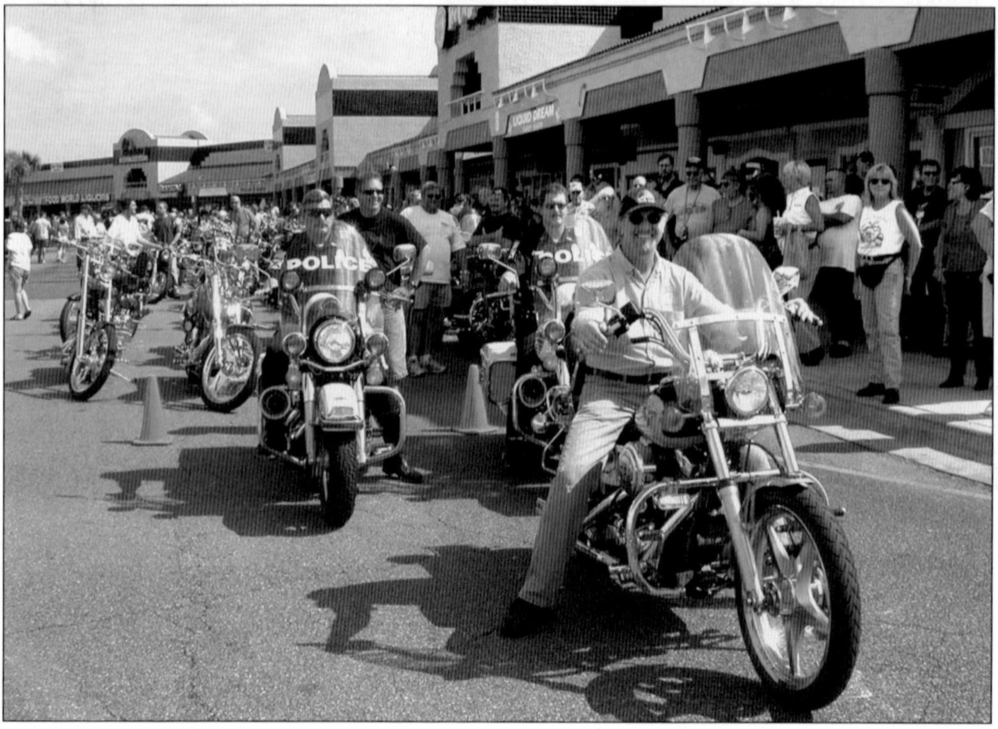

Panama City Beach police officers provide an official escort to Joe Biggs as he leads the annual Thunder Beach Motorcycle Rally parade in 2003. (Courtesy Walt Lumpkin.)

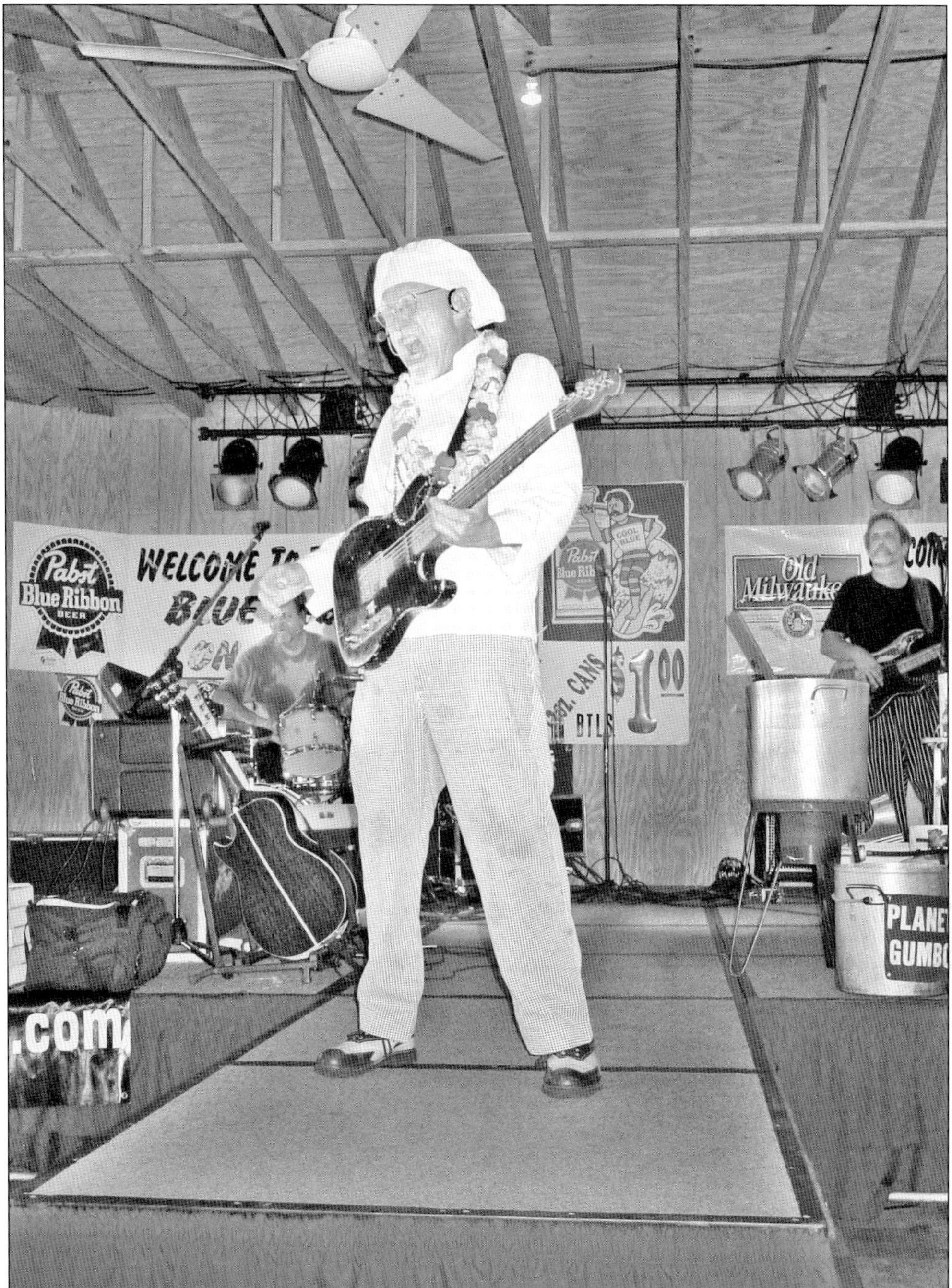

Bill "the Sauce Boss" Wharton performs annually at the Thunder Beach Motorcycle rally to the delight of his fans. Shown here in 2003 onstage at the Boardwalk, Bill has cooked up his own unique style of blues and spicy food for over 100,000 people over the years. After each show, the audience gets to eat. A portion of the money goes to Planet Gumbo, a non-profit foundation started by Bill and his wife Ruth to feed the homeless. (Courtesy Walt Lumpkin and Ruth Wharton.)

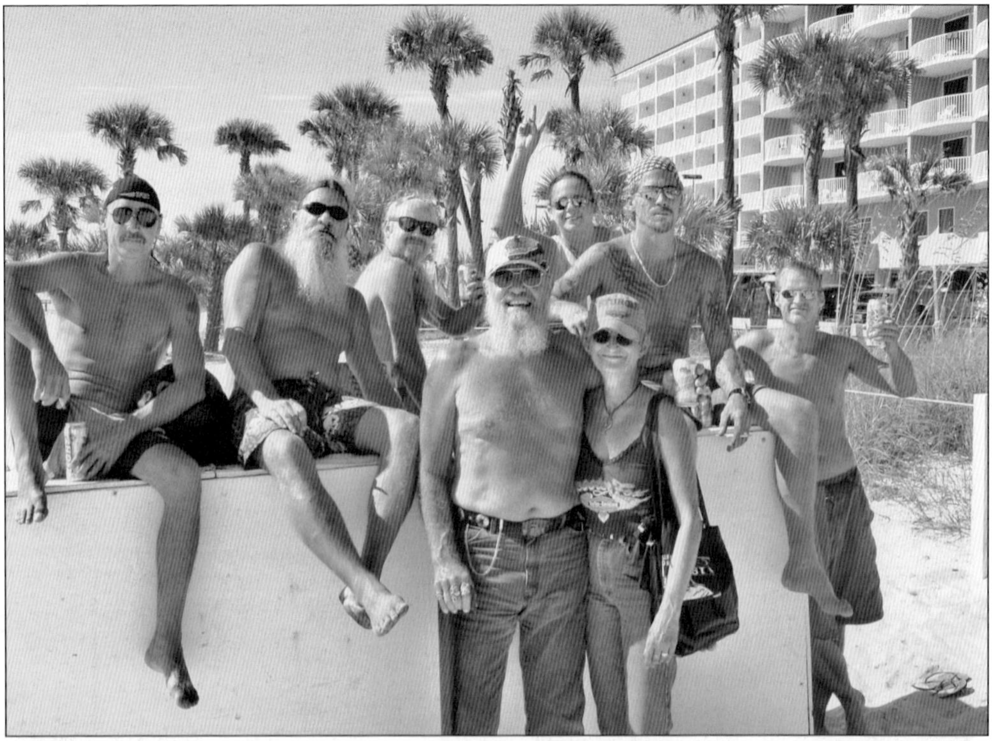

Taking a break from their "rides," these Thunder Beach Motor Cycle Rally participants take time to pose for a photograph. (Courtesy John "Scubajon" Metcalf and *Southland's Full Throttle Magazine*.)

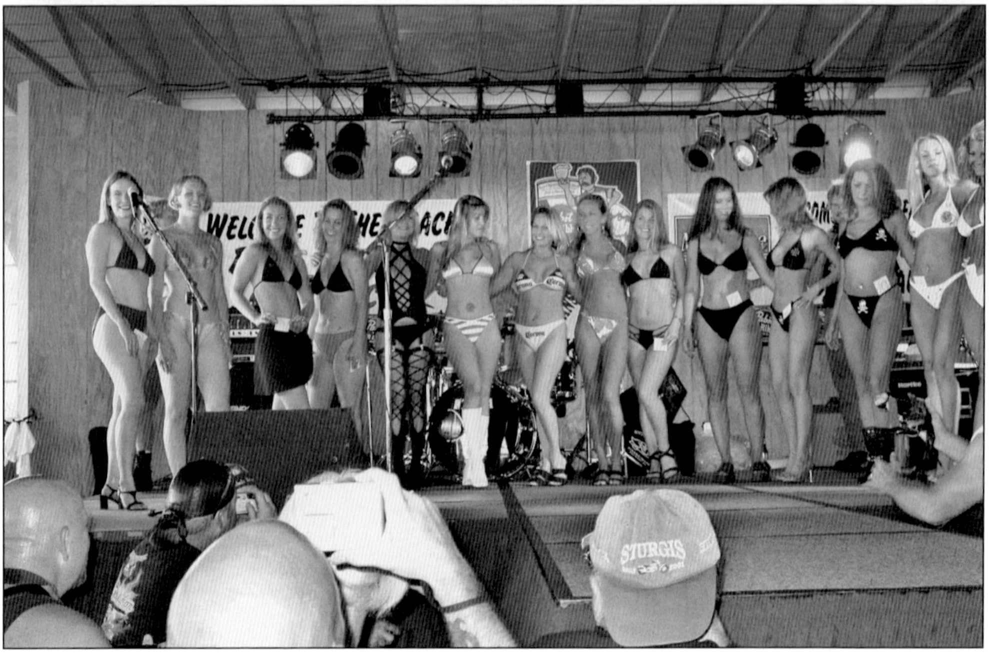

Contestants await the results of the Miss Thunder Beach beauty competition in 2003. (Courtesy John "Scubajon" Metcalf and *Southland's Full Throttle Magazine*)

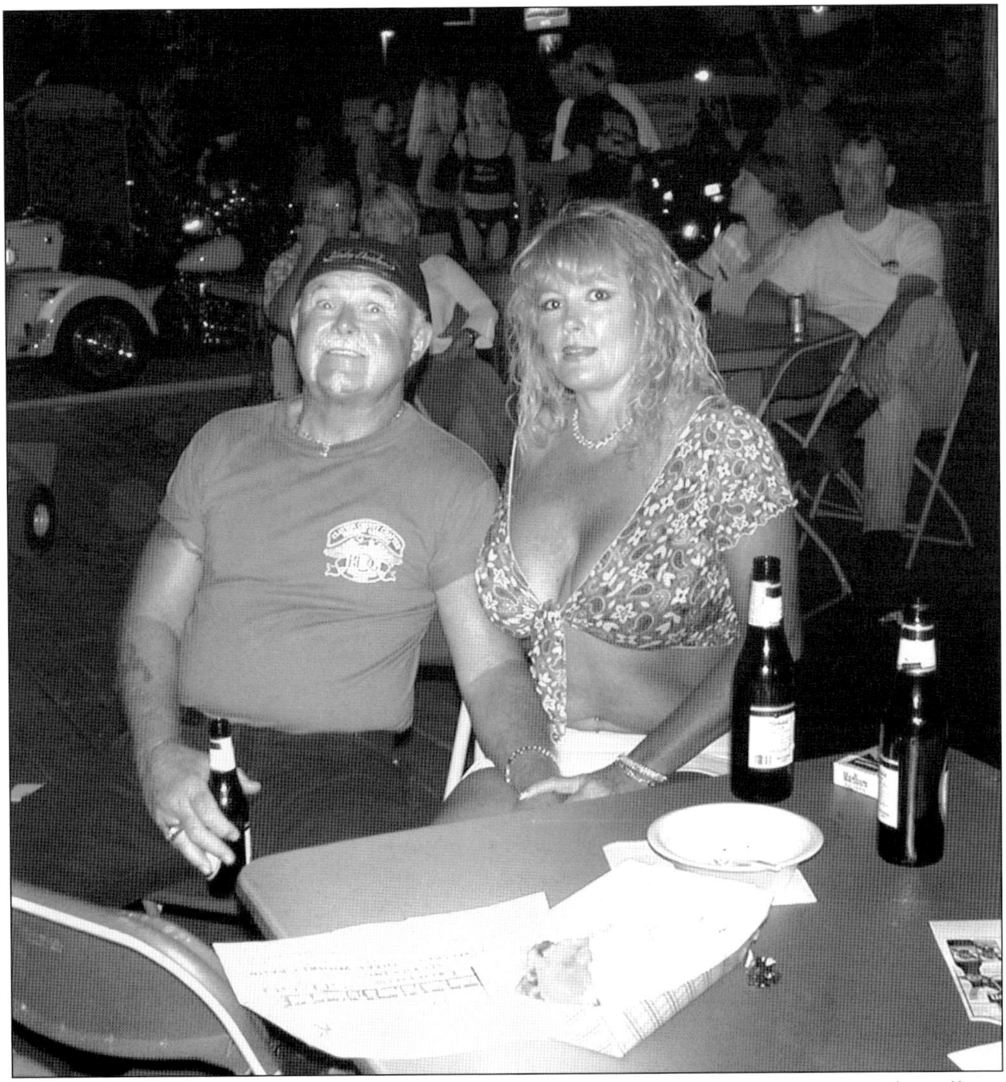

Visitors enjoy the sights and sounds that accompany the Thunder Beach Motorcycle Rally in this 2003 photo. (Courtesy John "Scubajon" Metcalf and *Southland's Full Throttle Magazine*.)

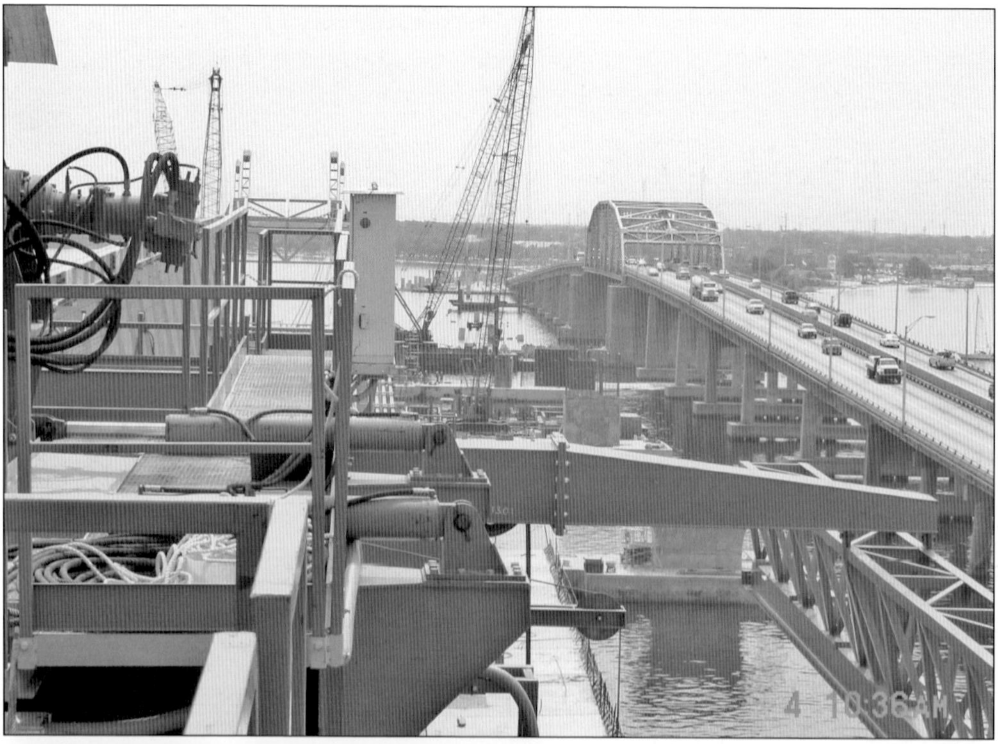

Shown is a unique perspective of the new Hathaway Bridge as construction begins. The old 1959 bridge is to the right. (Courtesy Reynolds, Smith, & Hills, CS, Inc.)

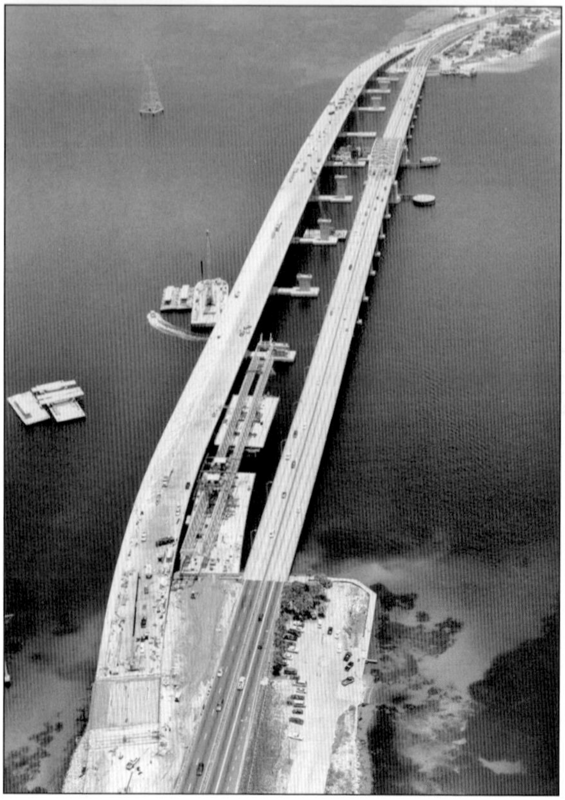

This aerial photo shows the two Hathaway Bridges side by side prior to the demolition of the older bridge (right). Almost completed, the new Hathaway Bridge can be seen at left. (Courtesy Reynolds, Smith, & Hills, CS, Inc.)

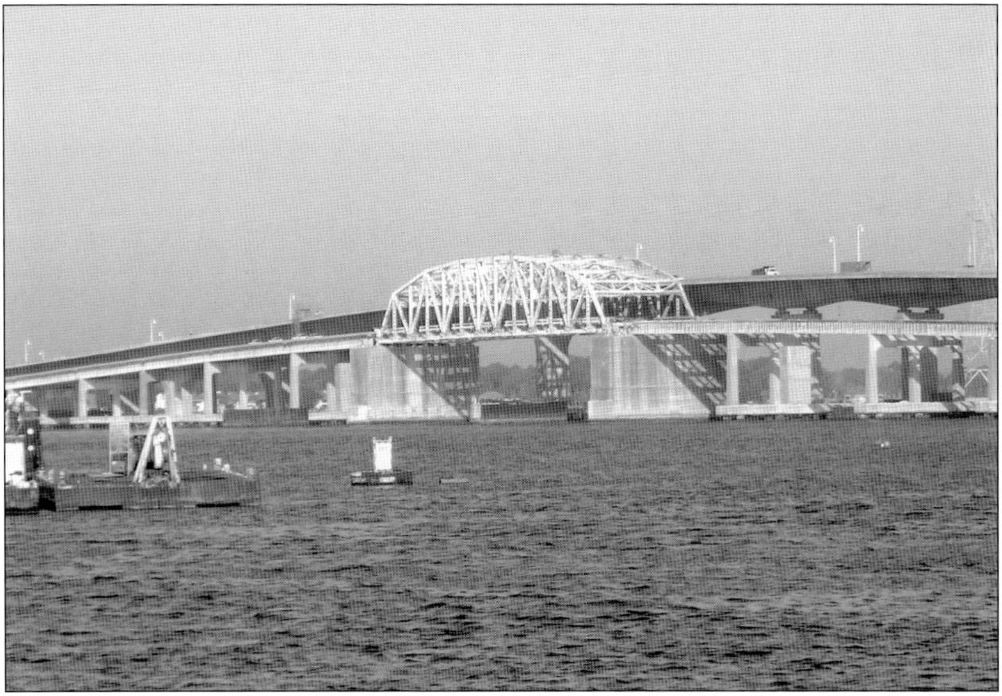

The old Hathaway Bridge is seen moments before its demolition at 9:47 a.m. on February 18, 2004. (Courtesy John van Etten.)

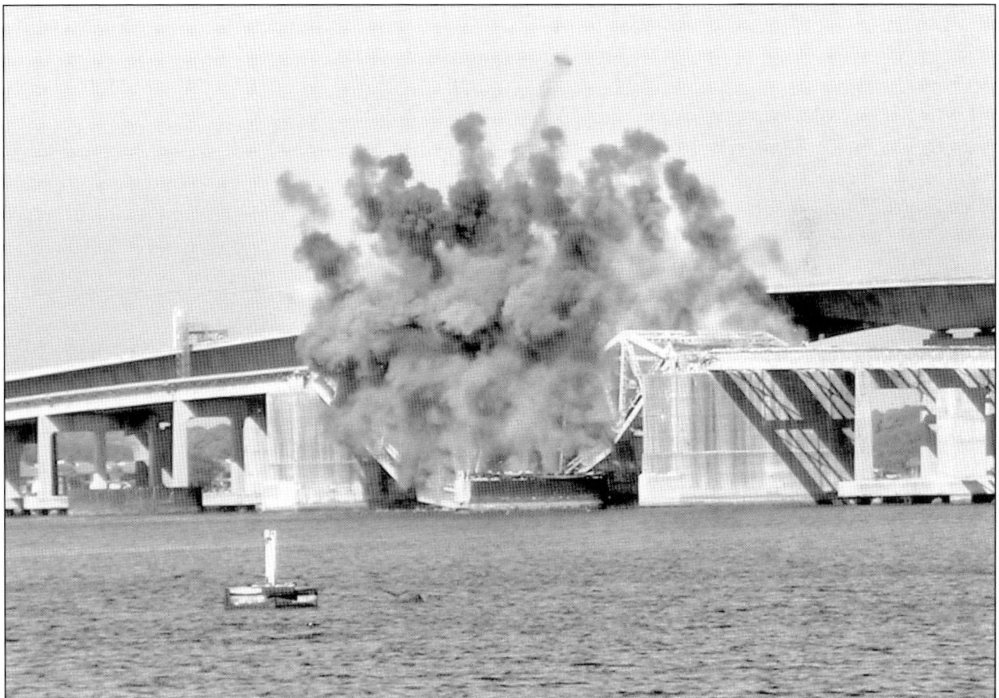

Captured at the moment of destruction, the old Hathaway Bridge explodes in a large cloud of smoke. (Courtesy John van Etten.)

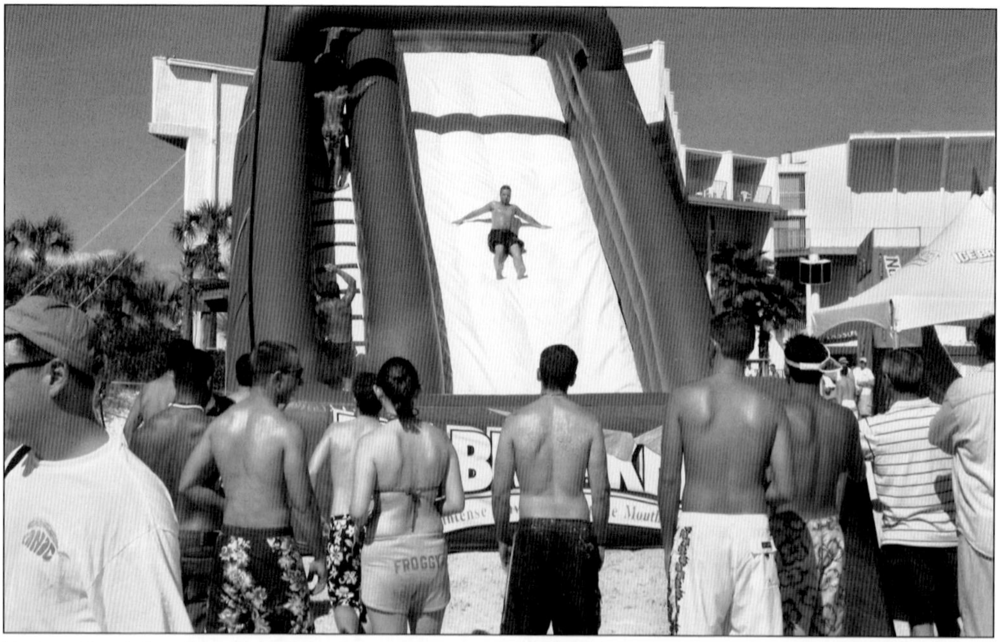

Spring Break has become a chief revenue source to the Panama City Beach community. Local merchants go all-out each year to make the event bigger and better than the season before. Clubs like La Vela provide all sorts of activities, from wet T-shirt contests to beer chugs. This oversized slide is just one of many such attractions set up along the beach for kids who "just wanna have fun." (Courtesy Jayna Leach and the Panama City Beach Convention and Visitors Bureau.)

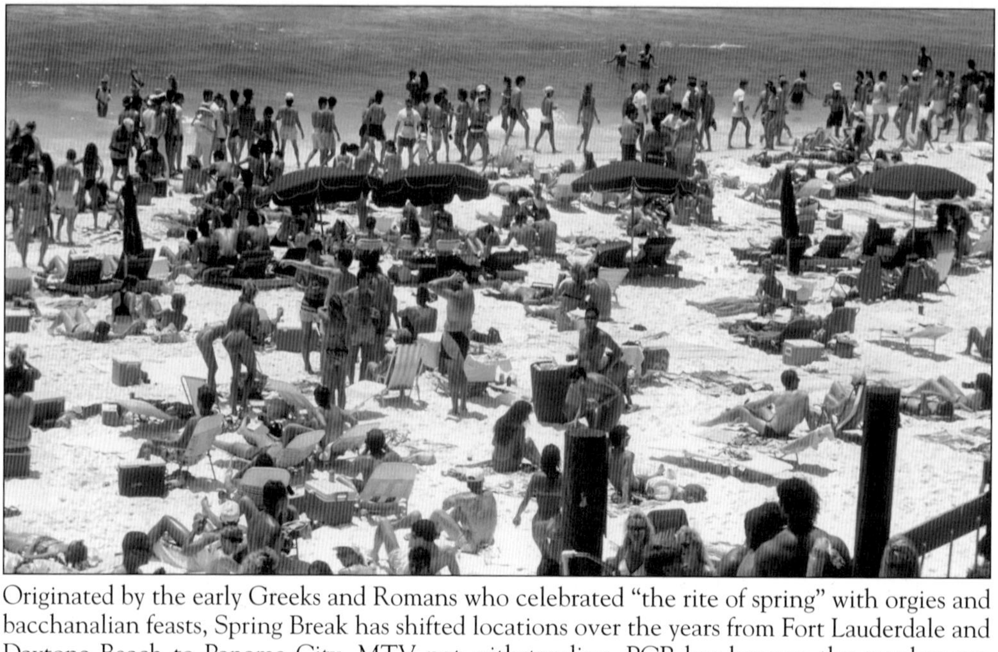

Originated by the early Greeks and Romans who celebrated "the rite of spring" with orgies and bacchanalian feasts, Spring Break has shifted locations over the years from Fort Lauderdale and Daytona Beach to Panama City. MTV not withstanding, PCB has become the number-one Spring Break destination in the world. (Jayna Leach and the Panama City Beach Convention and Visitors Bureau.)

Nine

Restaurants and Motels

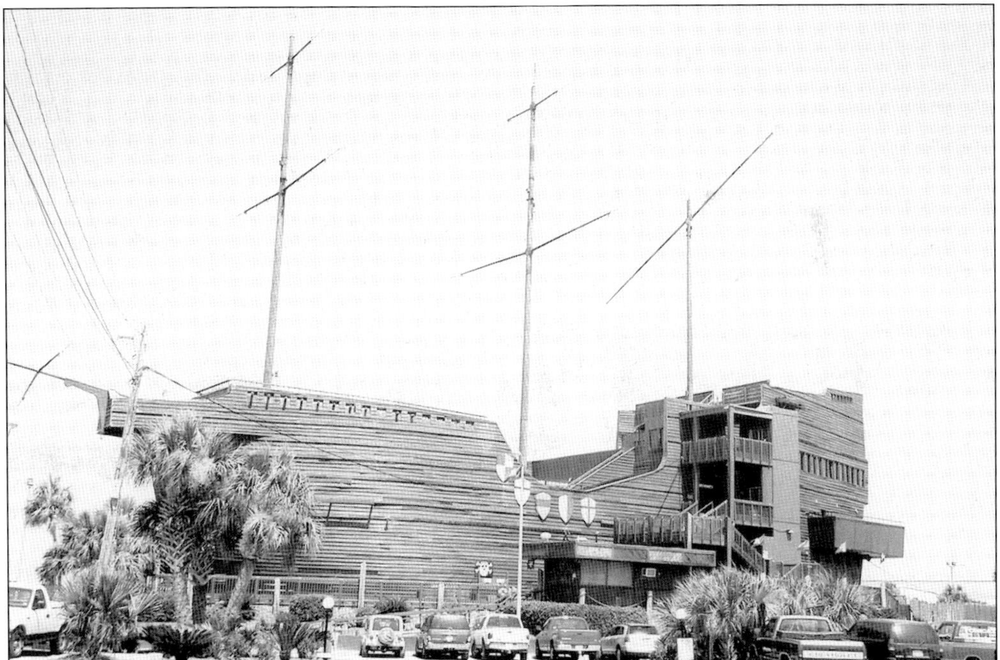

A Panama City Beach landmark since the early 1980s, the Treasure Ship restaurant features three eateries: Captain Crabby's, The Hook and Grille, and the Main Dining Room. A gift shop is also located on the premises. (Courtesy Carolyn Insley.)

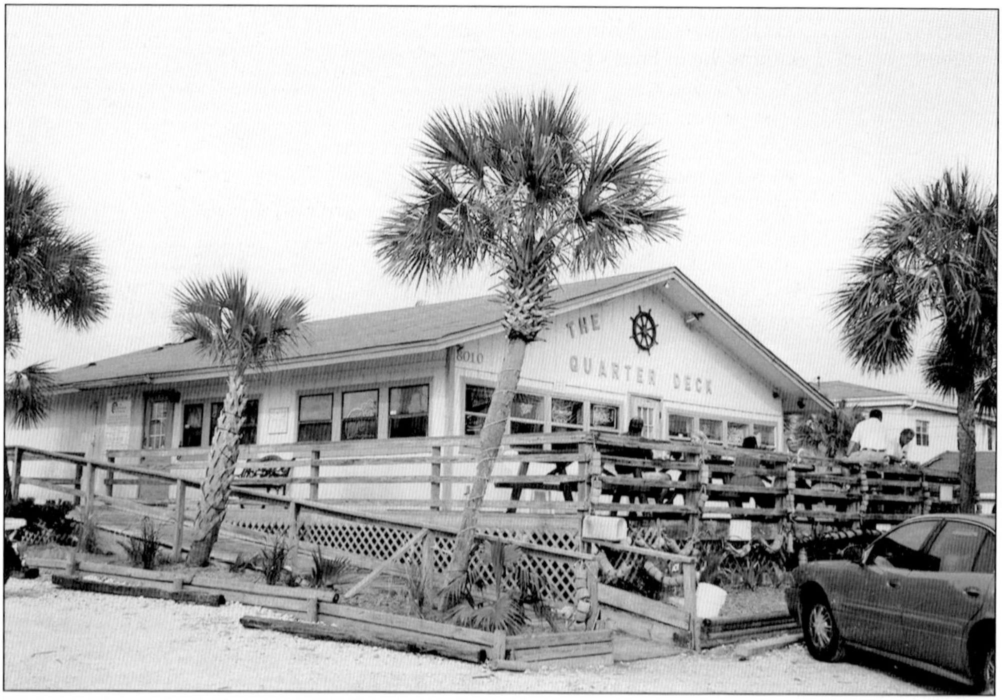

License plates deck the walls of the Quarter Deck as a testament to the restaurant's standing offer of a "free beer" for every license plate donated. (Courtesy Carolyn Insley.)

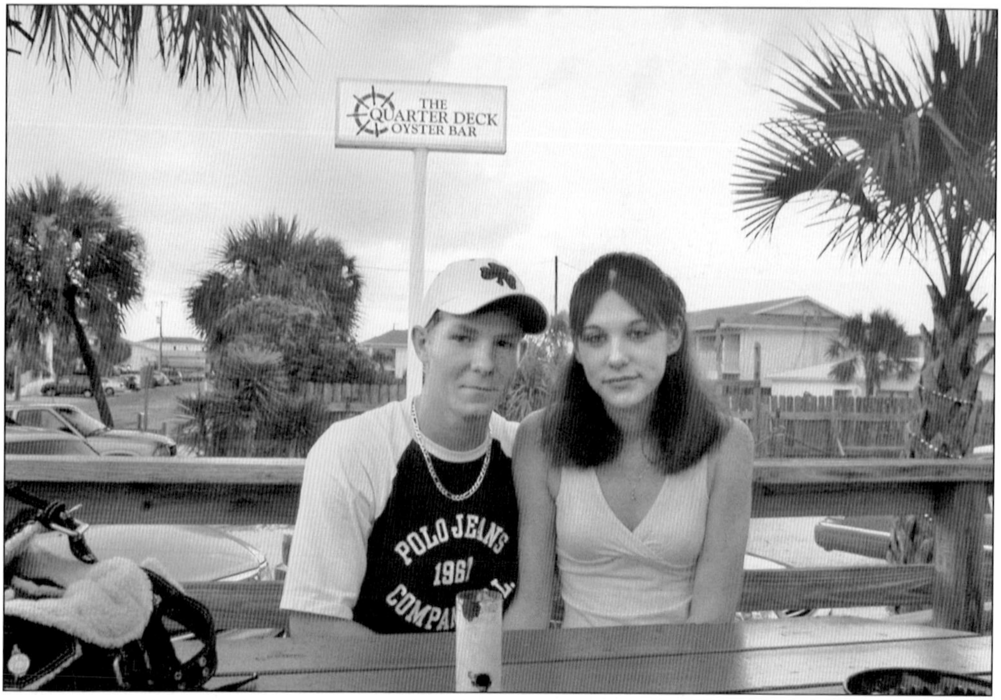

Ramanda Nichols and Buck Myers, both of Panama City Beach, are pictured enjoying a night out at the Quarter Deck on Surf Drive. Ramanda's sister is a manager at the restaurant, which features great oysters and nightly karaoke.

When Mike and Neil Bennett and Rob Hammer opened Hammerhead Fred's in 1995, at the site of the old Buffalo Rings and Things store on Thomas Drive, they were already seasoned restaurateurs. Known for their fresh local seafood and signature "Voodoo Punch" (a heady rum concoction from Fred's secret recipe files), Hammerhead's "shark" is a Panama City Beach landmark. (Courtesy Hammerhead Fred's.)

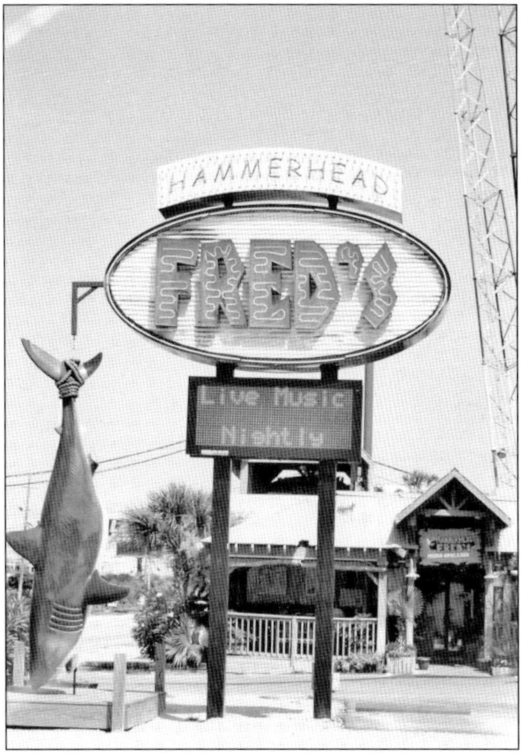

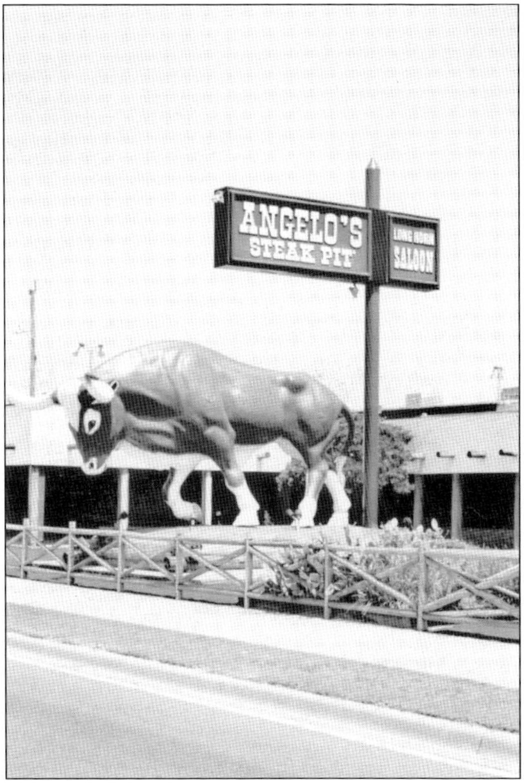

Located where the old 98 Club once stood, an enormous steer statue today stands in front of Angelo's Steak Pit. In an area where seafood reigns supreme, the restaurant is a haven for vacationing carnivores. (Courtesy Carolyn Insley.)

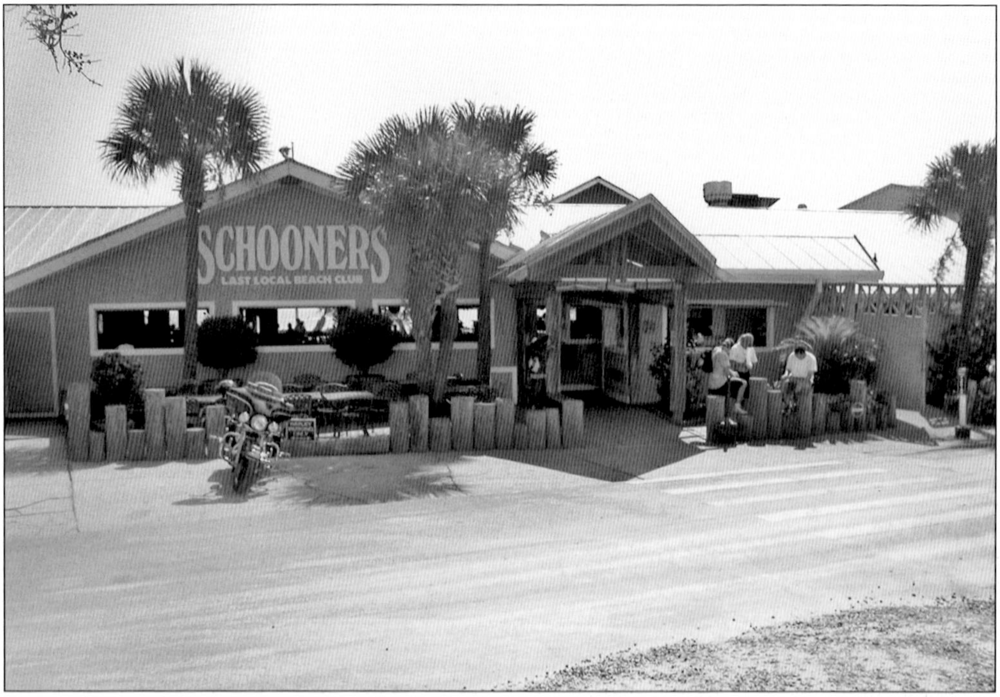

Famous for its great view of the beach, wonderful seafood, and lively entertainment, Schooner's remains a favorite venue for locals and visitors alike. Many enjoy Schooner's traditional salute to the sunset—a cannon is fired just as the sun goes down. (Courtesy Scott Smith.)

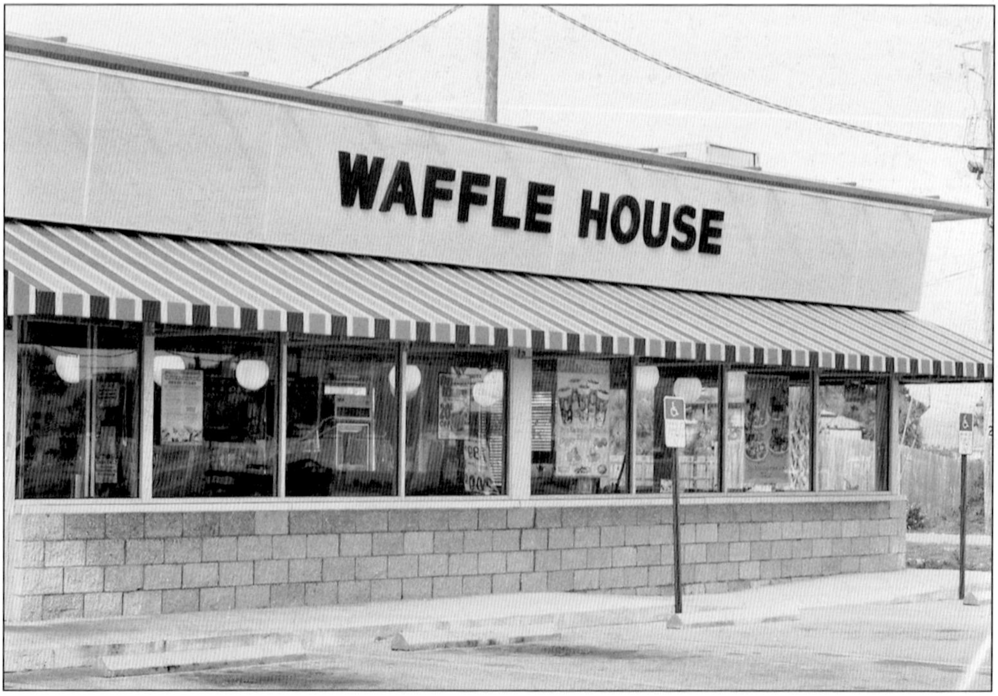

It wouldn't be a true Southern resort area without a Waffle House or two. This well-known restaurant is located on Thomas Drive. (Courtesy Carolyn Insley.)

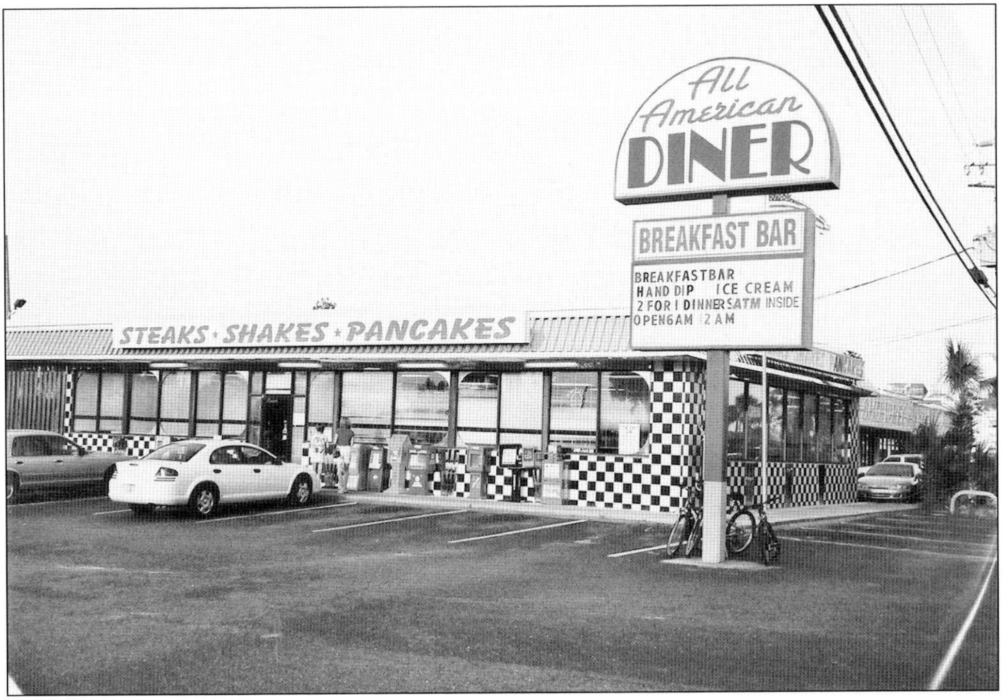

Famous for its breakfast bar, the All American Diner is a big hit with tourists and Spring Breakers. This picture was taken in 2004. (Courtesy Carolyn Insley.)

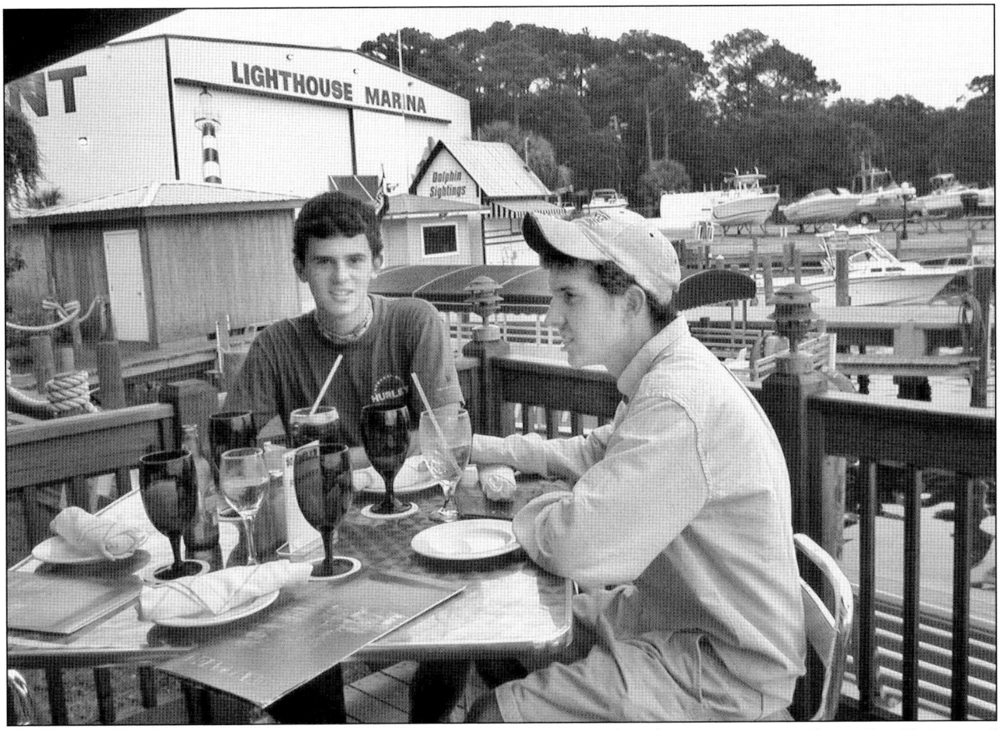

Scott Smith (right) and Colt Pierson of Towson, Maryland, enjoy a meal at the Boatyard restaurant overlooking St. Andrew's Bay. This picture was taken in July 2004.

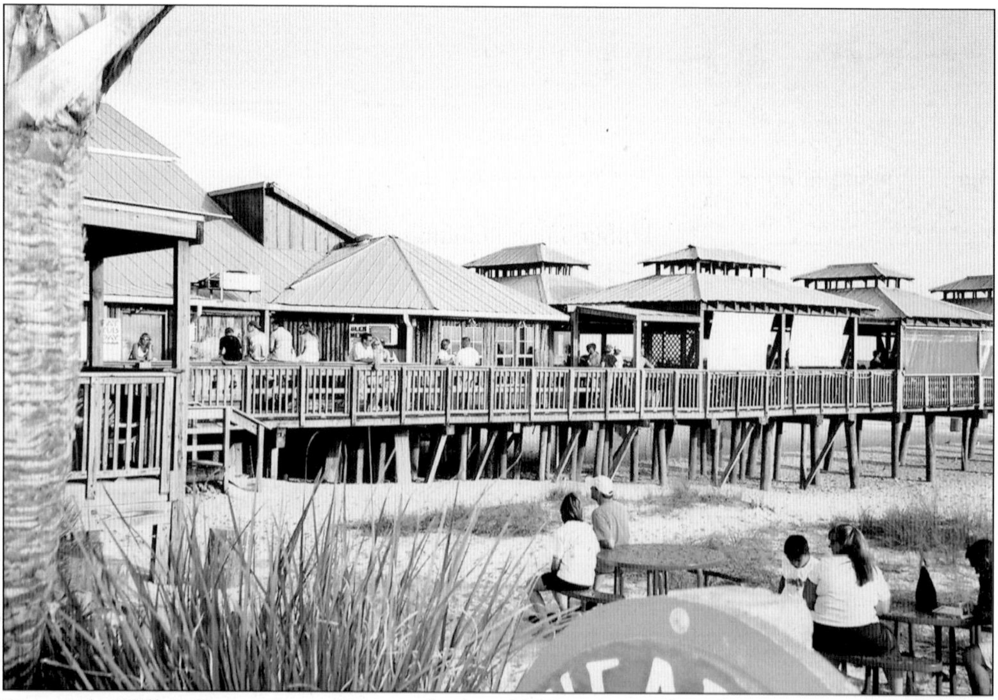

Pineapple Willy's Restaurant, photographed in 2004, is located at the site of the old Panama -City Beach resort and 1000-foot pier. Owned by the descendants of Gideon Thomas and A.W. Pledger, the restaurant sits atop a portion of the famous pier. (Courtesy Carolyn Insley.)

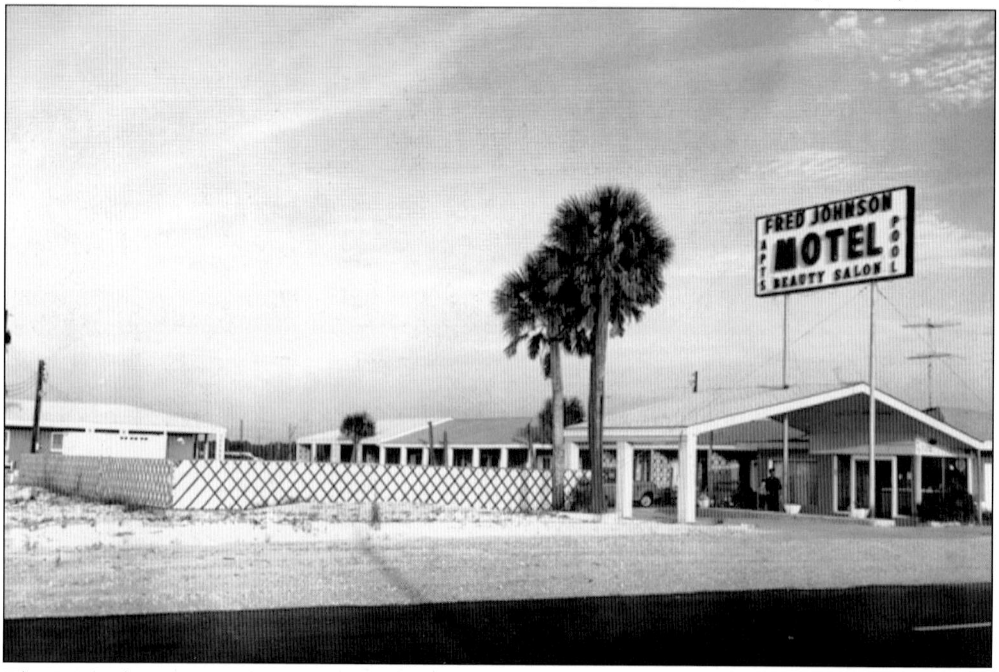

The Fred Johnson Motel had a decided advantage over the competition with its in-house beauty salon. Women were able to get their hair done and schedule a manicure without ever leaving the premises. (Courtesy Bay County Library.)

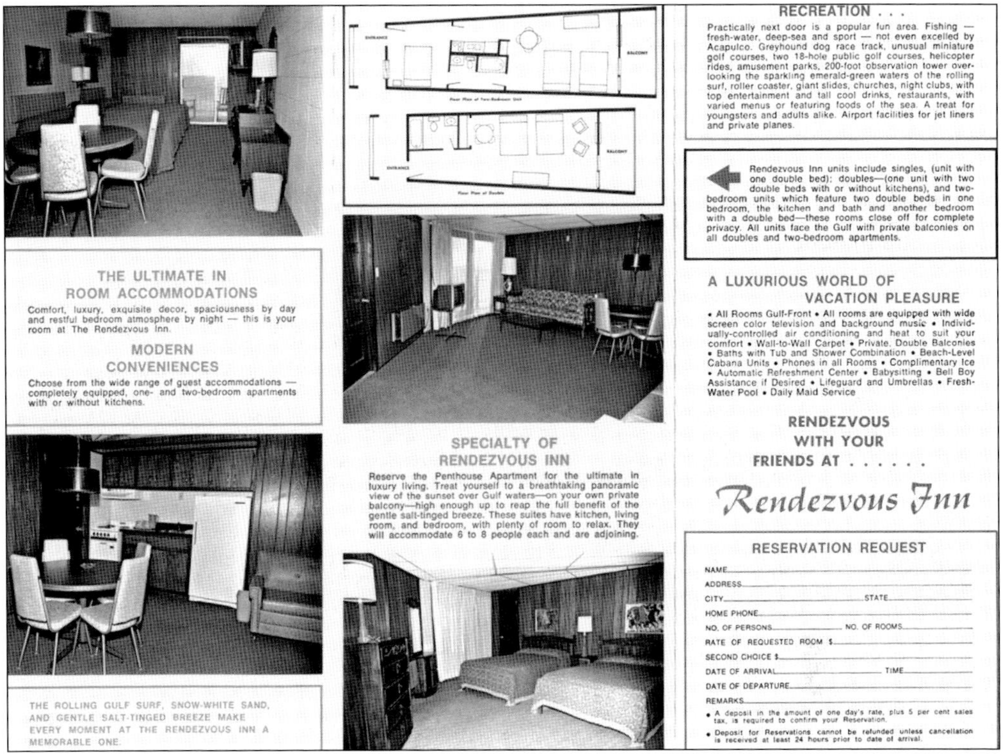

A brochure for the Rendezvous Inn shows two available floor plans. The advertising at bottom right claims that "the rolling Gulf surf, snow-white sand, and gentle salt-tinged breezes make every moment at the Rendezvous Inn a memorable one." (Courtesy Louie Walker.)

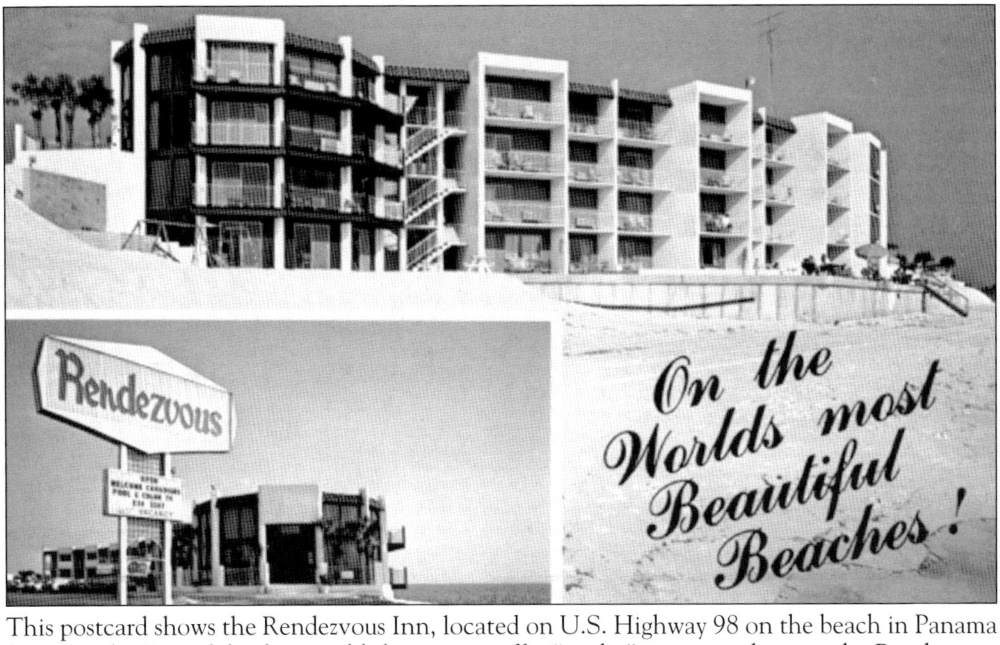

This postcard shows the Rendezvous Inn, located on U.S. Highway 98 on the beach in Panama City Beach. One of the first establishments to offer "studio" accommodations, the Rendezvous featured a kitchenette in its deluxe units. (Courtesy Louie Walker.)

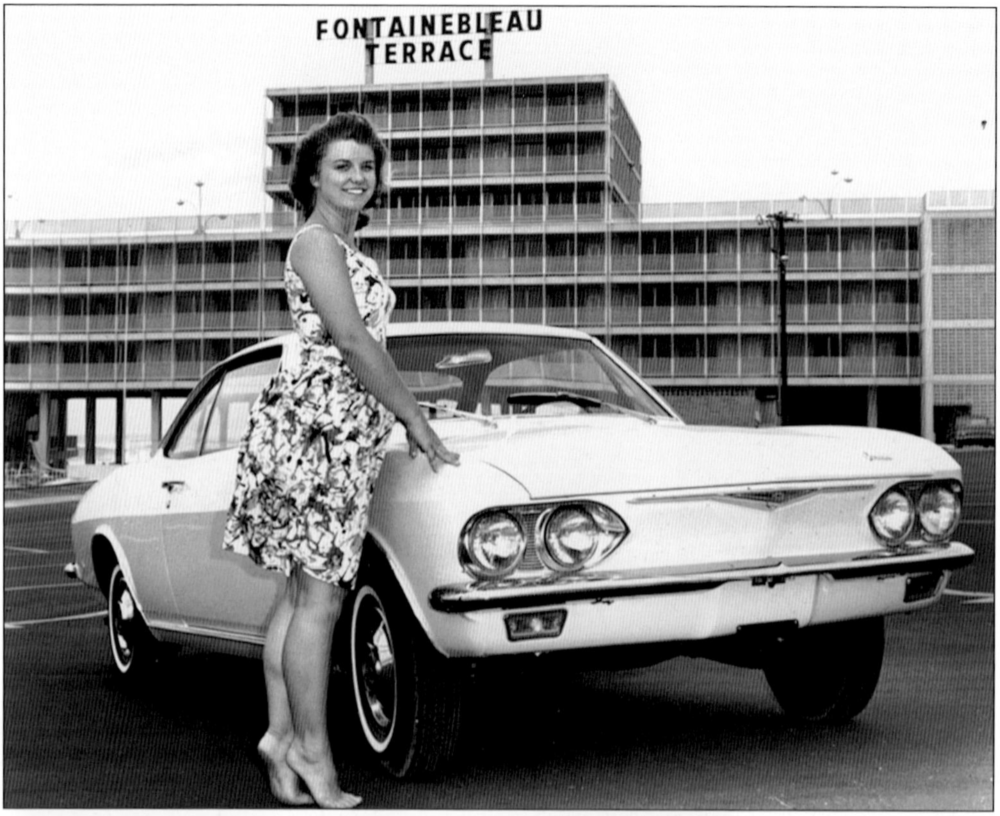

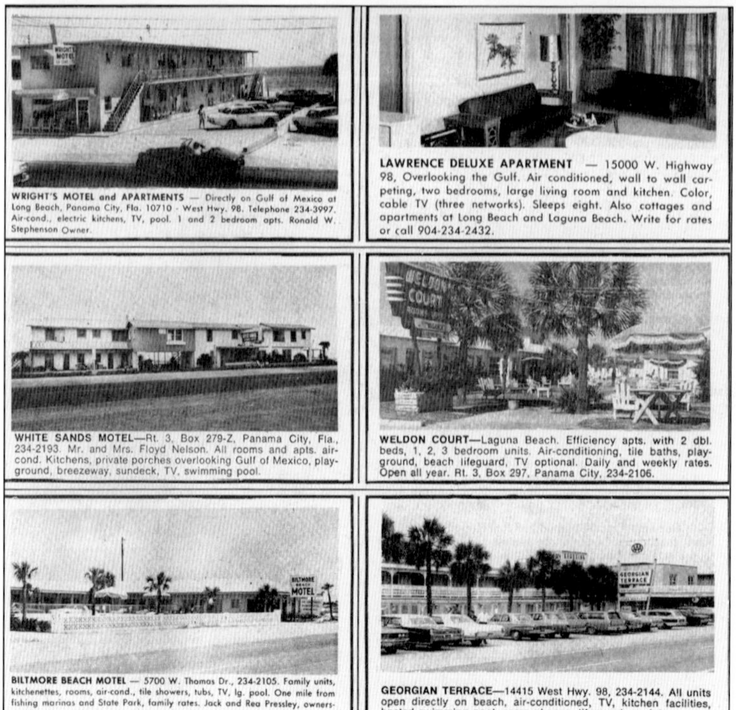

Janice Branning is photographed in 1960 standing outside of the Fountainbleu Terrace Motel in Panama City Beach. (Courtesy Bay County Library.)

This 1970s multi-motel advertisement includes Wrights Motel and Apartments, the White Sands Motel, the Biltmore Beach Motel, the Lawrence Deluxe Apartments, Weldon Court, and Georgian Terrace. Note that air-conditioning is heavily promoted! (Courtesy Bay County Library.)

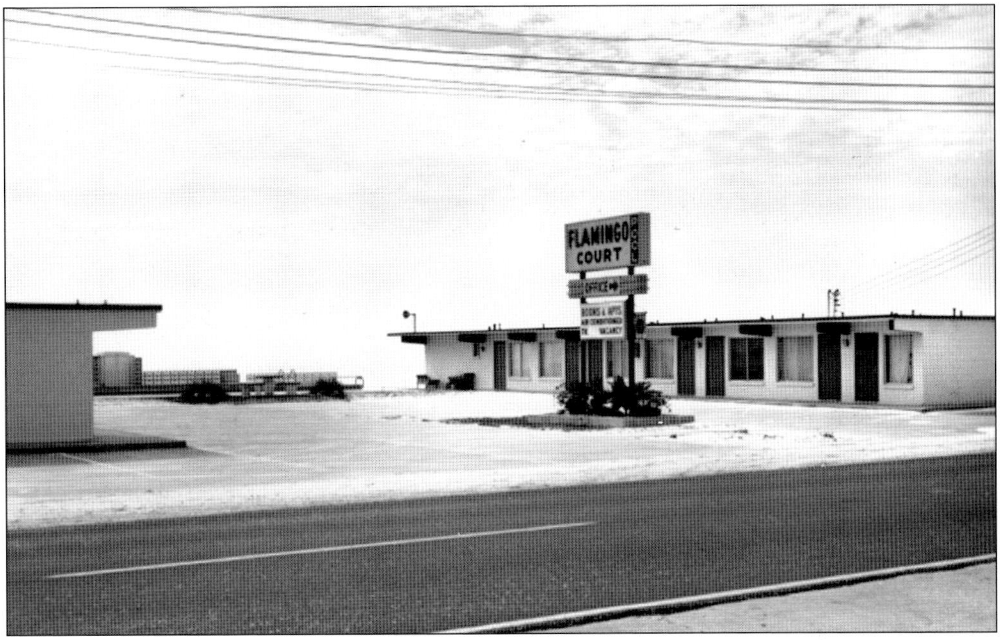

The Flamingo Court Motor Lodge is pictured here as it looked in the 1970s. (Courtesy Bay County Library.)

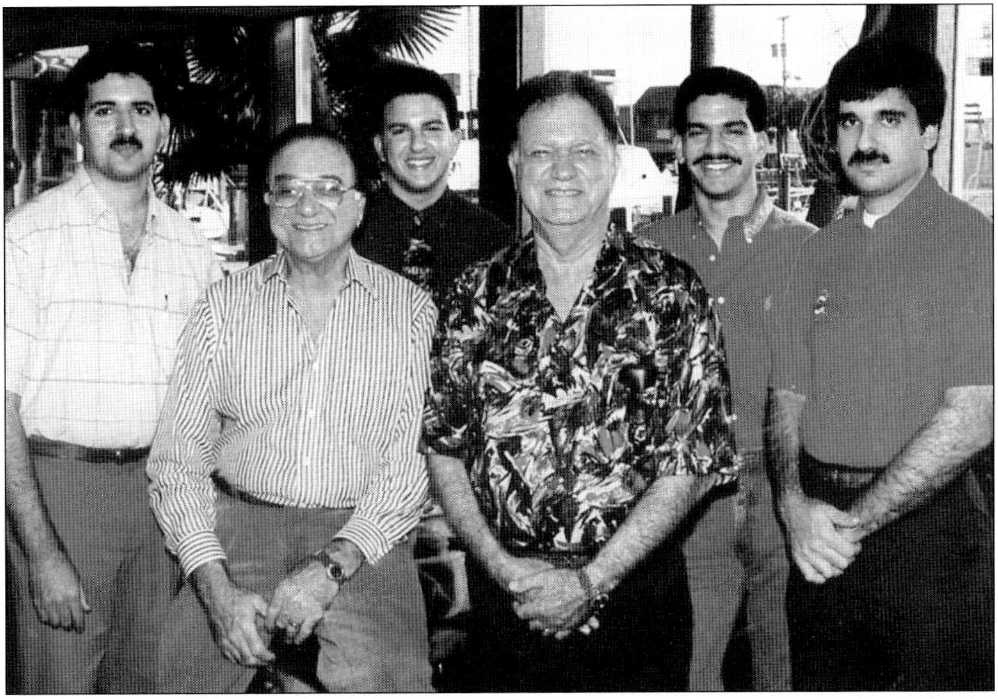

Johnny and Jimmy Patronis purchased Captain Anderson's in 1967 from the Anderson family. Overlooking the Grand Lagoon, the restaurant seats hundreds of people and was voted *#1 Seafood Restaurant* by *Southern Living* magazine for the years 1996 through 2001. Pictured here from left to right are Yonnie, Johnny, Jimmy Jr., Jimmy, Nick, and Theo. (Courtesy the Patronis family.)

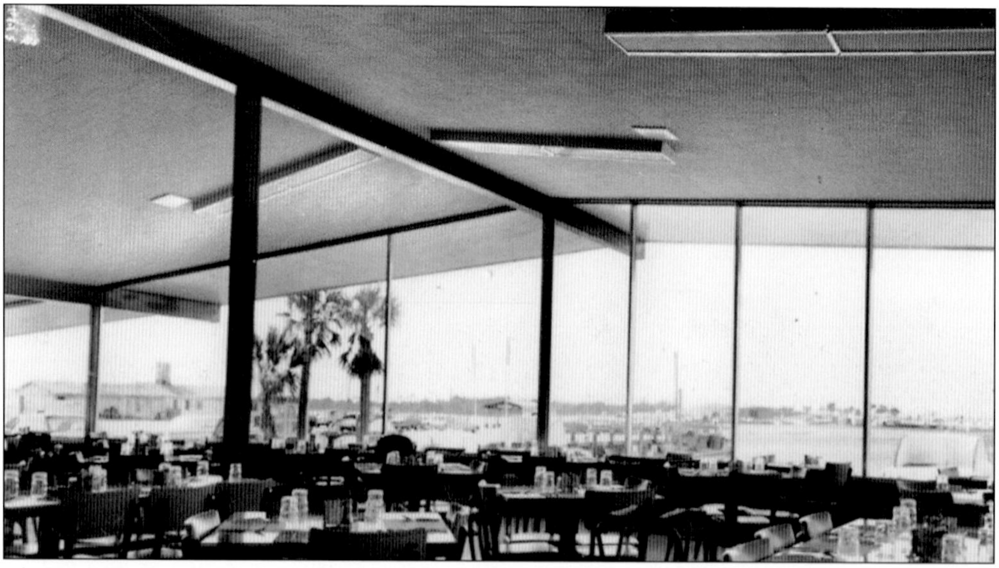

This Bob Hargis photo shows the interior of Captain Anderson's Restaurant as it looked in the 1970s. The restaurant has served many celebrities over the years, including Johnny Cash, Tanya Tucker, Jane Pauley, "Bear" Bryant, Ted Williams, and Morley Safer, to name a few.

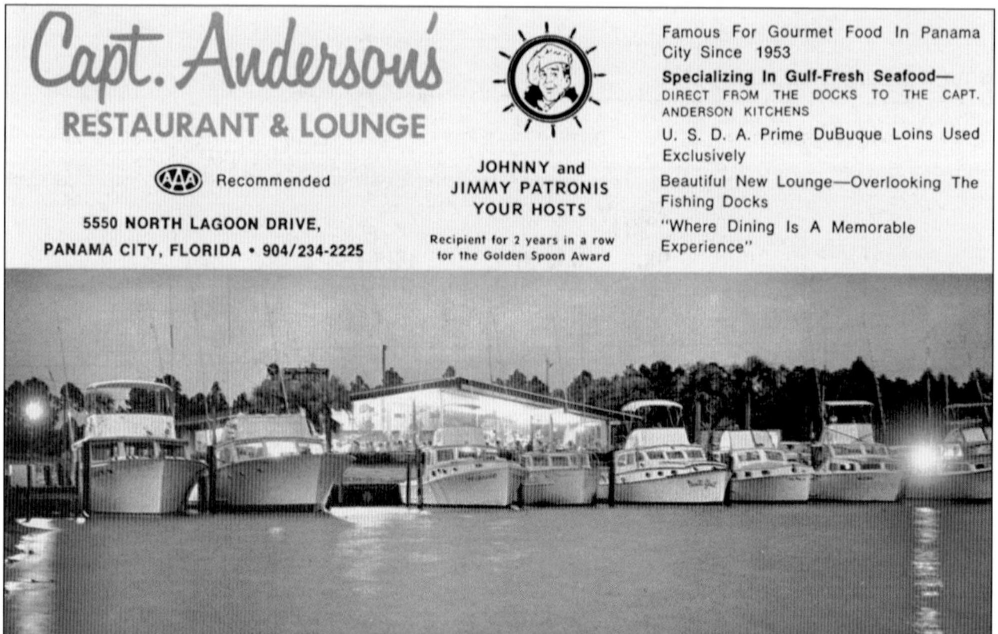

Captain Anderson's Restaurant has expanded over the years to include a market, marina, and sightseeing/dinner cruise trips along the Bay. (Courtesy Bay County Library.)

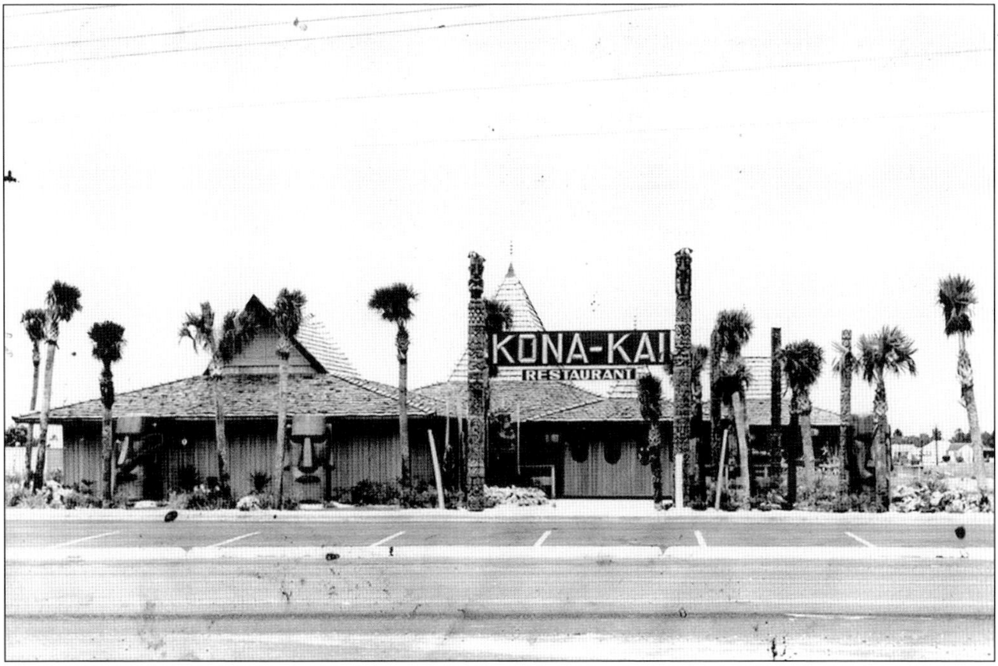

The famous Kona-Kai Restaurant provided an exotic dining experience in the 1970s. With its Polynesian-style interior and welcoming tiki statues, it was a landmark for many years. Pompano's Restaurant is there now. (Courtesy Bay County Library.)

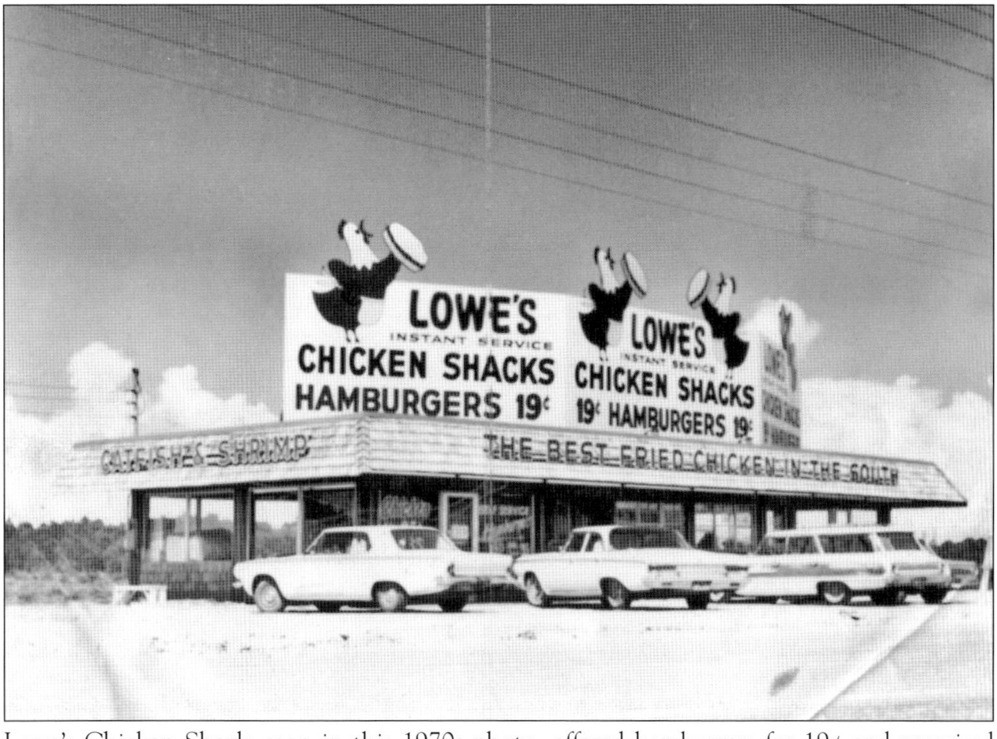

Lowe's Chicken Shack, seen in this 1970s photo, offered hamburgers for 19¢ and promised "instant service." (Courtesy Bay County Library.)

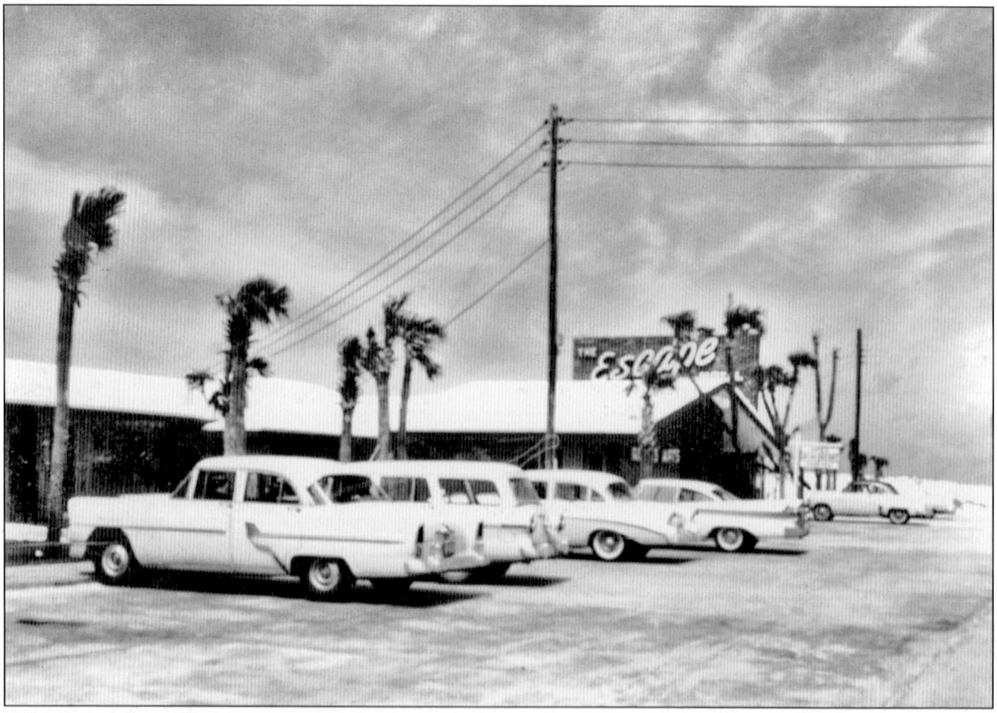

The Escape Motel is pictured in the late 1950s. Note the tail fins on those cars! Jimmie Jones took this photograph. (Courtesy Susan Moore and Nelson Jones.)

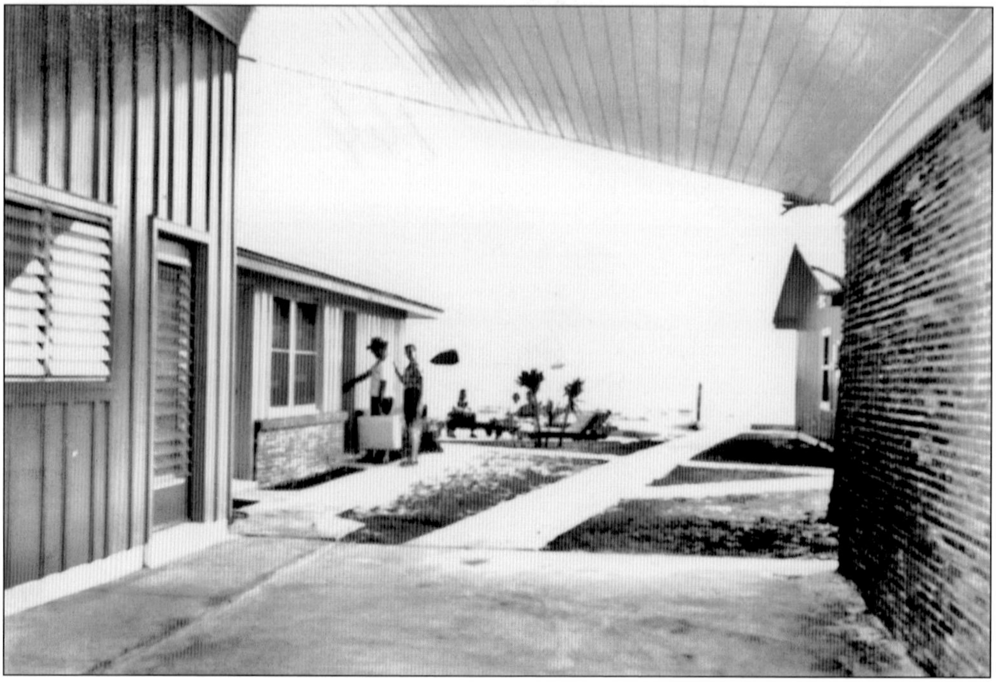

Vacationers prepare to enter their room at the Escape Motel in 1959. This Jimmie Nelson photo shows the breezeway and the outdoor lounge area next to the beach. (Courtesy Susan Moore and Nelson Jones.)

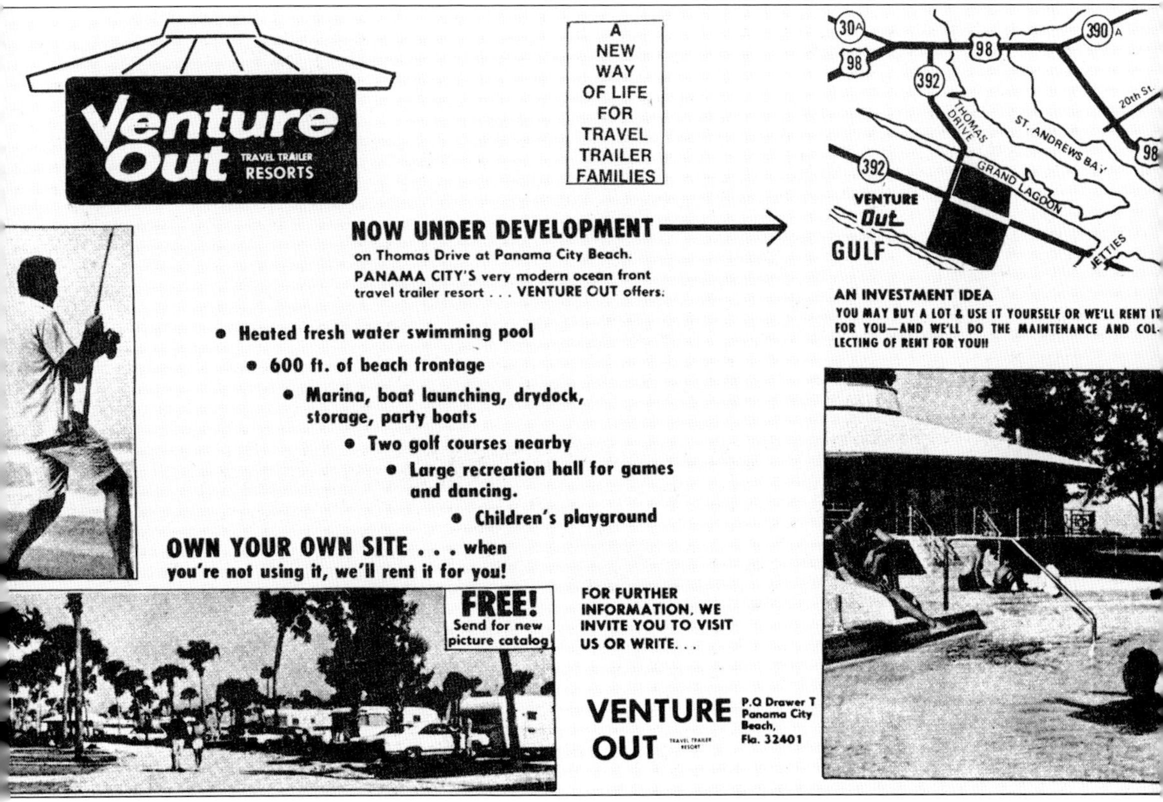

On July 3, 1970, the Gulf Oil company opened a travel-trailer resort park at Panama City Beach, boasting 100 acres with 300 feet on the Gulf of Mexico and 1,000 feet on the Grand Lagoon. The park, known as Venture Out, offered lots complete with palm trees for prices starting at $4,500. (Courtesy Venture Out.)

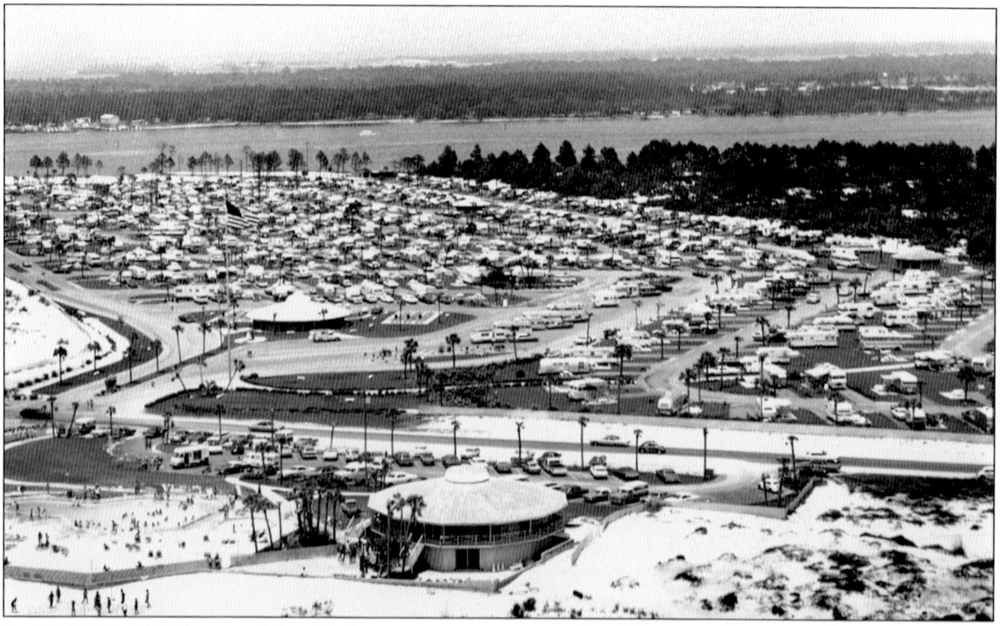

In 1977, Gulf Oil turned handed over management of its Venture Out Travel Trailer Resort to the Condominium Association, which consisted of 735 owners. Over the past 30+ years, Venture Out has evolved from a travel-trailer park to a gated residential community, complete with two swimming pools, tennis courts, a putting green, boating facilities, and a large clubhouse. (Courtesy Venture Out.)

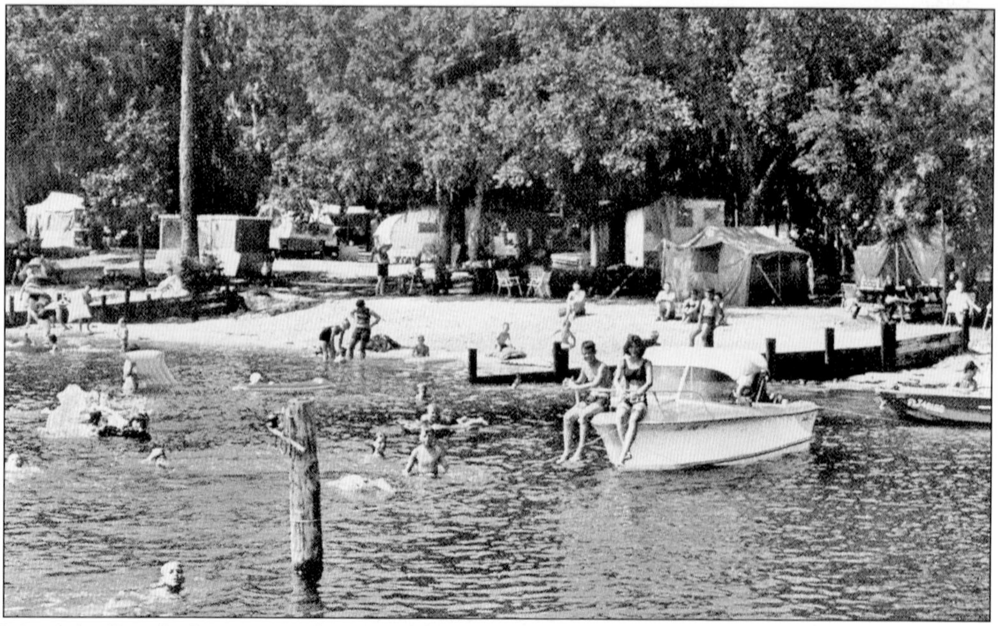

Magnolia Beach Campgrounds, owned by Mr. and Mrs. James E. Smith, offered "first-rate" campsites and recreational facilities for those who chose to take a camping vacation at Panama City Beach. Barbecue grills, showers, boat rentals, ice, and washers and dryers were just some of the amenities campers could look forward to at the site. Today, Magnolia Beach is a RV park. (Courtesy Bay County Library.)

Ten

HERE TODAY . . .

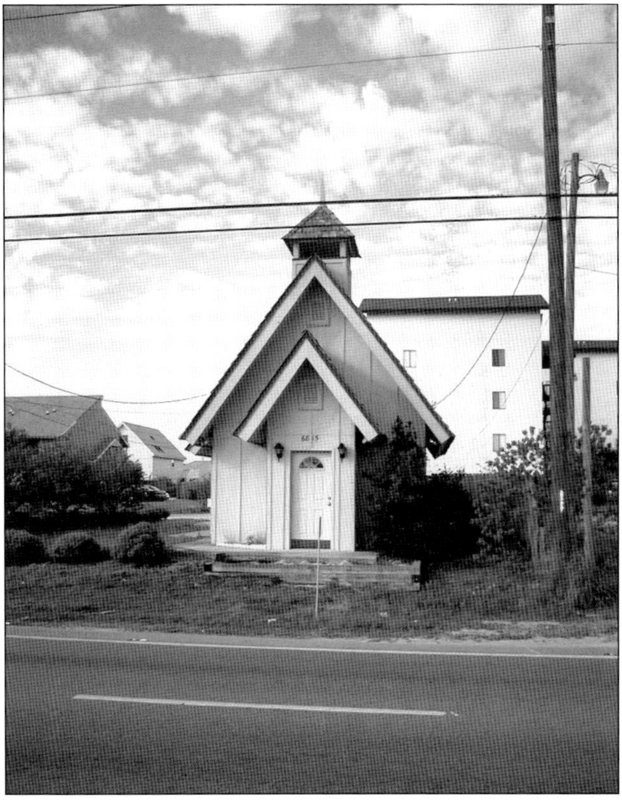

A familiar sight on Thomas Drive, this little chapel has seen many weddings over the years. It was recently sold, and one can only hope that it will not become a parking garage. (Courtesy Carolyn Insley.)

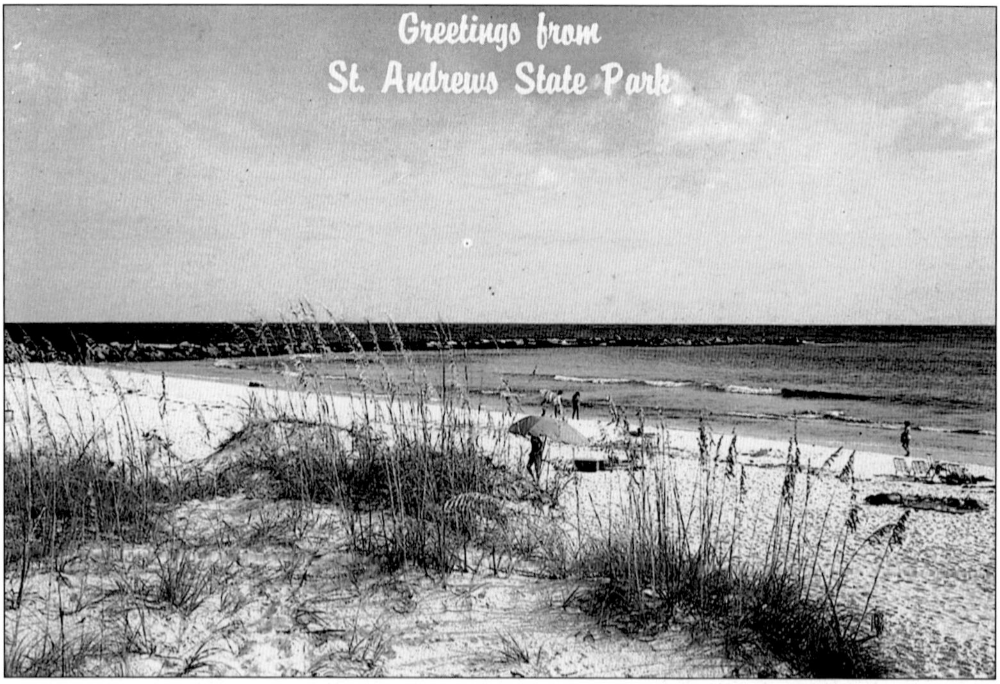

Named by *Travel Magazine* as "The World's Best Beach" in 1995, St. Andrews State Park is known for its white, sandy beaches and gin-clear water. In addition to camping, boating, fishing and, swimming, the park offers live history demonstrations and guided tours. (Courtesy St. Andrews State Park.)

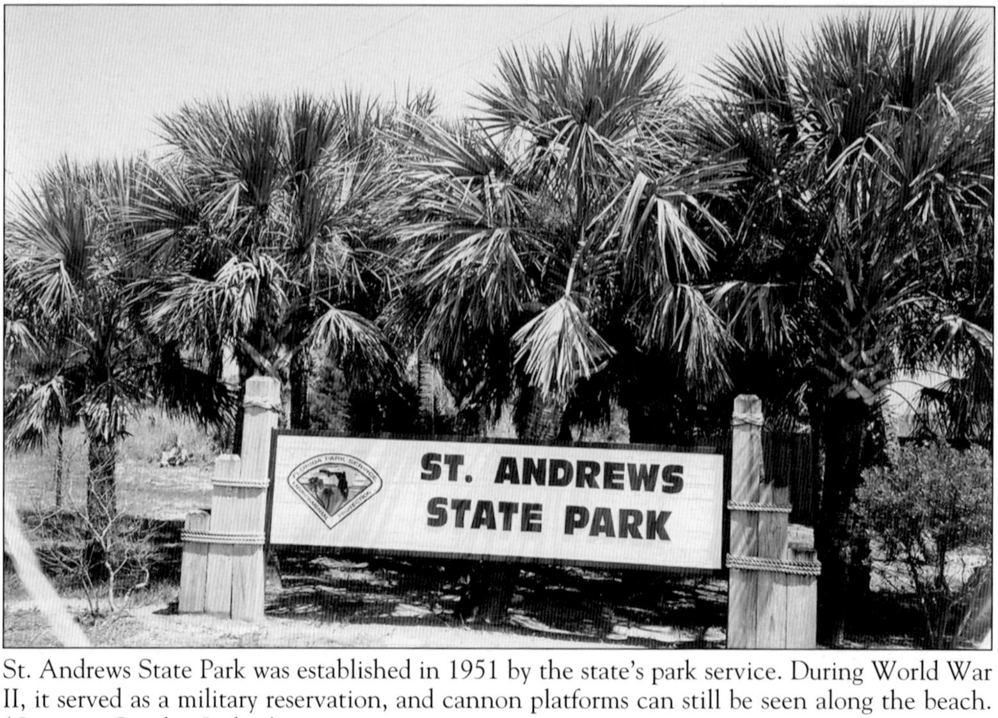

St. Andrews State Park was established in 1951 by the state's park service. During World War II, it served as a military reservation, and cannon platforms can still be seen along the beach. (Courtesy Carolyn Insley.)

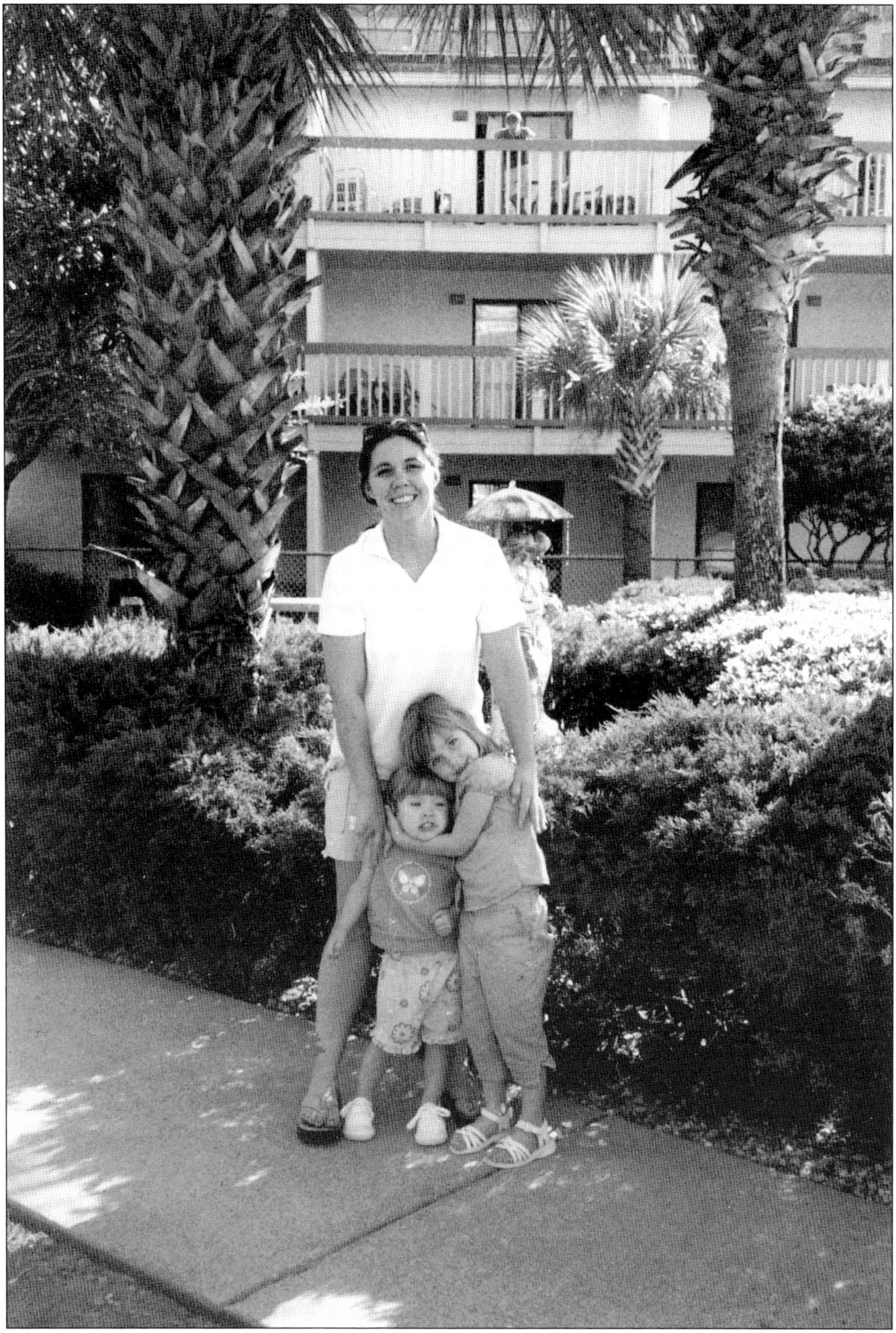

Shannon, Kelsey, and Callie Knight are posed beside the Fountain at Sunswept Condominiums. Shannon, a Panama City Beach native, helps to manage the complex.

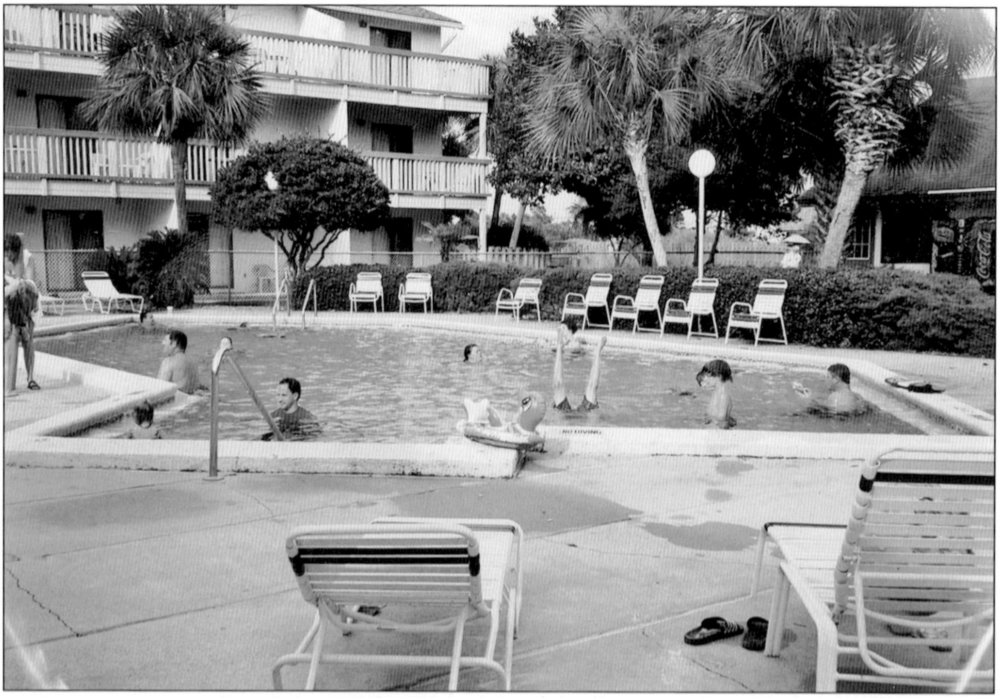

This picture is poolside at the Sunswept Condominiums. With high-rise complexes popping up all along the beach, this 60-unit "mom-and-pop" remains much the same as when it was built in 1985. (Courtesy Carolyn Insley.)

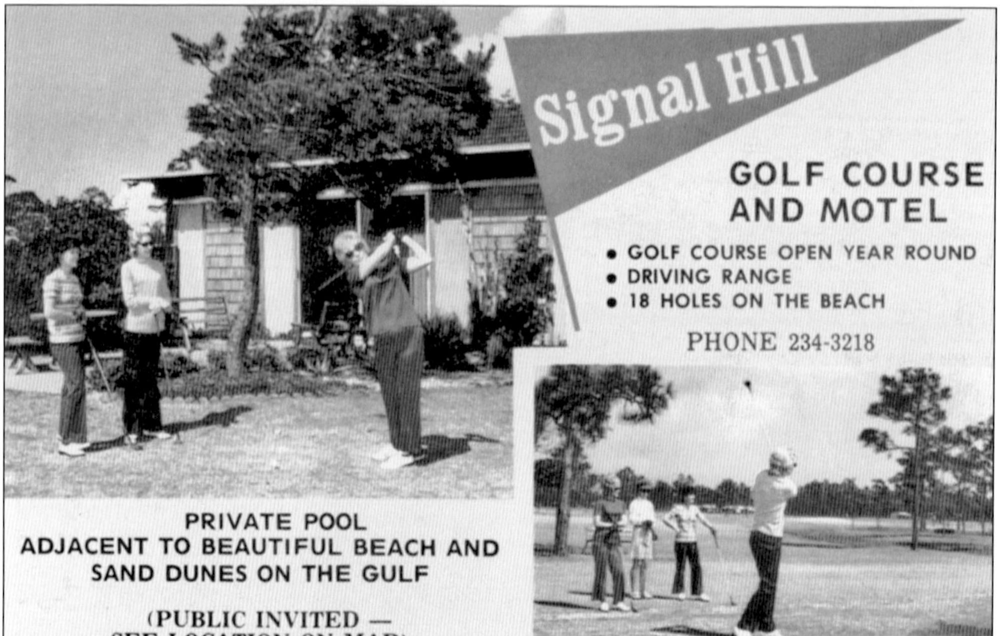

Signal Hill Golf Course is seen in a magazine advertisement in the 1970s. (Courtesy Bay Hombre Golf Club, located in Panama City Beach, is home to the PGA Tour School Qualifier. This

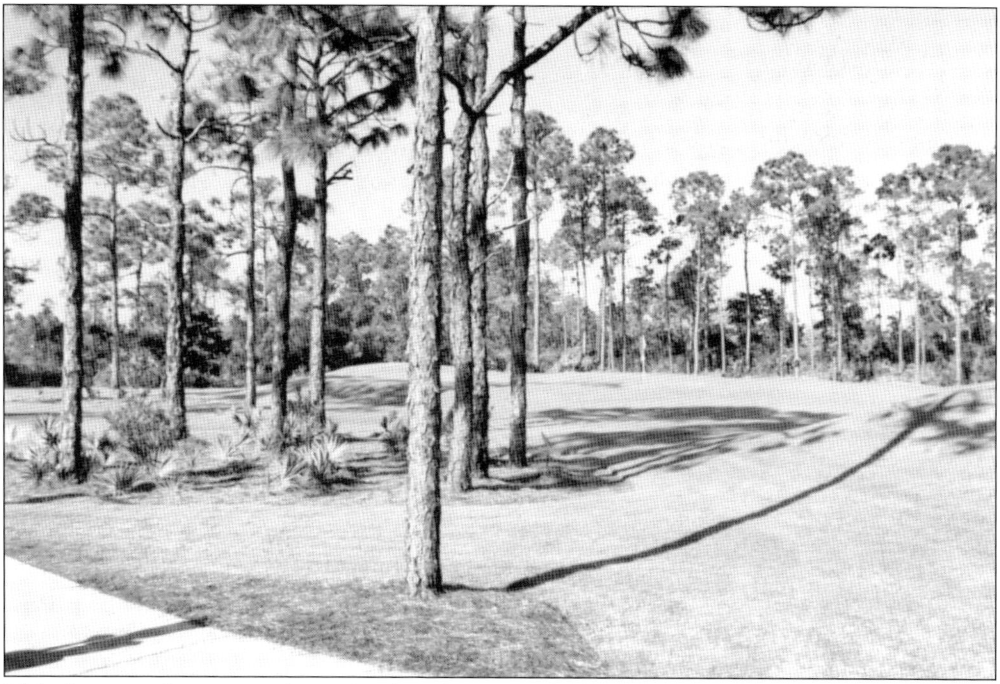

27-hole course has names for each of its three nine-hole layouts—the Good, the Bad, and the Ugly. It opened in 1995. (Courtesy Hombre Golf Club.)

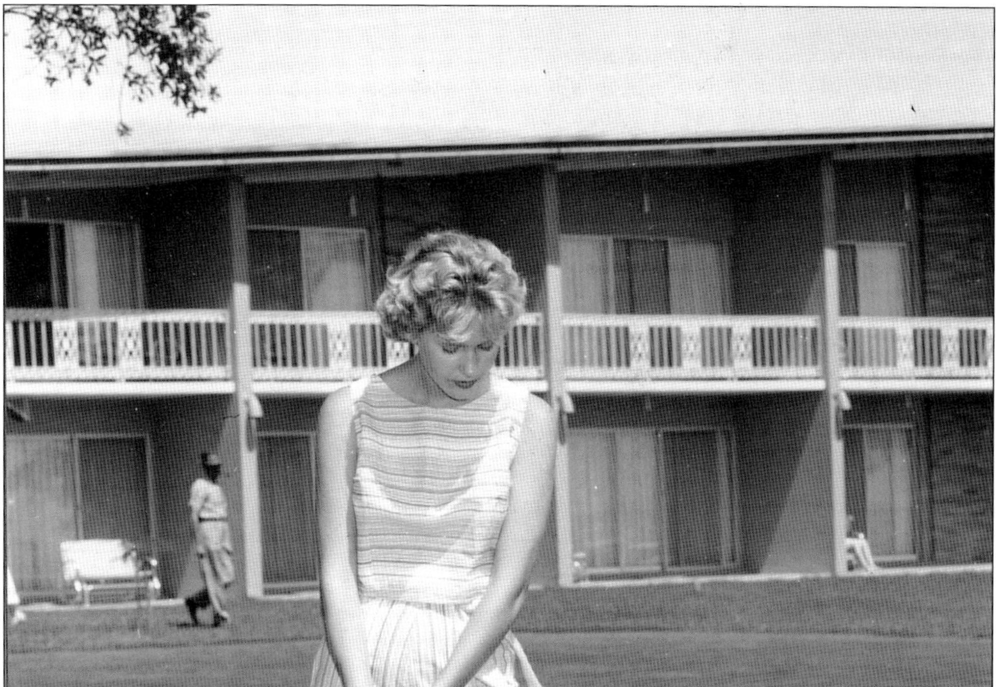

Judy Palmer and Sally Stockton are seen here in this 1959 photo playing golf at the Holiday Lodge. (Courtesy Florida State Archives.)

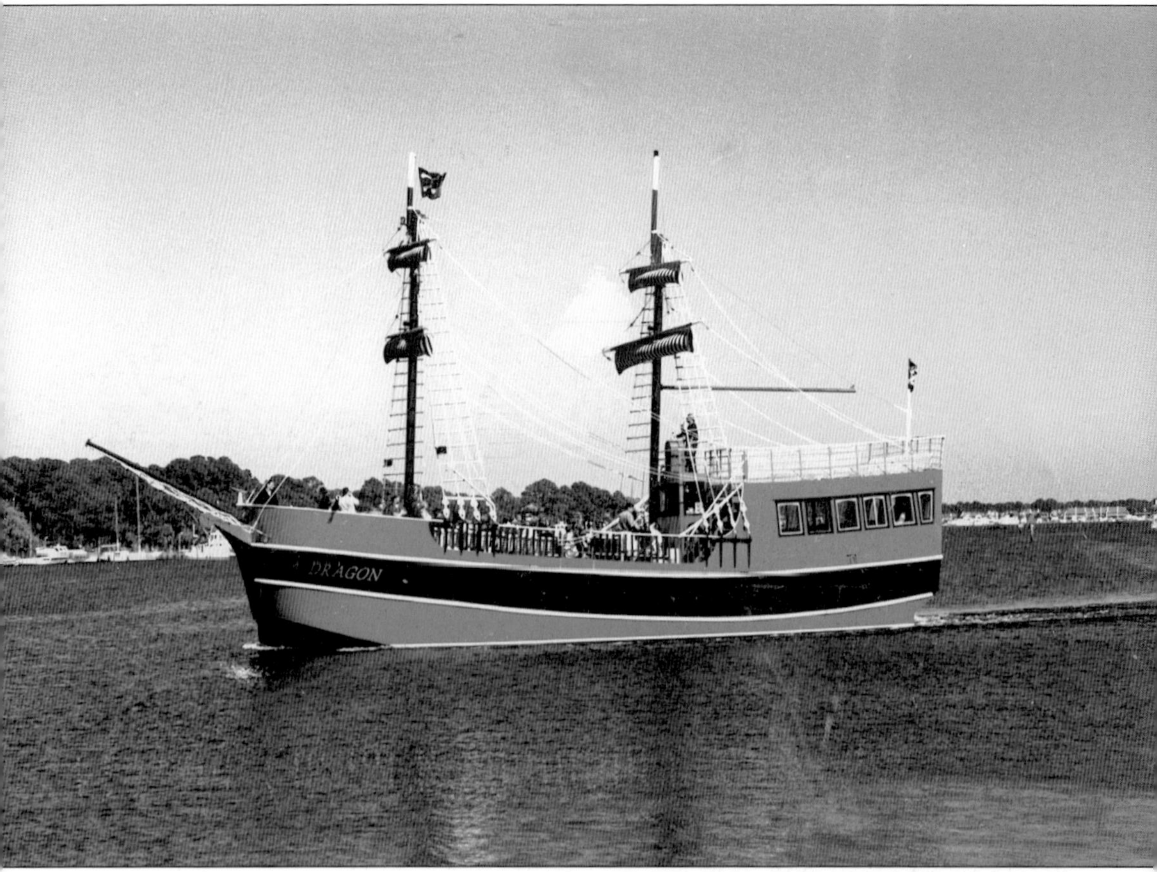

The *Sea Dragon*, owned by Capt. Andy and Celia Redmond, was originally built by Larry McNeil at a plumbing supply house off Harrison Avenue in Panama City. The vessel took over eight years to build, and during that time friends and neighbors speculated as to what form the boat would take. It emerged a perfect replica of a pirate ship. First named the *Golden Eagle* in 1992 and launched as a sightseeing boat, the replicated pirate ship was later put into dry-dock for several years. In 1997, Captain Andy and his wife Celia purchased the vessel and re-christened her the *Sea Dragon*. In 1998, the Redmonds put their boat into service as a thematic pirate cruise-ship that provides daily sightseeing tours. (Courtesy Capt. Andy and Celia Redmond.)

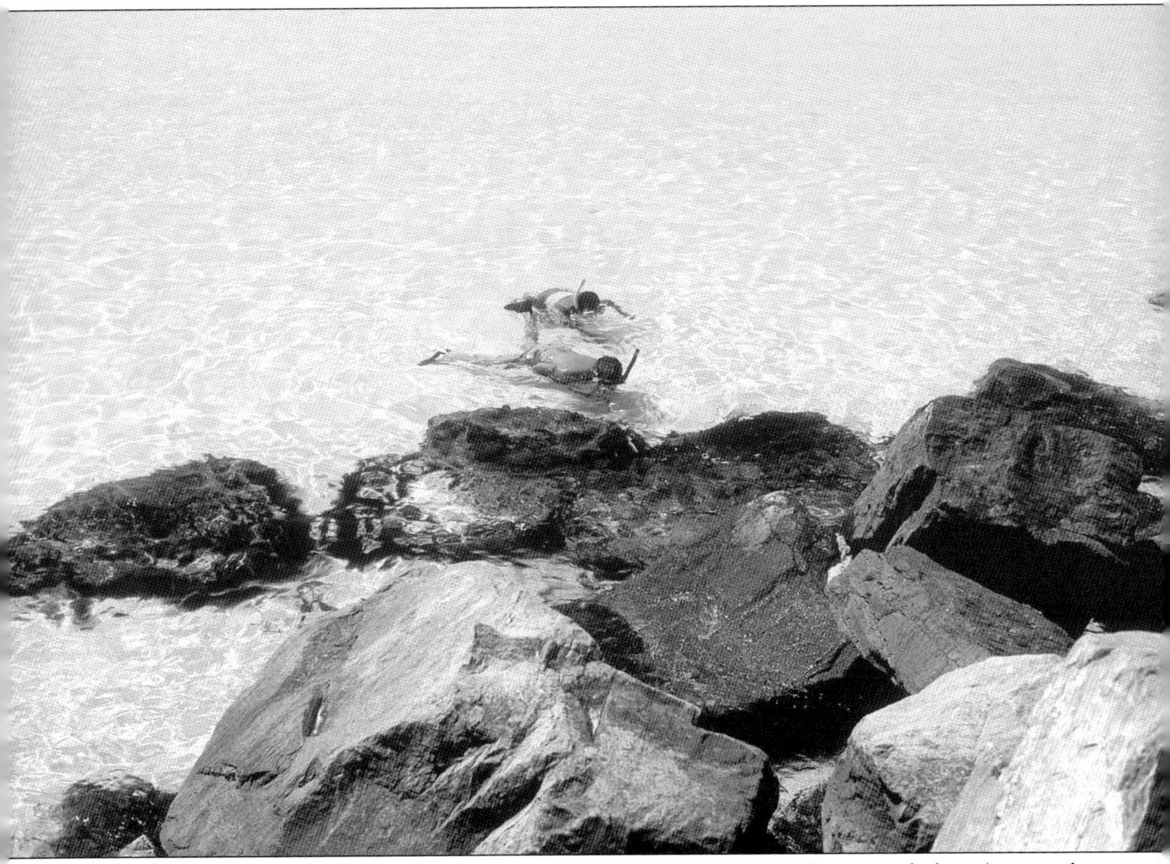

Easily accessed by boat, Shell Island provides a myriad of activities, from snorkeling (pictured here) to shell seeking. Many local entrepreneurs have built businesses providing Shell Island sightseeing excursions. (Courtesy Jayna Leach and the Panama City Beach Convention and Visitors Bureau.)

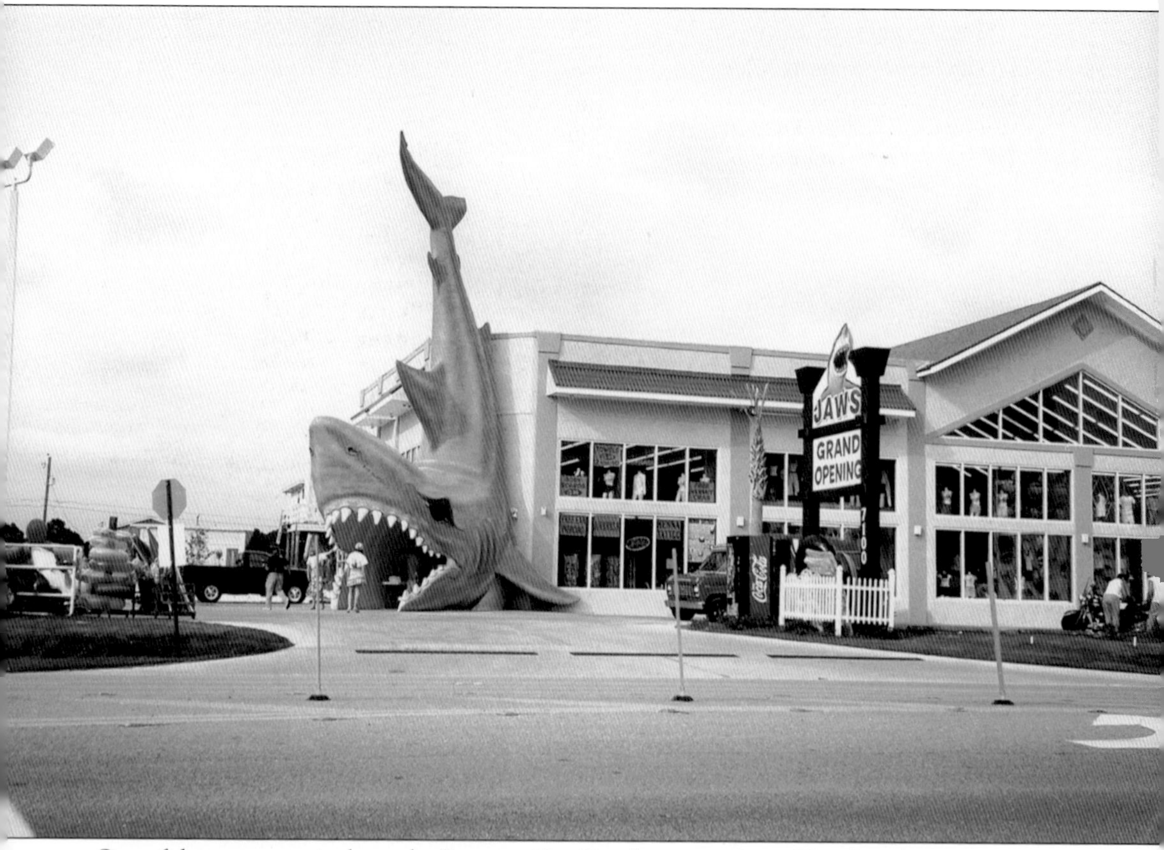

One of the newest arrivals on the Panama City Beach scene is Jaws. This "toothsome" swimwear and surf gear shop opened on Thomas Drive in 2004. (Courtesy Carolyn Insley.)

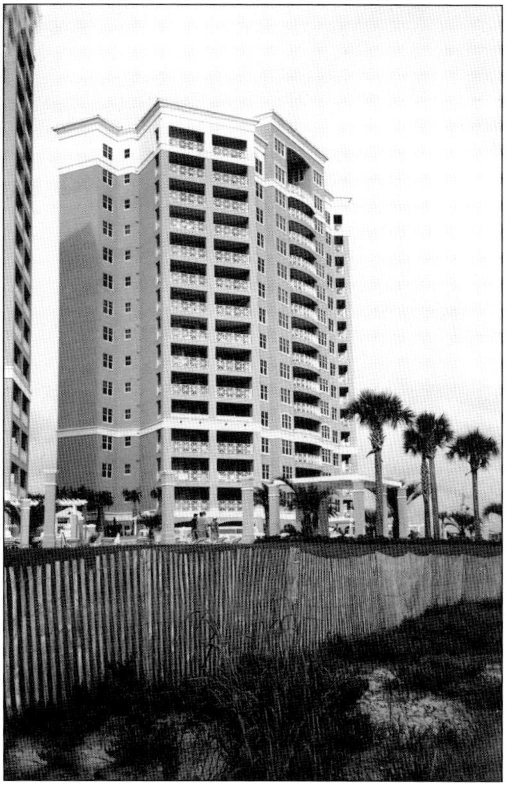

Recognized by its distinctive yellow and seafoam green Mediterranean colors, En Soleil resort is located next to the Rick Seltzer Community Park in Panama City Beach. (Courtesy Carolyn Insley.)

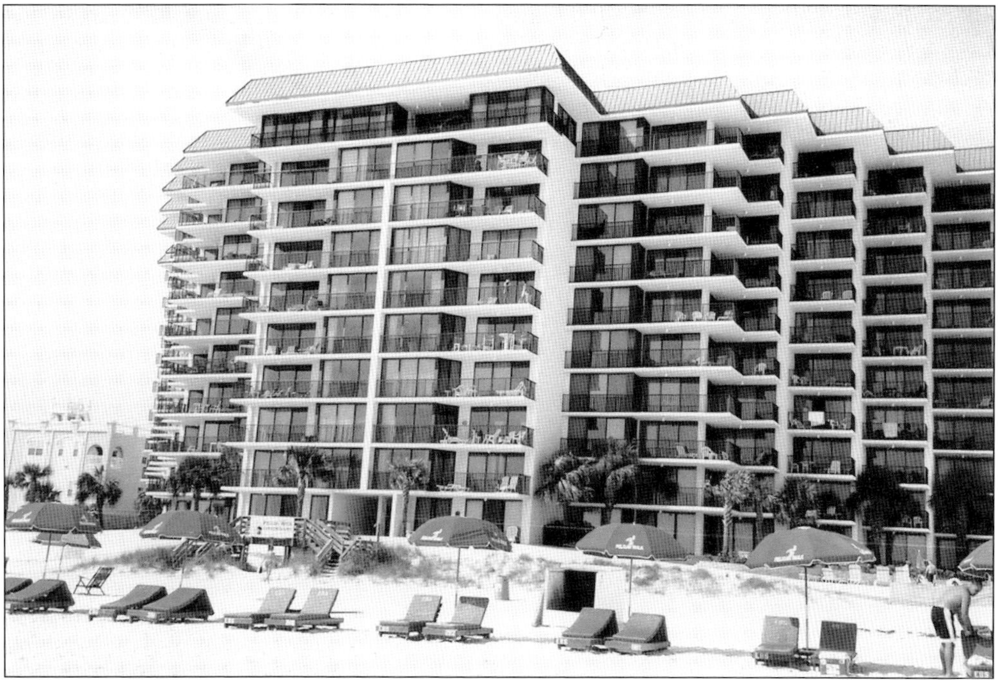

Pelican Walk is just one of the many new luxury high-rise condominiums to be built on the beach in the past few years. E.B.S. services this property by providing equipment and lifeguards.

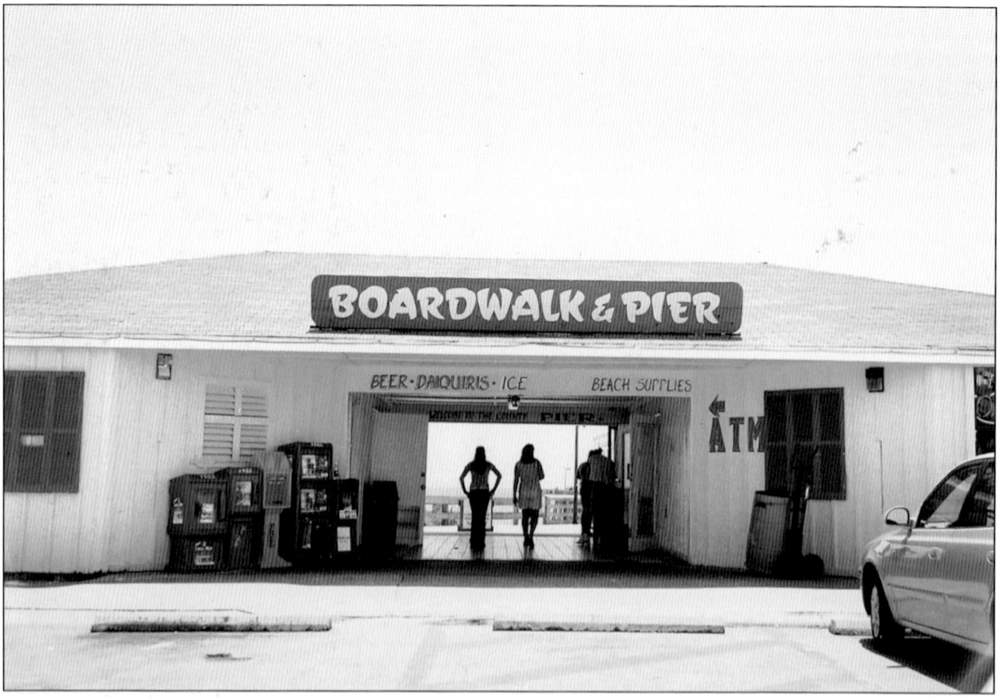

The Boardwalk and Pier is shown as it appeared in 2004. (Courtesy Carolyn Insley.)

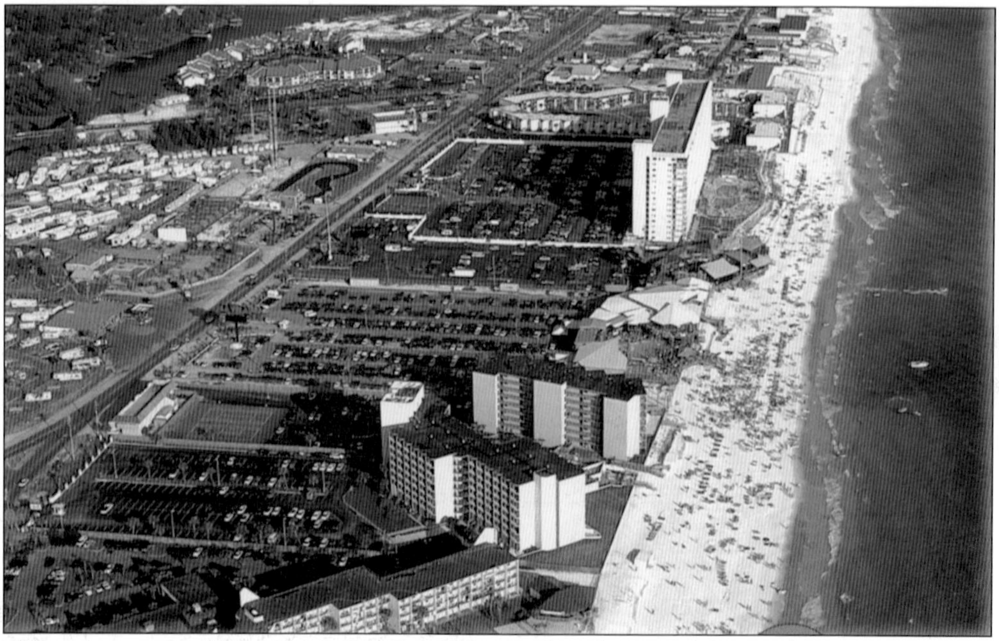
This is a view of Panama City Beach that is destined to change. Club LaVela is at right center. A mobile home park is seen at left near the "Y" formed by the Thomas Drive division.